KT-132-781

GLORY DAYS

BOOKS BY L. JON WERTHEIM

This Is Your Brain on Sports

Scorecasting

Blood in the Cage

Venus Envy

Strokes of Genius

Running the Table

Transition Game

Rookie Bookie

GLORY DAYS

The Summer of 1984 and the 90 Days That Changed Sports and Culture Forever

L. JON WERTHEIM

Houghton Mifflin Harcourt
BOSTON NEW YORK
2021

hmhbooks.com

Library of Congress Cataloging-in-Publication Data
Names: Wertheim, L. Jon, author.
Title: Glory days : the summer of 1984 and the 90 days that changed sports and culture forever / L. Jon Wertheim.
Description: Boston : Houghton Mifflin Harcourt, 2021. |
Includes bibliographical references and index.
Identifiers: LCCN 2020033845 (print) | LCCN 2020033846 (ebook) |
ISBN 9781328637246 (hardcover) | ISBN 9780358449058 | ISBN 9780358449393 |
ISBN 9781328637901 (ebook)
Subjects: LCSH: Sports — History — 20th Century. | Nineteen eighty-four, A.D.
Classification: LCC GV576 .W45 2021 (print) | LCC GV576 (ebook) |
DDC 796.09048 — dc23
LC record available at https://lccn.loc.gov/2020033845
LC ebook record available at https://lccn.loc.gov/2020033846

Book design by Chloe Foster

Printed in the United States of America
1 2021
4500825104

Part of the introduction was first published, in different form, as the 2014 article “Rare Air Time: Michael Jordan, the ’84 U.S. Olympic Trials and Me,” by Jon Wertheim for *Sports Illustrated* online.

To my family family

To the *Sports Illustrated* family

Glory Days, well, they'll pass you by.

—BRUCE SPRINGSTEEN,
from *Born in the U.S.A.*, released June 4, 1984

REPORTER: "Is it true you can fly?"

MICHAEL JORDAN: "No. Well, maybe for a little."

Contents

GLORY DAYS

Introduction

Though dripping with modest Midwest charm, my hometown, Bloomington, Indiana, was — and still is — a somewhat sleepy college town. Especially so between semesters at Indiana University. When the students aren't around, the population plunges by half.

But in the late spring of 1984, when I was 13 years old, the usual quiet was ruptured. Bloomington was enlivened and invigorated that April because the circus had come to town. The attractions, though, weren't tightrope walkers and jugglers and trapeze acts; the menagerie instead featured a collection of extraordinarily tall and extraordinarily athletic young men, ages 18 through 22.

Bob Knight — Indiana University's famously unyielding coach and the most powerful figure at the time not just in the Hoosier State but in all of college basketball — was tasked with putting together the roster of the U.S. men's basketball team that he was going to guide that summer at the Los Angeles Olympics. These were still the days when the Games demanded amateurism, before NBA players were eligible to compete.

And these were still the days when coaches were absolutists, wielding their authority like unchecked dictators.

The players weren't *asked* to be on the team; they *auditioned* for a spot. And there was no national training center. The hopeful applicants came to Knight's domain and worked on Knight's timetable. They went through a series of tryouts for Knight and his staff. Like Roman emperors assessing gladiators, the assessing coaches either gave performers a thumbs-up or sent them home.

In keeping with Knight's entire mode of being, the players were not exactly coddled. Joe Kleine, a Missouri kid who played at the University of Arkansas, recalls flying into the Indianapolis airport. "We all picked up our own bags and then piled into these buses. It was like going to Camp Wong-a-Monga or whatever. Except you'd look around the bus and it was Michael Jordan across the aisle and Charles Barkley in the row behind you and Patrick Ewing in the row ahead of you."

When the players arrived in Bloomington, they were assigned spartan rooms at the Indiana University student union. They mostly ate cafeteria food. They were transported around town in maroon vans, three players per row. The tryouts were held at the IU Fieldhouse, a no-frills gym, redolent mostly of Ben-Gay wintergreen and an indifference to showering.

When practice was over, the players were on their own, ambling around town, sometimes accepting rides to the movies from strangers. Soon everyone in town had a tale. They watched an already rotund Charles Barkley devour an entire pizza, somehow smiling and laughing and talking the whole time. They drove Patrick Ewing home from a screening of *The Karate Kid* at the College Mall Cinema when his scheduled van ride didn't show up. They played pool against Chris Mullin or *Pac-Man* against Wayman Tisdale.

Up and down the roster, the players were exceptionally cool. They were uncorrupted by fame and wealth, but, then again, they had little of either back then. What they had instead: a giddiness about the Olympics and, more generally, their luminous futures. Many would be drafted by

NBA teams that summer. But they came across as college kids, with college tastes.

Even so, one player projected a different level of magnetism and charisma.

Wearing Bermuda shorts, collared shirts, leather Top-Siders, and a generous smile, Michael Jordan walked around with an easy confidence. Like everyone else, Jordan didn't know what successes awaited him — that he would eventually drive every other athlete on the planet into the shadows. But his disposition alone suggested that, at least at some level, he sensed that his future brimmed with possibility.

Jordan always looked up and out, happy — or at least not annoyed — to be recognized. He joked easily, in a deep voice, and often offered a rich laugh that originated in the depths of his belly. Though he was a proud son of North Carolina, his voice was flecked with only the slightest southern accent. He was quick to dispense nicknames. And not just to his teammates. One day he spotted me, age 13, carrying a tennis racket. "Hey, John McEnroe!" he said, miming tennis strokes. "When are we gonna play?"

Most of Bloomington looked at Michael Jordan somewhat indifferently in the summer of 1984, as he ordered a smoothie at the Chocolate Moose ice cream joint, or lost 18 holes of Putt-Putt, only to shoot the winner a scalding stare and demand an immediate rematch. *This time for real, no more playing around.*

Of course, Jordan possessed sport's ultimate trump card: talent.

He'd just finished his third season at the University of North Carolina — ironically, losing to a Knight-coached Indiana team in his final college game — and most experts pegged him as a high lottery pick, provided, that is, that he would skip his senior season and go to the NBA.

During the Olympic Trials, Jordan's aura grew as he distanced himself from the others. Shod in powder-blue Converse high-tops, leftovers from his North Carolina basketball wardrobe, Jordan executed moves other players wouldn't think to attempt, much less pull off.

Knight, not one prone to insincere praise, much less to gushing, could not conceal the admiration he had for his shooting guard. Knight warned that any NBA team foolish enough to pass up drafting Jordan would regret the decision. "Jordan's game is made for the NBA," he declared. When he raved about Jordan, it was as much about his competitive resolve and comportment as it was his quickness or the moves that defied the laws of physics and geometry.

Here was Knight on Jordan that summer, long before MJ played his first NBA game: "The kid is just an absolutely great kid. If I were going to pick the three or four best athletes I've ever seen play basketball, he'd be one of 'em. I think he's the best athlete I've ever seen play basketball."

Knight wasn't entirely prescient that summer; the players he would cut from his team included Barkley, Karl Malone, John Stockton, and Joe Dumars, all of whom would go on to become NBA stars. But he sure had Jordan pegged.

In all his tongue-wagging glory, Jordan breezed through the various rounds of cuts as the roster was winnowed, first to 20 players, then to 16, and finally to 12 players and two alternates. The team was now practicing at Assembly Hall, then—and, improbably, still now—home arena of our beloved Indiana Hoosiers.

Hoping to catch Jordan in action, a few of us hoops-happy middle schoolers hatched an elaborate plot to sneak into a team practice. It was totally unnecessary. When we made our approach, it was clear that every door was unlocked. We entered and sat in the bleachers, watching in awed silence.

At one point, Jordan blew by four men, including Ewing, and threw down a howlingly fierce dunk. Even Knight let loose an admiring whistle that pierced the air. That afternoon, I saw Jordan at the Chocolate Moose. I told him what I'd seen. "You know what, John McEnroe?" he said, smiling as ever. "That wasn't even my best dunk."

Michael Jordan strolling through town, happy to make small talk, whiling away the days before the Olympics? It didn't seem especially remarkable or portentous at the time.

Yet looking back, it was the perfect prelude to the summer of 1984. Those three months would be filled with signature events, sweeping social trends, and outsized personalities — and, like a photograph that would develop before our eyes, would take on greater significance the more time elapsed.

That entire year, all American schoolkids worth their acid-washed jeans and Lacoste shirts (collars upturned) and black rubber bracelets stopped feeding quarters into arcade games long enough to read George Orwell's chilling novel *1984* — which had been assigned that year by every English teacher in America. Orwell's dark and dystopian vision warned of repressive Big Brother and the Ministry of Truth and the creep of government.

But *1984* was published in 1949. And the reality of 1984 — the year and not the book? It was dominated by forces and sensibilities almost entirely antithetical to the ones predicted by Orwell. The Reagan era was in full tax-cutting, free-market bloom, and as he approached reelection, the president offered the hopeful, invigorating slogan "It's morning again in America." Reagan had his critics, especially those rightly skeptical of supply-side trickle-down economics, doubtful that the gains of the wealthy would redound to the less fortunate.

Still, unemployment and inflation were on the decline. Plenty of other indexes — from life expectancy to worker productivity — were surging. Interest rates from the Federal Reserve stood at 10.75 percent, rough if you were buying a home — average new home price: $87,000 — but agreeable if you invested in a certificate of deposit that paid 7 or 8 percent annually. Wall Street didn't budge much — one of the few darling stocks of 1984 was Tootsie Roll Industries — but, as the public was constantly reminded, the "fundamentals" of the economy were strong.

Contrary to Orwell's *1984,* this was an era of less government, not more. Reagan himself first won election while stating, "Government is not the solution to our problem; government *is* the problem." At odds with the fictional *1984,* the nonfictional 1984 was, for Reagan's voters anyway, a time flush with optimism and a certain faith in the future.

As Reagan ran for reelection against Walter Mondale that summer, he re-asked the question that he had first posed when he beat Jimmy Carter in 1980: "Are you better off than you were four years ago?" This time it was a rhetorical question. He assumed, safely, that most voters would answer yes. And he would be right. He ended up winning the Electoral College by a run-up-the-score blowout of 525–13, with only Mondale's home state of Minnesota preventing the incumbent from pitching an unprecedented shutout.

Even Reagan's harshest critics had to admit: the man never seemed upset, even when confronting those dastardly Soviets. Reagan was, as Alistair Cooke, the BBC journalist, characterized him at the time, "the chucklingest president in history." *This* seemed to trickle down. Reagan's image as both a breezy, upbeat guy *and* the candidate most willing to take on Russia and avoid nuclear apocalypse may have been what won him the election.

Beyond politics and world events, the summer of 1984 was a season of sunshine, not darkness. At the time, it felt like a typically benign and pleasant American June-July-August, all heart and soul. It was a summer soundtracked by sugary pop songs blaring from car speakers on the radio. A string of blockbusters and action movies cycled through the theaters. Americans read glossy magazines and bought books, those authored by Stephen King and Robert Ludlum in particular. In the summer of 1984, U.S. newspaper circulation hit what is still its highest level in history.

In the span of three weeks in June, Bruce Springsteen released *Born in the U.S.A.*, Prince released his sixth studio album, *Purple Rain,* and, in between, *Ghostbusters* and *Gremlins* and *The Karate Kid* all opened in the theaters, where the average ticket cost $2.50. John Hughes released the first film in his angst-filled canon. Written over a single weekend,

Sixteen Candles spoke to teenage anxiety and status envy and pushback against authority. And with that, the teen movie genre took off.

That summer, an old woman inspecting a hamburger asked, persistently and ubiquitously, "Where's the Beef?"—an accusing question that, unlike the hamburgers, somehow never seemed to congeal or go stale. It was suggested that Clara Peller, the unlikely star of this commercial for Wendy's hamburgers, was the closest we got to Winston Smith, the anti-establishment figure of Orwell's *1984.* Here, after all, was a woman unafraid to question authority, who saw through artifice and resisted the bullshit she was being peddled by mass marketing.

Meanwhile, 41 percent of American homes—a huge jump from even a year earlier—were blessed with a cable box, a magic cube that unlocked a world of television viewing options. Each month that summer, cable systems added roughly 300,000 new households. As my friend and colleague Steve Rushin—who grew up around the same time in Bloomington, Minnesota, not Bloomington, Indiana—described it perfectly, cable was the equivalent of a Trojan horse, "sneaking into our house through Bananarama's 'Cruel Summer' video and Atlanta Braves telecasts and scrambled soft-core movies on premium channels that Mom and Dad scarcely knew existed."

As for the channels Mom and Dad *did* know, the three dominant broadcast networks—ABC, NBC, and CBS—took their usual extended summer vacation and restocked their arsenals. As reruns reran, America would have to take a break from new episodes of *Dallas, 60 Minutes, The A-Team,* and the other popular prime-time shows.

A remake of a 1970s game show titled *Jeopardy!* filmed throughout that summer and premiered on September 10, 1984, hosted by a slick Canadian, Alex Trebek. A new kind of cop show that married drug crime with rock music, *Miami Vice,* premiered the following week. A new kind of sitcom, *The Cosby Show,* entered American living rooms four days after that.

Thanks, though, to a new appliance, Americans were starting to watch television shows on *their* terms. The videocassette recorder, or

VCR — slogan: "Watch whatever whenever" — gave viewers the ability to record programs for future use. By the summer, Sony had a backlog of orders for VCRs, even as factories were at full capacity manufacturing the machines. In 1984, VCRs outsold personal computers by 1.5 million units. "It's freedom!" Barbara Walters enthused about the VCR on the ABC network's news program *20/20.* "I hear it's the biggest craze since the Hula-Hoop!" (She was right about the freedom. She was, of course, dead wrong likening on-demand media to a fad.)

Americans also spent the summer of 1984 acquainting themselves with two other hot appliances. One was the handheld video camera, a contraption that enabled users to make their own recordings — and then insert the mini-cassettes into their VCRs and watch. In Orwell's *1984,* the government recorded the citizens. In the actual 1984, the *citizens* did the taping, presaging the YouTube culture. People were now able to create and control their own content, beyond the reach of the usual cultural gatekeepers.

The second appliance that found favor in the summer of 1984: a new personal computer that was less a cold piece of technology than it was a warm household appliance. Some likened it to a pet. It even smiled at you when you turned it on. The Macintosh, it was called. The man behind this lovable beige cube, Steve Jobs, was so personable and almost evangelical in his fervor for technology — so counter to the archetypal computer nerd — that in May of 1984 he reached perhaps the pinnacle of pop culture when he was featured on . . . the *ABC Afterschool Special,* hailed as the father of this supercool piece of technology.

That summer, for the first time ever, a major political party selected a woman to run for national office. When Geraldine Ferraro accepted the vice presidential nomination from Walter Mondale at the Democratic Convention that July, she announced, "By choosing a woman to run for our nation's second-highest office, you send a powerful signal to all Americans. There are no doors we cannot unlock."

Two nights before that, an African American man from Chicago took the podium and spoke with the cadence of a southern preacher. His voice hoarse and his shirt saturated with sweat, Jesse Jackson declared that he was representing "the desperate, the damned, the disinherited, the disrespected, and the despised." He marked what *Time* magazine called "the first black to play a pivotal role at a major party convention" and stirred, for the first time, speculation that Americans might elect an African American president one day.

Less happily, in the summer of 1984, an unhinged, middle-aged white man, armed to the hilt, walked into a McDonald's in Southern California and began spraying bullets. Mass shootings would become commonplace in the United States in the decades to come, horrors that would unfold with almost numbingly predictable frequency. At the time, it was such an aberration that customers in the McDonald's didn't even think to duck, believing that the commotion was all a practical joke.

History doesn't send out invitations in advance. Which is what makes this summer special. Unlike, say, the summers of 1968 or 1969 or 1972, all of which felt momentous in real time, the summer of 1984 unfolded at such a leisurely and summery pace, few Americans considered it remarkable.

Like the vision of a carefree Michael Jordan ambling — alone — through the town square, only in retrospect was the moment so pivotal.

This broader theme was mirrored in the cultural theater of sports. The period between Memorial Day and Labor Day of 1984 didn't, in the moment anyway, seem especially transformative. But now, as time has galloped by, we can look back and appreciate those days as a critical pivot point.

With hindsight, it's easy to make the case that the summer of 1984 would set the course for sports for the next half century. Name a resonant issue in sports today and, odds are, it figured prominently in the summer of 1984. This was the summer that sports officially became entertainment. That the television lazy Susan better known as cable — and the rights fees it would pay to televise games — would forever change the balance sheets of teams and leagues. That a struggling all-sports network, ESPN, would be sold to ABC, putting it on firmer footing and the path to profitability. That the Olympics would turn a profit. That the WrestleMania franchise was, effectively, hatched. That Michael Jordan would become a professional basketball player and a professional pitchman.

That summer, a sleek, skilled, and mulleted young hockey player, Wayne Gretzky, won the Stanley Cup for the first time, the final certification before fulfilling his nickname, the Great One. He was 23. A few weeks later, Magic Johnson (age 24) and Larry Bird (age 27) opposed each other in the NBA Finals for the first time. One could not have scripted a more compelling series, a drama with a seven-game arc, featuring two storied teams — one from each coast — led by a pair of rivals who would be bracketed together for their entire careers.

Rewatch those 1984 NBA Finals and you might notice a man with large glasses and a caterpillar of a mustache — "I wanted to look older than I was!" — seated in the stands, watching delightedly. David Stern, five-foot-nine and then 41, had just been anointed as the NBA's fourth league commissioner and was overseeing his first championship.

Stern got the job for a variety of reasons, not least his clairvoyance, his knack for glimpsing where sports were headed. "David," Magic Johnson said in the eighties, "has this unbelievable gift for seeing around the corner before anyone else."

Magic was right. Stern was quick to see the opportunity presented by the growing media landscape, with the explosion of cable television, and to grasp how sports could benefit from selling rights to their games. Stern recognized that as people were recording their favorite TV shows and buying cassettes of movies to watch on *their* schedules, sports were immune from this. Unpredictable, unscripted, and unchoreographed, sports were best watched live, a feature that brought with it huge value. Stern also saw the world flattening and the ability to sell the NBA not only in Ojai but also in Shanghai, Dubai, and Mumbai — and everywhere in between.

One week after Bird and Magic met for the first time in the NBA

Finals, Stern returned to New York and presided over the NBA Draft. Michael Jordan would be joining the workforce. So would a sui generis player, the charismatic and convex-shaped Charles Barkley. For good measure: that same summer in Ohio, a young woman, Gloria James, would learn that she was pregnant with her first child, a son. She would name him LeBron.

Yet even Stern, the visionary, had no idea at the time just how pivotal the summer of 1984 would become — to his sport and to all of sports. It was like one of those sequences in a game or a match or a race that passes without much fanfare. Only later would its transformational importance — its role as a *game-changer,* we would later call it — become obvious.

1

BE LIKE MIKE

He was, at once, the immovable object *and* the unstoppable force. And now he was bounding downcourt, a semi with no brakes, all that forward momentum. He was the human embodiment of the physics equation $F = ma$, force equaling mass times acceleration. Charles Barkley—all six feet, six inches and (at least) 275 pounds of him—was on his way to the basket. And only one man was in a position to stop him.

A senior-to-be at the University of North Carolina, Michael Jordan could score in abundance, and everyone knew that. But Jordan wanted to show the decision-makers and the gatekeepers at the Olympic Trials that he could also make a difference by stopping *others* from scoring. That would be the best way to survive this winnowing process and make the Olympic team.

Now, here was Jordan's chance. Spotting Barkley 75 pounds, sacrificing his body, and stopping all that forward progress . . . Jordan figured that would be the ultimate signifier of a hard-nosed team player. But as Barkley thundered in, Jordan's internal risk-analysis department reached a firm conclusion. Jordan got the hell out of the way, unwilling to absorb an impact akin to getting hit by a car. He watched passively as Barkley, who'd just finished his junior season at Auburn University, took one more dribble and dunked the ball through the hoop.

A whistle filled the air of the Indiana University Athletic Fieldhouse, where the Trials were being held. Mike Krzyzewski, the head coach of Duke, had been named an assistant coach for the Olympic Trials, tapped by Bob Knight, his onetime mentor and, at the time, close friend. Krzyzewski had yet to coach a team to a national title. In fact, at age 37, he was lucky to have a high-profile college coaching job, having survived a miserable 11-17 season in 1982–83, which ended with calls for his firing. The Duke power brokers decided to keep Krzyzewski, and "Coach K," as he was inevitably called — a merciful simplification of that Scrabble rack of a surname — made the most of his reprieve, improving to 24-10 in 1983–84, securing his position at Duke for at least a few more years.

But now Krzyzewski was stopping the scrimmage to confront Jordan, a player he knew from a series of Duke-Carolina games. "Michael, get in his way and take the charge!" Krzyzewski said firmly. Jordan arched an eyebrow and smiled wryly, wordlessly replying in the forceful yet gentle manner that Jordan had already perfected, *Man,* you *stand in his way.*

For the first round of the 1984 Olympic Trials, Barkley was the talk of the camp. He was a one-man rebuttal to every coach, parent, and teacher who preached optimal nutrition. Having heard about Knight's unyielding ways, Barkley went on a crash diet before the Trials, drinking mostly juice. When he ended up in the hospital, he said the hell with it and went back to eating everything and anything. It didn't seem to exact a price on his basketball. However improbable, he could still jump, still dunk, still rebound in traffic, still run the floor.

Barkley's physique had become both a curiosity and a source of great amusement in college basketball. Curry Kirkpatrick of *Sports Illustrated,* the glossy sports weekly that carried unrivaled institutional clout in sports media, had recently profiled Barkley. Kirkpatrick spent much of the piece describing the player's pillowy physique. A sample: "Charles Barkley, all 6'6", 272 pounds of him (before breakfast, snack, lunch, snack, supper, snack, dinner, snack, dessert, snack and midnight munchies, by which time he might be up around 400), plays the game like Porky Pig gone berserk on a trampoline."

At the Trials, Barkley was at his Barkleyest. During one of the first practices, Mark Halsel, a six-foot-six, 214-pound forward from Northeastern, made the regrettable decision to attempt blocking a Barkley dunk. "I was going to jump," Halsel said that day, "and he grabbed my face, pushed me down and dunked it in with one hand. He didn't want me to interrupt him. After that, I've been trying to be his friend."

Reporting from the Olympic Trials, Kirkpatrick, the acid *SI* scribe, was still at it. He quipped that Barkley's defender was "caught between a rock and a lard place." The players were equally amused. Joe Kleine, the center from the University of Arkansas, had heard about Barkley but was otherwise oblivious, never having seen him play, not even on television. "I wasn't alone here," Kleine recalls. "After our practices and scrimmages were over, the first thing we did was check to see where Barkley was, and hope he was still playing. 'Hey, there's a guy who weighs 300 pounds and goes coast-to-coast.' We gotta check this out."

Perhaps because he was so damn good, Barkley wasn't just fat; he was unapologetically fat, immune to the jokes. When people called him "Round Mound of Rebound" or "Leaning Tower of Pizza" or "Boy Gorge," he laughed along with them.

At the Trials, Barkley was asked about his girth and explained, "People say I eat a lot. I really don't. More or less, I just eat all the time." He mocked other players as "morbidly skinny." He put on an eating display, asking who made the best pizza in town and then eating an entire pie from Mother Bear's. The next morning, he laid waste to the breakfast buffet at the Indiana University student union, where the players were staying.

Like moths attracted to a flame, the other players were drawn to Barkley—his dorm room, his pool table. Players who had bumped against Barkley during the three daily practice sessions would race to sit at his table during meals. For those in Barkley's orbit, he seldom disappointed.

One of his favorite jokes at the time entailed telling others that he might be even better at basketball if only he had learned two important words.

After waiting a beat for the listeners to lean in and speculate on what gnomic wisdom was about to be imparted, Barkley delivered the punch line: "I'm. Full."

The Olympic head coach — the man who would ultimately be selecting the team — was less amused. Asked if he had ever had a fat player on one of his teams, Bob Knight deadpanned, "Not for long."

Apart from his weight, Barkley and Knight were, to understate it, a study in contrasts. "Uncoachable" was the word Knight muttered to his assistants, who were dazzled by this most unusual player, gibbous in shape but possessing the agility of a dancing bear. To Barkley, Knight was "a bully."

One afternoon, Knight called a meeting for 5:00 p.m. Throughout the entire camp, Knight and his assistants had stressed the virtue of punctuality. Knight arrived late to this meeting. When he finally walked in, Barkley thought he'd poke him good-naturedly. "You're ten minutes late! Where the hell have you been?" Barkley asked Knight, drawing laughs from the other players.

Anger sprung from Knight's face, which matched the color of his trademark red sweaters. Cartoon puffs of smoke may as well have come out of his nostrils. "Let me tell you something, you fat s.o.b., there's only one general in this army!"

When the first round of cuts was announced and the field of 72 players was pared to 20, Knight pulled Barkley aside to let him know personally how impressed he was with his play. And how unimpressed he was with his presentation, especially his weight. Barkley had survived this round of cuts, but then Knight added a caveat: "You can't be that heavy and play the way we want you to play. Come back at 268 pounds."

Barkley nodded.

And then Barkley went home to the South and its lard-based diet. When he returned to Bloomington three weeks later, he weighed *more* than before. But then there was this tally: when the statisticians added up the numbers, Barkley was the leader in points, rebounds, and assists.

When it was time to whittle the roster further, Knight asked the team's three assistant coaches — George Raveling, C. M. Newton, and Don Donoher — to list the players they wanted to keep on the roster. Independently, they made their lists. Independently, all three indicated that they wanted Barkley to remain. Knight hissed. "Too. Damn. Uncoachable."

A day or two later, everyone gathered for a team picture. The twenty remaining players were to stand in the middle, with the coaching staff bracketing them on the left and the right. Knight arrived wearing a pair of wing-tip shoes that Barkley deemed unfashionable. "Where did you get your granddaddy's shoes?" Barkley asked.

This drew raucous laughter from the players, (a) because it was funny and (b) because of the dynamics, the portly and charismatic 21-year-old dressing down the famously authoritarian coach. "I've never heard anyone talk to Coach Knight like that," Jordan later said. Knight was not amused. He lit into Barkley, calling him a jackass, among other epithets.

The following day, Barkley was cut. Though not by Knight. It fell to Raveling — then the head coach at Iowa and, pointedly, the only African American on the staff — to break the news. To Raveling's relief, Barkley was philosophical. He explained that all he wanted from the Olympic Trials was to play well enough to become a top-five pick in the upcoming NBA Draft, validating his decision to leave Auburn early. "I think I did that," Barkley told Raveling. "Now I can go back to Alabama. And get a good meal."

Barkley wasn't the only player who announced himself at those 1984 Olympic Trials. John Stockton looked less like an elite young basketball player than an elite youth pastor, what with his modest physique, his close-cropped jet-black hair, and shorts so short that they looked like they were purchased in the boys' department of the local sporting goods store. He played for tiny Gonzaga University, in his hometown of

Spokane, Washington. Operating in the upper left-hand corner of the country, Stockton had never competed against most of the other players at the camp. He'd averaged more than 20 points his senior season, but, it was even suggested, he was invited as much for geographic diversity as anything else.

Immediately, the players and coaches alike were impressed with the crispness of his game, and amused by just how thoroughly his appearance belied his toughness.

Draggan Mihailovich, a Chapel Hill native, had graduated from UNC the previous year. His first job out of college was as the assistant sports editor for *The Chapel Hill Newspaper.* He was assigned to cover the Trials, because two UNC players, Jordan and Sam Perkins, were both expected to be selected. After one session, the cub reporter sidled up to Jordan and asked who had impressed him the most.

"Man," Jordan said, "if I had this one little guy as my point guard, I'd score fifty points a game!"

Mihailovich was taken aback, especially since Jordan's point guard in college, Kenny Smith, was top-notch. Mihailovich wondered who it was that had impressed Jordan so deeply.

"I think they said 'John Stockton' was his name."

Mihailovich then headed over to another familiar face, Dean Smith, the venerable North Carolina coach, who, like Kyzyzewski, was on hand to help Knight. Mihailovich asked Smith the same question. *Anyone in particular catch your eye?* "This guy John Stockton is unbelievable. You see him?" Still, like Barkley, Stockton survived the first round of cuts but not the second.

Ironically, Stockton's future collaborator—another unsung player from a little-known school—called attention to himself as well. Karl Malone was a strapping power forward from Louisiana Tech, then best known for its women's basketball program. The son of a general store owner who chewed tobacco (and that was his mother), Malone was, by his own admission, a "country kid."

At the Trials he projected a sense of awe at the collection of talent.

"They said they was gettin' the best 72," he announced, in his trademark country twang and diction, "and they wasn't tellin' no stories."

But he held his own against far more prominent—that is, far more televised—talent. Only a sophomore, Malone didn't make the cuts. But coach after coach told him that if he continued working hard, he stood a real chance of making it to the NBA one day.

Still, one player, unmistakably, soared above the others, literally and figuratively. Michael Jordan arrived with an aura. And it was undiminished when he left. It started with the basketball itself. Jordan wasn't merely *good;* he was effortlessly good. He hit shots that other players would never attempt, much less make. He saw angles unapparent to everyone else. He could handle the ball and penetrate as well as the point guards. He could score from any coordinate on the court, shooting as well as the best of the shooting guards. He could drive to the basket and elevate better than any of the small forwards.

Barkley had put on a show. But even Barkley conceded that if you considered any dimension of basketball—speed, quickness, explosiveness, hang time once airborne—Jordan was a superior species. Before the three-point shot rose to prominence, the dunk was the coin of the basketball realm. As every hidebound coach—ever—has pointed out, the dunk is worth no more points than a simple layup. But, especially to players, it has always come with extra-emphasis style points that may not register on the scoreboard but count nonetheless.

And here, too, Jordan was a singular talent. He could dunk in transition, dunk in the half-court set, dunk after clearing out his side of the court like a traffic cop and beating his defender off the dribble. After the scrimmages, Jordan would continue dunking, winning impromptu contests and coming up with new and creative ways to elevate, press his wrist to the rim, and stuff the ball through, violently yet elegantly.

In 1984, print media was at its height. Newspapers were operating on 35 percent profit margins and spent lavishly, dispatching journalists on assignments. More than 200 sportswriters from all over the country had descended on Bloomington to cover the Olympic Trials. Mark

Heisler, basketball writer for the *Los Angeles Times,* was among the media contingent. Awed by watching Jordan in a scrimmage, he turned to a colleague and declared simply, "That is the most beautiful, graceful basketball player I have ever seen."

To the coaches, Jordan may have been at his most impressive on the defensive end. He may have chickened out by declining to sacrifice his body to impede an oncoming Charles Barkley, but otherwise he was, critically, as adept at preventing points from being scored as he was at scoring them himself. He would use his wingspan — which, distorting Vitruvian Man, exceeded his height by five inches — to steal the ball. He relied on quickness to prevent his man from driving. He called upon his jumping ability to contest shots and rebound. When the coaches at the Trials wanted to test the offensive prowess of other players, they assigned Jordan to guard them.

What really made Jordan *Jordan,* though: his disposition. Jordan projected ferocious competitiveness. He played as though his very salvation rested on the outcome of every scrimmage, never mind game. But he also discharged his duties with such joy, smiling and winking and playfully slapping the backs of teammates and opponents. "Even then," says Barkley, "Michael smiled while he killed you."

This mirrored his temperament away from basketball. He was cool, but not too cool. Just when it seemed that Jordan might scan cocky, he would pull back. Friends recall him driving a 1976 Grand Prix — emblazoned with a vanity plate, MAGIC JORDAN — around the UNC campus that spring. But he would honk at classmates when he passed and, without inhibition, wave out the window.

Jordan invested in his appearance, wearing gold chains and collared Polo Ralph Lauren shirts and Bermuda shorts and shoes without socks, then the height of preppy vogue. When he spoke to the media in his rolling voice, he would start with prescripted pablum; but he could never stay in character and soon began smiling expansively and launching missiles of candor.

At the Trials, he was both god and mortal. He was perceived with a sense of awe, but he was happy to shoot pool with other players, swap good-natured insults, and generally stitch himself into the social fabric. As *Sports Illustrated* put it, "It was almost eerie how Jordan passed through the Trials virtually unmentioned. The North Carolina junior is so marvelous a talent, possessing such a perfect basketball body that his status high above the rest was simply taken for granted."

It was, in fact, such a given that Jordan would make the Olympic team that, in April, ABC Sports sent a crew to Chapel Hill to shoot a profile piece that would air during the network's coverage of the Games in August. Draggan Mihailovich, the cub Chapel Hill newspaper reporter, had known Jordan from covering UNC. He also knew Jordan's parents, who, reliably, were in the stands to watch their son, from the UNC home games to the Cable Car Classic in San Francisco. So it was that ABC asked Mihailovich if he could assist with the shoot. Happy for the experience in television, happy for the extra cash, and happy to spend some time with Jordan, Mihailovich agreed.

One of the segments entailed shooting Jordan as he dunked. As the crew scampered off to find the right camera equipment, Mihailovich sat with Jordan at midcourt of Carmichael Auditorium, the UNC basketball venue. They chatted easily, and Jordan was generous with his time. But eventually he grew antsy waiting for the crew to set up. And, as Jordan tended to do, he broke up the boredom with competition. Specifically, a wager.

"Want to bet I can make a half-court shot?" Jordan asked.

From his time covering the Tar Heels, Mihailovich knew that Jordan was a heroic gambler. He recalled card games in airports, watching Jordan steal glances at his teammates' concealed hands, only to accuse *them* of cheating.

Mihailovich also remembered the time that three Carolina players were marooned in a Charlottesville hotel room, relaxing the night before a game against Virginia by playing a casual game of bridge. When it was suggested that Jordan join the group as a fourth, the other players waved off the idea. Jordan was playing poker with another teammate, Curtis

Hunter. This was an entirely different level of gambling, and their game would extend into the a.m. hours. Or at least until the UNC assistant coach in charge of bed checks, Roy Williams, walked by.

That afternoon in Chapel Hill, Mihailovich knew that he had to keep Jordan engaged. He responded, “What do you want to bet?”

“How about a grape soda?” said Jordan.

“Sure.”

With that, Jordan stood, grabbed the ball, took a few dribbles, and let loose something that was neither a heave nor a jump shot.

Swish.

Jordan circled the court, jumping and punching the air with his fist.*

Then MJ grinned tightly and waited a beat. “Let’s go double or nothing.”

“Two grape sodas?” Mihailovich asked.

“Nah,” said Jordan. “Dinner this time.”

Mihailovich considered the prospects. Two straight half-court shots — that was highly improbable. And, worst-case scenario, he was eating dinner with Michael Jordan.

“Deal.”

Smiling coyly as if this were a con and he knew the outcome in advance, Jordan took the ball and began dribbling. Again he put up a heave/shot that seemed to lick the rafters of the arena. Again the ball flitted through the hoop, without so much as brushing against the rim.

Swish.

“Okay,” Jordan said. “Now, this time —”

“No ‘*this time*,’ Michael,” Mihailovich said, cutting him off. “We’re done.”

---

* A half decade later, Jordan would famously hit a hanging, buzzer-beating jump shot over the hapless Cleveland Cavaliers defender Craig Ehlo. Jordan would celebrate in a manner that Mihailovich, watching at home, recognized instantly from that day at Carmichael.

2

THE GREAT ONE

Designating an athlete as "great" suffers from laziness and vagueness. There are no parameters for *great,* no agreed-upon definition. *Great,* like beauty, resides in the eye of the beholder. Over the accrued years, all of the great plays and great games and great shots and great seasons have weakened the word's descriptive powers, weak to begin with.

Yet in the case of Wayne Gretzky, he was conferred the perfect nickname: "The Great One." Simple and elegant, with the "One" doing the heavy lifting.

Gretzky's primacy was almost predestined. Unlike so many kids who ultimately grow and evolve to become exceptional hockey players, Gretzky was a prodigy. At age two he first skated, dashing around a rink that his father, Walter, had fashioned in the garden of the family home in Ontario. At age six, he held his own playing alongside the best 10-year-olds in the area. When Gretzky turned 10, he scored 378 goals in one Pee-Wee season. At 16, he was the world's best player under 20. When, at 17, he signed his first professional contract, it was before a crowd of 12,000.

His skills were luxurious, but in a numinous, abstract way. He was not especially fast. At six feet tall and 160 pounds, he was not much of a physical presence. Power? He would finish dead last in team strength tests. *Sports Illustrated* described him as being "as normally proportioned as the newspaperboy."

But there was magic to his play. His instincts, his hand-eye coordination, his decision-making, his intelligence, his poise . . . they were immediately and manifestly obvious. Gretzky scored goals ritually, almost devotionally. He distributed the puck masterfully, giddy about finding open teammates when he was double-teamed. He performed trick after trick, his blond mullet poking out from under his helmet and trailing like a kite's tail, just above that quirky jersey number, 99, that he had chosen in double honor of his idol Gordie Howe's number 9.

Gretzky turned pro in the old World Hockey Association (WHA), first (briefly) playing for the Indianapolis Racers and then with the Edmonton Oilers. The Great One played his first game, and an essay in the program sold in the arena gushed, "Watching him play hockey [is] probably a little like hearing Mozart play a piano at five or Einstein recite mathematical tables at seven."

Born as he was on January 26, 1961, Gretzky turned 18 in the middle of this historically surpassing season, making him the youngest professional athlete in North American team sports. In 1979, four WHA teams — the Hartford Whalers, Quebec Nordiques, Winnipeg Jets, and Edmonton Oilers — were absorbed by the NHL, transforming it into a 21-team league. The Oilers' crafty owner, Peter Pocklington, had not signed Gretzky to a conventional WHA player contract, but rather a "professional services" contract, so Gretzky remained in Edmonton and was not eligible to all teams, as the other WHA players were.

Inevitably, there were questions about how well Gretzky would make the transition. Specifically, was he strong enough and tough enough for the best hockey league in the world?

But again, Gretzky's performance didn't suffer against this higher class of competition. And again, he delivered a fusillade of goals, 51 of them, in the 1979–80 season on an Oilers team that was quickly on the rise, thanks largely to its transcendent young star. Often, Gretzky set up more goals than he scored, complementing his 51 goals with 86 assists.

Since Maurice "Rocket" Richard achieved the feat in 1945, decades had passed with no NHL player scoring 50 goals in 50 games; it was thought to be one of those never-to-be-broken records on the order of Wilt Chamberlain's 100-point game in basketball. Then, during the 1980–81 season, Mike Bossy scored 50 goals in 50 games. In 1981–82, Gretzky scored his 50th goal in his *39th* game. He finished that 80-game season scoring 92 goals and distributing 120 assists, for a record 212 points. Mike Bossy of the Islanders, the NHL's second-leading scorer that season, had the fourth-highest point total (147) in league *history*, and he *trailed* Gretzky by 65 points.

In 1982–83, Gretzky registered "only" 71 goals and 125 assists, for 196 points. Before he turned 22, Gretzky had been named league MVP three times and held 27 NHL records. Gordie Howe was next, with 14 records — and he had played 26 NHL seasons over four decades.

"He was great to cover; and sometimes he was so great that he was hard to cover," says Terry Jones, sports columnist for the *Edmonton Sun*. "Every night he'd do something and you'd say, 'Now I've seen it all.' Then he would do something just as amazing the next night. And you'd say, 'I just used *incredible* or whatever last game; how can I possibly describe this game?'"

Most accounts and profiles of Gretzky from the time simply cited his statistics, letting math rather than prose tell the story. But when the hockey salon took to exploring what, specifically, made the Great One great, it turned to the fine arts (*maestro, artist, ballet dancer on skates*), to the supernatural (*magician, sorcerer*), to meteorology (*Hurricane Gretzky touched down in Chicago, scoring three goals*).

Yet, familiar as Gretzky was becoming to hockey fans, he was also operating at a remove. Some of this was Gretzky's own doing. He was thoroughly pleasant, but thoroughly free of friction, the antithesis of what journalists call "a good quote." His discomfort with air travel was about as sensational a storyline as you could hope to find. Jones recalls that the Oilers would win a game, say, 4–2, Gretzky scoring a hat trick and a "plumber" knocking in the other goal. Afterwards, Gretzky would emerge last from the showers, ensuring that the teammate got the post-game glory from the media.

Beyond Gretzky's modesty, the Oilers played their home games in Alberta, far geographically and, almost immeasurably, far culturally from tastemakers in New York and Los Angeles. And the team played in the mountain time zone, two hours removed from the two major Canadian media markets of Montreal and Toronto. American hockey fans had to dig in the corners to find televised games. *Hockey Night in Canada* did not yet have a western doubleheader. (Canada's The Sports Network, or TSN, didn't launch until September 1, 1984.) A thought exercise: What would the profile of Gretzky — young, blond, handsome, strenuously inoffensive — have been had he spent his prime in Toronto, never mind New York, instead of bracingly cold Alberta?

Unless Gretzky was playing against your team and you attended the game in person, you were unlikely to see him play — and dazzle and change the game. That Gretzky was a player of the imagination, a mythical figure whose incredible statistics — literally straining credulity — only added to the folklore. Michael Farber would become a dean of hockey writing. But in the early eighties, marooned on the East Coast of the United States, his coverage of Gretzky mostly entailed grabbing a newspaper, hoping the Oilers' result had made the late-edition deadline, and then scouring the scoring summary, much as he had scanned the newspaper baseball box scores as a boy in the late 1950s and '60s to check whether Hank Aaron had hit a home run the night before.

With each successive season, though, Gretzky's star brightened. In their (and Gretzky's) first season in the league, the Oilers were the NHL's worst road draw. Within two years, thanks overwhelmingly to Gretzky, the Oilers were the NHL's strongest road draw.

Eventually, Gretzky was discovered by sports marketers and landed endorsements with brands like Mattel and General Mills, which enabled him to double his $1 million playing salary. He hired an assistant — the mother of his girlfriend at the time, the Canadian singer Vikki Moss — to help make inroads with the 5,000 pieces of fan mail he received each month.

In 1982, he was named the *Sports Illustrated* Sportsman of the Year, an honor that had recently been bestowed on the likes of Jack Nicklaus, Terry Bradshaw, Sugar Ray Leonard, and the Miracle on Ice U.S. Olympic hockey team. Gretzky was only 21 years old. Then again, he had already cracked the top 10 on the NHL's *all-time* scoring list.

In Edmonton, he moved into a penthouse duplex on the 17th floor of a building not far from the arena. There was no hot tub or pool table or large-screen television. The great extravagance? A baby grand piano. Two works of art figured prominently on the walls: an Andy Warhol portrait of Marilyn Monroe and a Warhol painting of Gretzky himself. Before the 1984 season, Gretzky had met Warhol. They first struck up a deal — Warhol would create six paintings of Gretzky, who was allowed to keep one of them for himself — and then struck up an unlikely friendship, a source of ribbing from his teammates.

For all of Gretzky's slowly blossoming celebrity, by 1984 it had started to come with a tinge of skepticism. He was the Great One, no doubt. But could he make his team a great one? The NHL betrays a reflexive — almost pathological — bias toward the team over the individual. From Pee-Wee league to the NHL, countless locker rooms come adorned with some variation of this bromide: "It's not the name on the back of the sweater that's important; it's the name on the front."

For all the records Gretzky was not simply breaking but mocking, there was this inconvenient truth: he had won zero Stanley Cups.

Foreshadowing the challenge Michael Jordan would confront a few years later, the tension was over whether Gretzky could achieve something more profound than mere video-game stats, astonishing and compelling as they were. Could he win — or, more optimistically, how *quickly* could he win — the Stanley Cup?

Already there had been, by turns, moments of encouragement and discouragement. In 1982, Edmonton was upset by the Los Angeles Kings in the first round of the playoffs, losing three games, including the "Miracle on Manchester," in which the Kings scored six unanswered goals, five in the third period, consecrating the greatest (that word again) comeback in hockey history. A year later, Edmonton progressed to the Stanley Cup Finals but lost to the Islanders, who won for the fourth-straight year.

The clinching game of the 1983 Stanley Cup was played at the Nassau Coliseum, a charmless, featureless sweatbox in suburbia that, even in the early 1980s, was starting to show its age. The cramped dressing rooms for both the Islanders and the visitors dotted the same corridor, only 20 or so yards apart. Gretzky recalled that after the game, he walked dejectedly past the Islanders' dressing room. He expected to see raucous celebration. And he did — from the players' friends and family members. The Islanders themselves were tending to their injuries, icing bruises and walking gingerly. They had finished a marathon and were more relieved than they were giddy.

"After they won, they were too beat up to really enjoy it and savor the victory at that moment," said Gretzky. "We were able to walk out of there pretty much scot-free. We had so much respect for the Islanders players and the Islanders teams that we learned immediately you have to take it to another level in order to win a Stanley Cup. And that's what we did. We learned from it and often credit the Islanders players and Islanders teams for teaching us exactly what it's all about and how hard it is to win."

By the 1983–84 season, the Edmonton Oilers had officially become the eye candy of the NHL. An upstart all-sports network, ESPN, began airing occasional Oilers games. Gretzky was, again, incandescent, scoring 87 goals and distributing 118 assists for 205 points. (He did this playing only 74 games of the 80-game schedule, so on a points-per-game basis, he actually exceeded his record 1981–82 rate.)

And during that season, Gretzky started a points streak, scoring a goal or dishing out an assist in 10 straight games. Then 20 . . . then 30 . . . then 40 . . .

Maybe the ultimate testament at the time: figures outside of the hockey ecosystem took notice. In January of 1984, Terry Jones, the Edmonton sports columnist, left the Oilers to cover the Super Bowl in Tampa. He was connecting flights in Minneapolis when someone yelled, “It’s Mr. Coffey!”

What the hell is the NHL star Paul Coffey doing in the Minneapolis airport? wondered Jones. Then he realized: he’d misheard. The passenger meant Mr. Coffee, as in Joe DiMaggio, the brand’s endorser, who also was headed to the Super Bowl aboard the same flight.

Jones was struck by inspiration. Why not approach DiMaggio—whose 56-game hitting streak for the Yankees during the 1941 season persists as a baseball record—and ask him about Gretzky’s streak?

When Jones approached him as the passengers were boarding, the 69-year-old legend demurred. But midway through the flight, a stewardess tapped Jones on the shoulder and mentioned that he had been summoned to first class. DiMaggio was waiting with an empty seat next to him, having reconsidered Jones’s request. He had been following Wayne and knew that his streak was extraordinary. Instead of Jones interviewing DiMaggio, Joltin’ Joe began peppering the reporter with questions. *What’s the kid like? How’s he holding up?*

Finally, after 51 games, Gretzky’s streak ended, leaving behind a record every bit as unbreakable as DiMaggio’s consecutive-game hit streak.

As for Gretzky’s orchestra, he was accompanied by Mark Messier, Paul Coffey, Glenn Anderson, and Jari Kurri, an embarrassment of offensive riches. Along with goalie Grant Fuhr, *five* Gretzky teammates would eventually make the Hall of Fame. The Oilers won 57 games; the next closest team, the Islanders, won 50. But now the entire team had been implicated in the Gretzky analysis.

The Oilers, like the Great One, were a joy to watch. But could they win? "Did they have the royal jelly, the grit to win tough games in the playoffs?" recalls Farber. "Everyone knew they could outscore you and [goalie] Grant Fuhr could make the big, timely save. But could they win tough, low-scoring games?"

Inevitably, the Oilers and the Islanders rematched in the Stanley Cup Finals. The contrasts were more vivid than ever. Champion versus ambitious challenger. Experience versus youth. Science versus art. Style versus substance. The Oilers dazzled. The Islanders were comfortable winning slogfests and, if need be, slugfests. Which is why the *tenor* of Game 1, as much as the outcome of Game 1, dictated the entire series. The Islanders again stifled Gretzky with their brutish, physical defense. But the Islanders committed a rare mistake, turning the puck over early in the third period. Kevin McClelland — who had scored only eight goals in the regular season — scooped it up and poked it past the left arm of Islanders goalie Billy Smith. It would stand as the only goal of the game.

After being swept in the previous Cup, Edmonton had finally won a game from the mighty Islanders. What's more, they won with "Islander-style" hockey — short on beauty but long on opportunism. With typical modesty, Gretzky says today that winning the first game turned the series, never mind that he was stifled every minute he spent on the ice.

The Islanders won Game 2 handily, 6–1. Gretzky did not have a point in the first two games. But the series was tied 1–1 as they headed to Edmonton for three games.* Northlands Coliseum was not a fabled NHL arena. Constructed in the early seventies for 17.3 million Canadian dollars,† it had little in the way of architectural charm. With a seating capacity of 17,498, it ranked among the NHL's smallest venues. But it was loud as hell. And playing amid a din that rivaled the rock concerts held at Northlands, the Oilers won the Cup. In Game 3, Gretzky tallied two

---

* The NHL switched from its 2-3-2 home format to its current 2-2-1-1-1 format in 1986.

† Even converted to 2019 dollars and U.S. currency, this is a risibly inexpensive $90 million.

assists as the Oilers showed their offensive firepower and won 7–2. He scored a goal in Game 4, another 7–2 victory. In the clinching Game 5, he scored a pair of first-period goals and assisted on a goal in the second. When Edmonton closed out the series, winning 5–2, ushers were distributing toilet paper so fans had the option of plugging their ears and preventing future hearing loss.

It was late on a Saturday night in May. The outcome didn't much pierce the American sports consciousness, but it was bedlam in western Canada. The fans were witnessing Edmonton's first NHL championship after just five years in the league. But, it turned out, they were also on hand for one of the great NHL plot points. The Islanders, somewhat overlooked by history, had finally been dethroned, losing their first playoff series of the decade, the run of titles stopped at four. But on this night, another dynasty was christened.

It's not simply that the Oilers would win four Stanley Cups between then and 1988. Here was the highest-scoring team ever to win the Cup. Here was the first team west of the Mississippi to win the Cup. Grant Fuhr, the goalie, was the first Black man to win a Stanley Cup.

But beyond the factoids, this title marked an aesthetic change. Here was a team that might not entertain with a brawl, or with the kind of violence that both gave hockey a bad name and made it relevant. Instead, the Oilers dazzled even casual fans with slick play and sorcery and offense — all being carried out by likable figures. "We proved that an offensive team can win the Cup," Gretzky said. "We showed you can win by skating and by being physical without having to fight all the time."

Gretzky had his scoring and his inexorable assault on hockey's records. He had his unbroken string of personal successes. But now he was officially certified. His name was to be engraved on the Stanley Cup.

Now — less than midway through 1984 and his 23rd year — the Great One was better than great. He was now something else entirely: a champion. And the greater sports world would start to pay attention.

In 1984, the Edmonton Oilers decided that, instead of passing the Stanley Cup around among themselves, they'd hold a show-and-tell around western Canada. It was the rare Canadian who didn't recognize the Stanley Cup as a totem, a symbol of excellence. But the object itself was seldom given real thought. Most fans never dreamed that they would ever see it in person, especially not in 1984 in Edmonton, which hadn't even had an NHL franchise a few years prior.

But suddenly the Cup was being passed throughout town and fans were seeing it, touching it, drinking from it, balancing it on their heads. This was the year "Lord Stanley's Mug" started to become the most traveled sports trophy in the world as winning teams went to great lengths to come up with new and creative ways to show off the trophy while "supervising" it during the off-season. All thanks to the Oilers in the summer of 1984.

When the Oilers' defenseman Randy Gregg married Canadian Olympic speed skater Kathleen Vogt on June 9, 1984, the Cup was prominently featured at the wedding. After the honeymoon, Gregg would take the Cup for a walk in his Edmonton neighborhood. Glenn Anderson, a right wing, took the Cup to Northlands Park, a local racetrack. Mark Messier took the Cup to his hometown of St. Albert, Alberta, 10 miles from Edmonton. He headed to the Bruin Inn, a local bar. It was the middle of the afternoon and only a half dozen patrons were in the joint; within an hour, the place was packed. The Cup toured senior citizen homes and funeral homes, golf clubs, and strip clubs, where it would appear onstage with an exotic dancer. One night it had too much fun and ended up dented. No problem: the guys who worked the body shop at Freedom Ford did the cosmetic repair work for free.

The NHL overlords did not hear about these adventures and misadventures until weeks — sometimes years — later. But if they preferred that the league's cherished trophy not get dinged up at a strip club, still they applauded the spirit. The Stanley Cup is a people's trophy, one that belongs to players and coaches and teams, but also to the fans. If seeing and touching the Cup strengthened the connection between a town and a team, between fans and a sport, why not take it on the road?

In the years to come, the Cup would cross countries and cross oceans.

It would show up in war zones, in the hope that its mere sight would elevate the morale of troops. (Once, in Afghanistan, the Cup passed through a military base just as it came under enemy fire.) It's been used for baptisms and as a feed bowl for a Kentucky Derby winner. It's been placed on late-night television show couches; atop floats during gay pride parades; alongside presidents and world leaders. It's seen the bottom of a swimming pool and the insides of many more strip clubs. The tradition was really hardened after the Oilers won their first Cup. "Stanley had had some episodes in the past," says Terry Jones, the longtime columnist for the *Edmonton Sun*. "But he'd never had half as much fun as he did that summer of 1984."

3

ARE THE GAMES DEAD?

It had to be the *least* compelling competition in the history of the Olympic movement. The bid to host the Games often becomes a pitched battle, pitting one world capital against another world capital — often with significant capital changing hands. But the derby to host the 1984 Summer Games came down to two disparate municipalities: Los Angeles and . . . Tehran.

L.A. was desperate to host, having submitted bids for the Summer Games in 1948, 1952, 1956, 1976, and 1980. When all of those were unsuccessful, L.A. still volunteered to serve as a "stand-by" if any scheduled host had to cancel unexpectedly. As for the Iranian bid, it was made when the shah was still in power. When he was overthrown in 1978, triggering great civil unrest, the bid was withdrawn. So it was that Los Angeles didn't *win* the right to host the 1984 Summer Olympics so much as the city got the Games by default.

Then again, at the time, the Olympic flame was flickering unsteadily. The Munich Olympics of 1972 were recalled foremost for the 11 Israeli athletes massacred by a group of Palestinian terrorists. The legacy of the 1976 Games in Montreal was not heroic athletic achievement but heroic expense: an event slated to cost $250 million carried a final price tag of $1.4 billion, and Canadians wouldn't discharge this debt until the fall of 2006, thirty years after the closing ceremonies. The United States was among the 65 countries to boycott the 1980 Games in Moscow, an incursion — however justified — of geopolitics into sports.

Some went so far as to predict that the 23rd Olympics would mark the *last* Olympics ever held. On May 21, 1984, *Newsweek* posed an existential question on its cover: "Are the Games Dead?"

Once L.A. was awarded the Games, in 1978, the discussion pivoted to who should run them. There was an entire slate of insider candidates. Tom Bradley, mayor of Los Angeles, had his man: Edwin Steidle, chairman of the May Company, a California department store chain. Other names bandied about included Lee Iacocca, the popular auto executive and globalist, NFL Commissioner Pete Rozelle, and Al Haig, who would not get the post but soon afterwards would settle for the position of U.S. secretary of state.

Then came another candidate.

An executive at Korn Ferry, an international consulting firm retained by the Los Angeles Olympic Organizing Committee (LAOOC), approached a local businessman, Peter Ueberroth, then 42, and asked if he would be interested. Ueberroth's first instinct: it was a prank. He looked over his shoulder suspiciously and asked, "Are you from *Candid Camera*?"

Ueberroth was both an inspired choice and an unusual one. His upbringing had been both unconventional and challenging in the extreme. His mother died of leukemia when he was four. His father, a salesman for Sears, broke his leg teaching his daughter how to skate; when he missed time from work, Sears let him go. As a teenager, Peter spent time living and working in an orphanage. It all instilled in him personal discipline, a serious, measured disposition, and the sense that life was a serious undertaking.

A skilled college water polo player — Ueberroth broke his nose five times during his career, never corrected the bend, and, later, allowed cameras to shoot him from only one side — he had a tryout for the 1956 Olympic team. Unsuccessful, he entered corporate America, in the travel services sector. By age 22 he was a vice president at Trans International Airlines, an Oakland-based charter. He moved to L.A. to start his own business, and, before he turned 40, he had built his travel company into an enterprise with 1,500 employees and $300 million in gross revenues.

A natural-born leader, Ueberroth was far more interested in building his company and hitting financial goals than in being a part of Hollywood royalty and the Southern California social scene. All of this appealed to the L.A. Olympic search committee. There were plenty of showbiz schmoozers in town. The organizers needed an ambitious, hard-charging, and, not least, disciplined business executive.

When Ueberroth got the job — receiving one more vote than Steidle from the board and the search committee — he was as surprised as anyone. He couldn't even celebrate with his wife, Ginny, as she had taken their four kids on a ski trip. "If I thought you'd win, I'd stay behind," she told him before departing. He sold his travel company for $10.4 million and took over as organizer, declining a salary in favor of a bonus.

Ueberroth's vast challenges were compounded by the political climate, both globally and in Los Angeles. He made it a goal to attract as many countries as possible. Some of this was philosophical: an international sporting event should be truly *international.* But there were also coldly rational considerations. The more countries that participated, the more valuable the Olympics would be in the marketplace. Avoiding a Soviet boycott was essential. If the Soviet Union and other Communist countries stayed away, it would not only undercut volume, but deprive the Games of rivalry and a sports prism for Cold War tensions.

More locally, Los Angeles voters had made it abundantly clear that if the city were to host the Games again — having done so once, in 1932 — it was not going to be on the public's dime. Unlike Montreal, which built new venues for the 1976 Olympics and was left with a herd of white elephants, Los Angeles was going to have to use 23 existing facilities.

In keeping with Reagan's America, Ueberroth wouldn't (and couldn't) rely on government. So he would rely instead on the private sector and free enterprise — "the magic of the marketplace," he called it.

If this had the effect of commercializing amateurism, of profaning something that had been perceived as pure and idealistic, so be it.

Ueberroth had a two-pronged plan. He would rely heavily on sponsorships. And he would rely heavily on television rights fees. When Lake Placid, New York, hosted the Winter Olympics in 1980, there had been nearly 400 sponsors — but only $10 million raised in revenue. If you were a toothpaste company, you would donate tubes for all the athletes and, presto, you were an Olympic sponsor. Ueberroth's model entailed far fewer sponsors for far more money. For a minimum of $4 million each, 30 sponsors would have exclusive use of the Olympics logo for their product lines.

With no real budget and no real office, Ueberroth held meetings in a Century Plaza coffee shop. He arranged to meet with Coca-Cola and Pepsi, but insisted that the CEOs show up. Finally, he asked them to submit sealed bids. Coke offered up a bid of $12.6 million and won the auction.

Kodak balked at the sponsorship price and offered only $2 million, daring Ueberroth to make a deal with a company based outside the United States. He obliged. Fuji, of Japan, agreed to pay $7 million to process all the new film on-site at the Games, and became an official sponsor. It wasn't the only time he called a bluff. When the Los Angeles Memorial Sports Arena dallied in signing an agreement to host basketball, Ueberroth called Lakers owner Jerry Buss and made the Forum, in Inglewood, the venue. The Sports Arena executives sheepishly agreed to host boxing instead.

When Ueberroth realized that there was no velodrome in Southern California capable of holding the cycling competitions, he hatched a plan and got 7-Eleven and its parent company, Southland Corporation, to agree to build a brand-new bicycle track. Ueberroth then called Don Gerth, president of California State University Dominguez Hills, with an offer: would his campus in Carson, California, 15 miles south of downtown L.A., be interested in hosting the Olympic velodrome? Gerth was thrilled to be part of the Olympic experience. "We'll take it!" Gerth said enthusiastically, before pausing to ask a reasonable question: "What is a velodrome?"

In keeping with the theme of sports in the summer of 1984, Ueberroth was also among those who grasped the power, the promise, and the profit of television. The L.A. Organizing Committee advisory board told Ueberroth that they expected to net $100 million from broadcasting rights. Ueberroth did not respond but took control of the bidding. He asked for $200 million plus equipment and facilities for international broadcasters. He insisted that the five bidding entities deposit $750,000 into an interest-bearing account while the process played out. ABC won the bidding for $225 million — plus they agreed to commit $75 million in production fees and facilities, in essence making it a $300 million bid.

A true insight into Ueberroth came next. The International Olympic Committee was entitled to $33 million of the broadcast fee. Ueberroth knew that the IOC's lawyer was about to leave on a business trip and wouldn't be able to deposit the check for another day. So he held off on sending the check for one day, knowing that the delay would net the L.A. Organizing Committee $9,000 in interest. As it turned out, the IOC didn't cash the check for 20 days.

Ueberroth was also committed to keeping the Games free of politics. He rejected proposals for a red-white-and-blue color scheme on the grounds that it scanned as too nationalistic. He went with pastel colors and hot pink instead* — "Festive Federalism," the assigned design team called it. Tacky as the design may have been to many, the colors were chosen largely because they did not appear in many national flags.

Above all, fearful that the Soviet Bloc countries would boycott the

* Though the Los Angeles Memorial Coliseum was painted magenta, the L.A. Organizing Committee promised that the surfaces would return to tan before the NFL's L.A. Raiders returned in the fall.

Games, Ueberroth made multiple trips to Russia and answered questions about everything from security to concerns about air quality.*

Ueberroth's other great triumph was the torch relay. In order to spread the gospel of the Olympics — and, of course, give the sponsors some added value — the LAOOC arranged for the Olympic torch to wend its way across the country. The torch would be lit in Greece, the ancestral homeland of the Olympics, then would arrive in early May in the United States. And for the 80 days before the opening ceremonies, a battalion of 3,600 runners (clothed in Levi's apparel and shod in Converse sneakers) would carry the torch across America — through gleaming cities, under spacious skies, to purple mountain majesties, above the fruited plains.

On May 8, the torch relay began on the East Side of Manhattan — symbolically, a block from the United Nations. There, Gina Hemphill, the 22-year-old granddaughter of Olympian Jesse Owens, and Bill Thorpe Jr., 27, the grandson of Native American Olympian Jim Thorpe, lit the torch and ran with it for the first kilometer.

And then, three hours later, TASS, the Russian news agency, issued a release. Timed for maximum embarrassment, dousing the spirit of the torch relay, the Soviet Union and most of the Eastern Bloc countries sent word that they were boycotting the 1984 Summer Games.

---

* When Soviet swimmer Vladimir Salnikov broke a world record in the 800-meter freestyle at a race in Los Angeles in July 1983, the Soviet complaints about bad air ceased.

4

JOHNNY MAC AND MARTINA

There's a great and abiding irony to the French Open. The august tennis venue in Paris is named not for a player but for a Gallic World War I aviator. The grounds are plastered with images of Roland Garros flying his prop planes, posed dashingly in his aviator goggles, themes of flight and elevation in abundance.

And yet the tournament itself is the essence of terrestrial: all ground, no air. The court surface is earth itself, a mixture of soil and crushed brick. And there is nothing ethereal about clay-court tennis. It is trench warfare, all toil and trouble, grinding and burrowing. Literally, dirty work.

June 10, 1984, marked a classic French Open tennis ground campaign — and one of the great upsets in tennis history. Having won the first two sets of the men's final, John McEnroe, in all his wondrous talent, was on the threshold of winning his maiden French Open title, another tournament in his celestial season.

McEnroe ruled the tennis roost. He was McBrat and McNasty, cleaving public opinion, helping the public grow familiar with the concept of the antisocial athlete. But in the summer of 1984, his "genius" was smothering his "tortured." He played with flair and artistry and creativity and angles, carving up the men's circuit on his way to 13 titles by year's end. On account of his singular game and singular temperament, he was approaching full-on global celebrity status.

In Paris, a camera crew was trailing him for what was being called a "sports documentary," a concept that was difficult for other players in the locker room to grasp. McEnroe was also trailed by a phalanx of representatives and middlemen and plenipotentiaries from Nike, the upstart and irreverent Oregon shoe company — a disruptor, it might be called in a later era — whose executives had realized that the cult of personality could help move product.

McEnroe was shod in Nikes but clad in a different brand (Sergio Tacchini), and Nike reps were tasked by their boss, Phil Knight, to make sure that McEnroe would be decked out in Nike clothes, head to toe. Nike had recently gone so far as to render McEnroe a tennis-playing, crossover-cool James Dean walking the streets of New York in posters — a chief form of marketing at the time — with the tagline "Rebel with a Cause."*

McEnroe's opponent in that French Open final, the dour Czech Ivan Lendl, had a reputation as an underachiever, having lost the previous four Grand Slam finals that he'd played. Ivan the Terrible Choker, he was called. It looked like he was at it again. Projecting nervousness while McEnroe played his precise-as-a-surgeon tennis, Lendl dropped the first two sets, 6–3, 6–2.

Inside the locker room, McEnroe's kid brother, Patrick, was preparing to play his match in the boys' doubles final on Court 1. (One of his opponents was a mop-topped German redhead, Boris Becker.) An official entered the room and said encouragingly to the four juniors, "If the [McEnroe-Lendl] match keeps going this fast, we're putting you on after them."

---

* McEnroe, ironically, would clad himself in Nike later that year but would never win another major after 1984.

Before 17-year-old Patrick McEnroe could get too giddy — about the prospects of his brother winning the French Open or the prospects of playing on Court Philippe Chatrier, one of tennis's seminal venues — Lendl stormed back to level the match at two sets apiece, summoning reserves of courage that had never before been in evidence and relishing the attritional battle.

Assigned to Court 1 after all, and playing in front of a half dozen fans, Patrick McEnroe could hear the roars emanating from the stadium and understand the French of the PA announcer. Midway through his doubles match, Patrick McEnroe deduced that his brother had lost. Which was confirmed a few moments later, when his parents arrived, "looking whiter than ghosts — and they were white to begin with." Lendl had beaten McEnroe, 3–6, 2–6, 6–4, 7–5, 7–5.

Patrick McEnroe and his partner, Luke Jensen, won the boys' doubles title, beating Boris Becker and another young German. But, as Patrick says gamely, "if the McEnroe family went one-and-one that day, this wasn't the one we wanted." At a postmortem dinner that night, John McEnroe was disconsolate. Every bit the doe-eyed teenager, Patrick tried to cheer his brother up. "You'll come back and win it next."

"No," said John, not in a self-pitying tone but as if he were simply speaking about an immutable truth. "That was it. That was my chance. And I blew it. I will never win this." And he wouldn't.

Suddenly emboldened, Lendl would go on to win seven more major titles, finishing his career with one more than McEnroe. Lendl's dramatic defeat of tennis's artistic, temperamental enfant terrible became the dominant storyline of the entire French Open tournament — which had the unfortunate effect of overshadowing the women's winner, Martina Navratilova. The day before Lendl's seminal victory, Navratilova — a fellow Czech exile — laid claim to her fourth-straight major singles title. In the final, she had thrashed Chris Evert Lloyd, 6–3, 6–1. As straight a shooter with her assessments as she was with her serve, Navratilova said flatly, "I have transcended another level."

She was, somehow, right. In the summer of 1984, Martina Navratilova was 27. It wasn't just that she stood (mulleted) head and (sculpted) shoulders above the rest of the field. It was as if she were simply playing an altogether different sport from everyone else. If her moment was being obscured . . . if the public embrace was of the arm's-length variety . . . if her portfolio of endorsements was badly out of proportion to her achievements . . . well, that was nothing new to her.

Martina Navratilova was 16 years old when she left her native Czechoslovakia and visited the United States for the first time. She came to compete in a series of tennis tournaments but was awed by her surroundings. The selection of candy in the airport convenience stores. The array of shows — in color! — on television. The diversity of fashion.

Most of all, there was the limitless possibility. In her autobiography, Navratilova would later write of this trip: "For the first time in my life I was able to see America without the filter of a Communist education, Communist propaganda. And it felt right . . . I honestly believe I was born to be an American. With all due respect to my homeland, things never really felt right until the day I got off the plane in Florida."

Two years after that first visit, Navratilova came back to play in the 1975 U.S. Open. Though she was only 18, she decided to defect. After losing to Chris Evert in the semifinals — the 14th of their 80 career matches — Navratilova headed to Manhattan from Queens, where the tournament was held. She went into the offices of the Immigration and Naturalization Service and applied for citizenship. Four weeks later, she had her green card.

As a new American, Navratilova resembled a new college student, gorging herself on every freedom — and sometimes American fast food. She read a variety of newspapers. She bought jewelry and designer clothes and sports cars. A Rolls-Royce Silver Cloud II came emblazoned on the side with Virgil's line *Amor vincit omnia* — "Love conquers all."

Navratilova exercised her new freedoms in less materialistic ways, too. At the time, athletes seldom used their platforms to amplify social and political causes. In parlance that would come decades later, they were content to "stick to sports," to "shut up and dribble," retreating quickly from any issue that could potentially divide the public and undermine their appeal.

Navratilova considered it as much a duty as a right to give her opinion on topics from defense spending to animal rights to her disdain for Ronald Reagan. As she saw it, she was a top athlete in the meaty years of her career, placed before a microphone after each match. Who better to call attention to injustice and hypocrisy and the afflicted?

What would be called "woke" today was largely dismissed as annoyingly opinionated. Athletes — recalling the old proverb about children — were there to be seen, not heard. Navratilova didn't care, dutifully avoiding pre-scripted talking points and instead delivering potent missiles of cultural commentary.

She says now: "I wasn't afraid of any kind of backlash or anything like that, because once you leave a Communist country, you are not going to censor yourself. I had already been censored in Czechoslovakia. In America what was going to happen to me? People wouldn't like what I had to say but I was not going to lose my job. And I didn't have to worry about it threatening my livelihood. Maybe it hurt me on the endorsement side, but that never came into my kind of vision. I always err on the side of saying something rather than being silent."

Navratilova knew that she was gay. She wasn't inclined to ignore her sexuality, to deny it or go to strenuous lengths to disguise it. It was an open secret in tennis circles. For years she had (loosely) concealed it, not because of social pressures but because of political ones. "Being gay was grounds to have your citizenship rejected; it could have disqualified me," she says today. "Can you believe that?"

As soon as it *was* approved, a reporter for the *New York Daily News* effectively outed her. Wrote Steve Goldstein: "Martina Navratilova, who admits to being bisexual though most of her recent relationships have been with women, says a chief sponsor of women's tennis will pull out if she goes public with her private life."

Navratilova debated whether to issue a denial, mostly to shield the women's tennis circuit from the kind of scandal that might indeed jeopardize sponsorship. Her response? *Screw it. Why not own and control the message?* So it was that, in the prime years of her career, already twice a Wimbledon champion, she came out, openly identifying as a lesbian, forcing fans and sponsors to confront her truth.

She did not have the benefit of a PR strategy or publicist to help "craft her message," as we might say today. (The species barely existed.) She did not have the support of a sympathetic media. Days after her announcement, Skip Bayless—an ambitious local sportswriter who lived in the same Dallas apartment complex as Navratilova—wrote a column that, while not overtly homophobic, made references to Navratilova's "tumultuous year" and loss of self-esteem. The headline: "Millionairess in Search of Happiness."

Navratilova also did not have assurances that her revelation would be well received among fans, colleagues, and sponsors. And, generally, it wasn't. Avon withdrew its support from women's tennis, at least partly on account of Navratilova's avowed homosexuality. Margaret Court, a 24-time Grand Slam champion who had retired to run a ministry in Australia, had launched a campaign against "predatory lesbians" in Women's Tennis Association locker rooms. A contemporary and fellow Czech tennis player, Hana Mandlikova, declared that Navratilova "must have a chromosomal screw loose somewhere." (The irony was lost on no one when, years later, Mandlikova would raise a family with another woman.)

And Navratilova further polarized with her political stances. Often conversations and interviews and press conferences would make their way to political and social topics. Agents and tour officials explained to Navratilova that alienating segments of the public was no way to build a brand and score endorsement bounty. She nodded. Then, the next time she was asked about the U.S. defense budget or South African apartheid or the wage gap between men and women, she would still weigh in.

"I didn't even think of it in terms of being political," she says. "I was just always a believer in fairness. Maybe that's a Czech thing. And so if I saw something unfair I would always try to do something about it. It was like 'I can't not go there.' Why would I say 'No comment' when I *do* have a comment to make?

"And tennis is such a democratic sport. It is about as fair a sport as you can get. Maybe that is where the sense of fairness comes from. Not necessarily right or wrong, but what's fair, you know? Not socialist. Just fair."

All of this dissonance and all of this change came at a price to Navratilova's image — to what would later be called her "marketability." While McEnroe, too, carried a bullhorn, he was getting paid millions — and receiving sports cars as gifts — to wear Nike and endorse razors. Navratilova was getting paid pennies on the dollar. A friend once asked her to imagine how she and McEnroe would be treated if they traded places — that is, if Navratilova were the Nike-branded rebel from the New York suburbs and McEnroe were a gay émigré and outspoken about political issues. Navratilova simply cackled at the thought. She was Ginger Rogers to his Fred Astaire, doing everything he did, only backwards and in heels.

At first, anyway, this dissonance and all of this change came at a price to Navratilova's tennis. The excess cargo from eating all that fast food restricted her speed on the court and dulled her natural athleticism and stamina. The attention to her sexuality drained time and energy from her tennis. For years, Navratilova's results did not keep pace with her innate talent.

Then Navratilova exercised another choice: she changed. For one, she changed her game. Though she had grown up on slow clay courts in Czechoslovakia, pinned to the baseline, she was eager to explore what is too often the undiscovered land of tennis: the area around the net, which was filled with uncertainty but also possibility. "I wanted to attack and go where the action was," she says. "Who wants to hang back?"

Navratilova changed her diet, cutting out the fast food and hiring a nutritionist. She gave up meat and went heavy on carbs. Based on the results from daily blood tests, she would adjust food supplements. In a way that other athletes hadn't, Navratilova considered the galaxy of training options at her disposal. She began working with a bodybuilding coach. In Dallas, she connected with Nancy Lieberman, the basketball star, who also became Navratilova's companion and lover.

The first time Lieberman saw Navratilova practice, she was appalled. *You call that training?* Lieberman declared that she should have chosen tennis over basketball. "You make all this money and you don't have to do any work." She watched Navratilova lose to Chris Evert and was disgusted. "You should be beating her every time. She's smaller than you, less athletic, older, and softer. Name one thing she does better than you do."

With Navratilova's buy-in, Lieberman embarked on an ambitious, sweeping plan to transform her into the most dominant player ever. Faster. Stronger. More flexible. Mentally impregnable. Lieberman didn't know tennis, but she knew self-improvement. Under Lieberman, Navratilova trained three hours a day, often without a racket in her hand. She would lift weights and run sprints and play basketball, all while Lieberman looked on, alternately approving and disapproving. "You stink, Martina!" she would bark in her Brooklyn-flecked accent. "Why don't you stop wasting our time?" Navratilova would return to her sit-ups or the interval training spurts, finishing off the set.

Navratilova, once so indifferent to off-court preparation, developed what, by her own admission, was an addiction — "really, truly a physical addiction" — to training. She hired a masseuse and an acupuncturist and an osteopath and a dietitian. There was another staffer who used a contraption — a personal computer — to analyze the patterns and play of Navratilova and her opponents, especially Chris Evert. The idea was that Navratilova could glean some useful insights from this information and incorporate it into her strategy during a match.

All this made Navratilova the subject of great derision. She was mocked for her "gurus" and "voodoo methods." In the individual sport of tennis, Navratilova was seen as violating a sort of social compact by building a team of experts. Far from being applauded for enterprise and for innovating and challenging a tired model of training, she was ridiculed for her "entourage." The idea of using computer data to analyze her game and the game of opponents? In the eyes of jealous opponents, skeptical media, and ungenerous fans, *it all bordered on cheating.*

Navratilova was also scorned for the tangible result of all that training and nutrition and attention to detail: her body. As muscle replaced fat, as smooth curves gave way to sharply defined angles, as cables of veins began lining Navratilova's arms and legs, she began not to *look* like a conventional female athlete. This was thrown into relief when her physique was contrasted with that of Evert, her less muscular (and unambiguously heterosexual) American foil.

"Everyone danced around it," says Navratilova. "But look at the facts. Muscles weren't ladylike. I came from a Communist country during the Cold War — never mind that I defected. I dated women. Then you had Chrissie. *The all-American girl, the girl next door. Chrissie America.* She was everything I wasn't. I was everything she wasn't. I could beat her at tennis, but I wasn't going to beat her as a darling with the public."

As for her tennis coach, Navratilova didn't exactly hew to convention there, either. Decades before Bruce Jenner would become Caitlyn Jenner, Navratilova grasped the concept of a woman feeling trapped in the body of a man, as if their gender had been assigned by mistake. Richard Raskin had captained the Yale men's team in the fifties; after finding some marginal success on the men's circuit, he went to medical school. In 1975, at age 40, Raskin transitioned to a woman, Dr. Renée Richards, who, after a legal battle, would join the women's tennis tour.

Predictably, this became a cause célèbre. (Richards even called *herself* "a controversial character.") And predictably, one player was especially supportive. After Navratilova beat Richards in the final of a tournament in São Paulo, she sidled up to her opponent in the locker room. "Stay with it, Renée. You'll make it." They both knew this solicitude went beyond tennis.

When Richards retired from professional tennis in 1981, she returned to her ophthalmology practice. But she was happy to moonlight as Navratilova's coach. When players asked about Richards, Navratilova offered an explanation that sounds empathetic today but drew sideways glances in the 1980s. "She felt like a woman trapped in a man's body. And she decided to do something about it. And I don't care about that. What I do care about is that I am lucky enough to benefit from her coaching."

That arrangement — the gay No. 1 player, dating the female basketball star, being coached by a transgender woman — only fueled the notion that Team Navratilova was, as the player herself says, "this traveling freak show." Navratilova used her wit to demystify. "Dr. Renée Richards is offering a free eye exam for all umpires and linesmen," she said.

It all worked. And in the summer of 1984, she was at the height of her powers. Bringing her muscular tennis to the forefront, she was overpowering. Bringing her fitness to bear, she had superior durability. Armed with data, she was more strategic. And her success begat confidence. For all the turmoil in her personal life — breakups, reunifications, relocations, political controversies — it did not slow her winning.

It wasn't just that Navratilova beat her opponents. She humiliated them. Matches seldom lasted more than an hour. When opponents walked into the locker room, colleagues would ask, "How many games did you win?" — bypassing the possibility that they might have beaten Navratilova. When players, including Evert, suggested that Navratilova ought to seek a challenge and play on the men's tour, they weren't entirely joking.

In time, other players — namely the Williams sisters — would storm through the door Navratilova had opened, showing that tennis was no demure pursuit, that power, wielded without apology, could be used to devastating effect. In time, other female athletes would proudly show off the veins and muscles that were the legacy of fitness training. And eventually athletes both male and female would emulate Navratilova and fully realize the power they wielded in addressing social issues. But that summer of 1984, Navratilova was out there alone. She was at her peak, not just winning matches, but setting precedents, blazing a trail, and approaching stereotypes as if they were short lobs and smashing them.

5

THE TRUMP CARD

The thermodynamics of celebrity makes for an inexact science. There are obvious paths to fame and recognition and aura. Play a starring role in a movie. Release a hit single. Win an election. Pull off an athletic feat. Other times, for no obvious or explicable reason, figures fit into the cultural moment and accumulate fame at escape velocity.

The summer of 1984 marked Donald Trump's elevation, his apotheosis from a regional celebrity in New York to a full-fledged American A-lister. In May of 1984, Trump graced the cover of *GQ* magazine. For the close-up, he wore a conservative suit, what would become known as a "power tie," a full head of brown hair (decidedly untinged by orange), and a look residing somewhere between supreme confidence and sneering smugness.

The accompanying article, charitable overall — written, ironically, by Graydon Carter, who would later become a leading Trump critic*

* *Spy* magazine co-founder Kurt Andersen and Carter, who were friends, are credited with coining the enduring Trump description "short-fingered vulgarian."

—was titled "Donald Trump Gets What He Wants." It detailed how the 37-year-old real estate magnate encapsulated success, at least by 1984's standards. "New York's brash landlord can afford to sit pretty. He has powerful friends, a beautiful wife, a football team, and some of the choicest turf in Manhattan."

That same week, Trump was featured, similarly, in *The New York Times Magazine* in a similar piece, "The Expanding Empire of Donald Trump," effectively introducing him to the country, local-boy-makes-good style. The writer, Bill Geist, left his nine-year-old son, Willie, and five-year-old daughter, Libby, at home and trailed Trump for a day. In what was either a nod to foreshadowing or a nod to the consistency of Trump's personality, Geist wrote:

> Donald J. Trump is the man of the hour. Turn on the television or open a newspaper almost any day of the week, and there he is, snatching some star from the National Football League, announcing some preposterously lavish project he wants to build. . . . Spending a day with Donald Trump is like driving a Ferrari without the windshield. It's exhilarating; he gets a few bugs in his teeth.

The precise source of Trump's newfound celebrity was something of a mystery. He was (notionally, anyway) wealthy. But no more so than thousands of other Americans. He was (notionally, anyway) a successful real estate developer and landlord. But that was hardly a well-trodden path to fame. Trump's contemporaries and competitors in New York—say, William Zeckendorf or Richard LeFrak or Jerry Speyer—could walk down Broadway unchecked. He was not, proudly, an intellectual or even particularly bright.

The fascination with Trump was a dramatization of the national mood. It would be three more years before another, fictional New Yorker, Gordon Gekko, appeared in the film *Wall Street* and uttered what may well be the catchphrase for the entire 1980s. "Greed, for lack of a better word, is good. Greed is right. Greed works. Greed clarifies, cuts through, and captures the essence of the evolutionary spirit."

Here was Trump—with the limo and the penthouse and the blond wife—the perfect exponent of the unregulated, risk-taking, market-driven, ego-driven Reagan 1980s. Here was an unapologetic capitalist, who dressed the part and viewed every action as a transaction. *Did you get the better of the other guy? Or did he get the better of you?*

And Trump garnished his persona by displaying a sixth sense for media exposure. He had his own publicist, a mysterious figure named John Barron, who would call the tabloids and furnish them with scoops and tips. (Barron was later revealed to be Trump himself.) Those in his orbit were also reliably available to furnish gushing quotes and testimonials. In 1984, Trump's lawyer, Roy Cohn, told *Sports Illustrated* that his client was "one of the most enterprising, ingenious businessmen on the American scene . . . a miracle man who can't seem to make a mistake even if he tries." Trump's wife, Ivana, added, "Donald's brilliant. A lot of people say, whatever he touches turns to gold."

Trump was not a political partisan. He was utterly pragmatic, siding with whatever candidate, mayor, or institution would help him get a permit or tax break. (If anything, he was partial to the Brooklyn Democratic machine that helped his father, Fred C. Trump, launch the family business.) In the 1984 *New York Times* piece, Geist asked Trump whether he had an interest in running for elected office. "Absolutely not" was his response. "All of the false smiles and the red tape. It is too difficult to really do anything." As Geist wrote, "He dislikes meetings and paperwork and is in the enviable position of being able to avoid both."*

Trump revealed a habit of taking the truth and twisting it in the manner of a Central Park performer making a balloon animal. "It is often pointed out that Mr. Trump is prone to exaggeration in describing his projects," said the *Times* story. Even his allies saw it more as an endear-

---

* Others felt similarly. A few years later, George H. W. Bush was preparing to run for president and was considering a running mate. Bush's campaign manager, Lee Atwater, threw out the name Donald Trump. Maybe Trump could be a businessman-politician crossover? Bush thought the idea was so preposterous that he declined to respond. "Strange," Mr. Bush noted in his diary. "Unbelievable."

ing personality quirk than a personality defect. "Oh, he lies a great deal," renowned architect Philip Johnson said, laughing. "But it's sheer exuberance, exaggeration. It's never about anything important. He's straight as an arrow in his business dealings." Not that Trump was ashamed about his truth aversion, his "truthful hyperbole," as he would call it in his ghostwritten 1987 autobiography *The Art of the Deal.* (Departing from facts, he noted casually, was a "very effective form of promotion.")

Trump also mastered the art of what would later be called "brand building." Slap your name on every inch of real estate and it gets repeated. Make gold your color of choice and you become a name brand. For years, Trump giddily recounted the trophy ceremony at the 1983 U.S. Open. Martina Navratilova had just won the title, and after she was handed the winner's check, she gushed, "Now I'm going to buy an apartment in Trump Plaza." (Which, to her great future embarrassment, she did.) To Trump, this was the equivalent of a free infomercial with a celebrity testimonial.

Members of the celebrity class who purchased the 268 condominiums in Trump Tower included Paul Anka, Sophia Loren, Steven Spielberg, and Johnny Carson. (Carson's neighbors across the hall installed a swimming pool in their unit, three apartments melded together, even though they planned to be there only one week out of the year.) Speaking, as ever, in superlatives, Trump explained that his eponymous tower was for the "world's best people."

He included himself in that cohort. On January 6, 1984, Ivana gave birth to her third child, Eric, who joined an older brother, Donald Trump Jr., and an older sister, Ivanka. The family of five would move into the building's $10 million triplex penthouse, a dee-luxe apartment in the sky, in eighties locution. Donald would move his offices to the 26th floor, with a sprawling view of Central Park.

For all that he had acquired — the celebrity, the possessions, the name brandished on buildings — Trump wanted more. More money, to be sure. But also more publicity, more fixes from the addictive drug of celebrity.

Trump also wanted social certification. Having won the *New York Post* crowd, he wanted the approval of the *New York Times* crowd. He wanted to be perceived not as a nouveau riche scrapper from an outer borough — he grew up in a 23-room home in the Jamaica Estates neighborhood of Queens — but as Manhattan establishment. In the 1980s, as now, there was no faster path to achieving this than owning a professional sports franchise.

And there was perhaps no better time to get into the business of franchise ownership. As a sector, sports was starting to make its transition from diversion to a full-fledged industrial complex. Cable networks were beginning to gain traction, looking to feed the maw of sports programming and previewing the rise in rights fees. Owners were becoming increasingly shrewd about tapping revenue streams beyond tickets and merchandising. Some were beginning to negotiate with (or to extort, as one might put it less charitably) cities to fund their arenas and stadiums. Others were recognizing the value in luxury seats and sponsored signs on every wall and every available inch of playing surface.

But for Trump, owning a pro sports team — unlike most of his transactions — was not chiefly about the financial upside. It was about what team ownership represented. He would be sanctified, joining the elite of the elite. Like an emperor in a modern-day Colosseum, Trump would sit in a stadium box, surrounded by toadies, watching the gladiators below.

While the man often bragged vaguely about his own sports prowess — even as there was scant evidence that he had ever played any organized sports, save squash and golf — the NFL appealed to him most. The league offered scarcity and exclusivity, qualities he cherished. And there was all that testosterone — real men colliding violently with each other.

There were, however, some minor hitches. For one, there were no available teams. At one point, Trump had made an offer to buy the Baltimore Colts. The owner, Robert Irsay, let it be known that the franchise was not for sale. Still more problematic: the NFL, starting with Pete Rozelle, the league's savvy, chain-smoking commissioner, held firm to its stance that Trump was unworthy and unfit for membership.

"I could have had four or five NFL teams," Trump breezily told *Sports Illustrated* in 1984. "People look at certain institutions, like the NFL, as being infallible when they're not. . . . Institutions are sometimes the most vulnerable elements of our society, and the NFL is very vulnerable." It was precisely this kind of statement—at once narcissistic, casual, and patently false—that repelled the NFL and incumbent owners.

Nothing if not resourceful, Trump saw another path to ownership. If he couldn't enter the NFL through the front door, he would try another point of entry. Specifically, he would buy a team in a fledgling football league, the USFL, which had launched in 1983 and played games in the spring and summer.

The USFL was everything Trump wasn't. It was whimsical and wild and took pride in both its bootstrapping creativity and its resistance to taking itself too seriously. The league was cost-conscious, hell-bent on austerity and containing expenses. The off-brand and off-season alternative to the NFL, it was the equivalent of a start-up that might one day compete with the blue chips if everything went right. In 1984, the league was not the biggest or the best. It was a tricked-out and quirky El Camino to the NFL's reliable and dignified, if comparatively bland, Lincoln Town Car.

No matter. Trump wanted in. Maybe the NFL would force a merger and absorb some USFL teams. There was precedent here: in the 1960s the NFL had merged with the AFL and acquired a number of its teams, including the Oakland Raiders, who, not coincidentally, were partially owned by the AFL's combative commissioner at the time, Al Davis. Or maybe Trump would try to pry open the door to NFL ownership with the crowbar of litigation. Specifically, the USFL could sue the NFL on antitrust grounds, accusing the incumbent of running an anti-competitive business.

But both scenarios—Trump becoming an NFL owner by league merger or by lawsuit—depended on one eventuality: the USFL playing in the fall, head-to-head against the NFL. If the league stuck to its spring schedule, the two leagues could coexist. There would be no reason to merge, nor a reason to sue. "It was a running joke," says Mike Tollin, then a head of the USFL's video arm. "From the word 'go,' all Donald could think about was moving the USFL to the fall."

Trump was supposed to be the original owner of a USFL team. The league's founder, David Dixon, was adamant about putting a team in the New York market and had tapped Trump as the owner. Trump agreed and paid the first installment on a franchise fee, but he allegedly backed out in order to try to buy the Colts. The USFL turned instead to J. Walter Duncan, an Oklahoma oil magnate who had originally planned to buy the Chicago franchise before shifting to the New York market. Duncan leased Giants Stadium — across the Hudson River from Manhattan — but his contract stipulated that the franchise was named "New Jersey" and not "New York." So it was the New Jersey Generals were born.

An unlikely owner, Duncan scored an unlikely coup when the Generals signed Herschel Walker, the 1982 Heisman Trophy–winning running back from the University of Georgia. Walker had been a junior at the time, and supposedly the USFL, like the NFL, forbade underclassmen from entering the league. But an exception was made for Walker, the son of a rural soybean farmer, who, quite understandably, did not want to risk an injury during his senior season, thereby jeopardizing future wealth.

Instead of signing a standard player contract, Walker agreed to a personal services contract with Duncan that was valued at $4.2 million and included a 25 percent share in one of Duncan's oil wells, far in excess of the league's $1.8-million-per-team salary cap that season. ("A few guys had a few beers and decided to start this league," Duncan quipped. "I had one too many and decided to sign Herschel.")

Walker was as good as advertised. As a rookie, he rushed for 1,812 yards and 17 touchdowns. The rest of the Generals were, unfortunately, not as good as advertised. The team finished its inaugural season with a 6-12 record, giving up 437 points, more than 24 points a game. After the season, Duncan, tired of pinballing back and forth between New Jersey and his home in Oklahoma, wanted out. If he found the right buyer, he could make a small profit for his year of ownership. Enter Donald J. Trump.

As usual with Trump, the deal terms were fuzzy. According to one account, the Generals' purchase price was $10 million; per another, it was $6 million. And Trump's friends claimed that the deal was structured so it was effectually less than $1 million. As usual, too, it came with a generous side helping of Trump bombast. "I bought the team for very little money — I paid much less than what is reported — and we've created value for it now. It's crazy what's happened. . . . I could have paid $40 or $50 million for an NFL team," Trump told *GQ*. "I could have bought Baltimore. I could have bought a number of teams in the NFL. But I wanted a team in New York, and I couldn't buy the Giants or the Jets. Besides, it's more creative this way. In a couple of years, maybe the two leagues will be equal."

Trump's timing was impeccable. The circumstances were ideal for a new figure in the New York sports tableau. Under first-year coach Bill Parcells — and his ambitious assistant coach Bill Belichick — the Giants were coming off a 3-12-1 season. The Jets weren't much better, slogging through another forgettable campaign and playing their games at charmless Shea Stadium.

That stadium's summer tenants, the New York Mets, were uncharacteristically hopeful in the summer of 1984, riding a rookie teenage pitching phenom, Doc Gooden; but they were still two years removed from making the playoffs. The Yankees, to the dismay of their autocratic owner, George Steinbrenner, were in rebuilding mode. Trump became a community steward. Or, as *New York Daily News* columnist Mike Lupica wrote at the time, "In a very short period of time Trump has become the second most recognizable [owner] of all pro football. He just wants to be famous. And he is."

In 1984, Charley Steiner was sports director for RKO Radio Network, a national syndicate with a talent roster that included John Madden and a precociously glib recent Cornell grad, Keith Olbermann. Steiner had a second job working as the morning sports anchor for New York's WOR radio station. When WOR acquired the radio rights to Generals games, Steiner and his rolling, deep voice became, in effect, the voice of the franchise. A native New Yorker, Steiner knew about Trump. And, immediately, Steiner had his concerns.

The first tip-off for Steiner came the day it was announced that Trump had bought the Generals. In his opening comments, the new owner immediately started referring to them as the *New York/New Jersey Generals*. Says Steiner, "It all began with him and his bullshit. And for those of us that were again blissfully ignorant little anarchists trying to tweak the NFL and make it a more exciting league and all that, here is a guy who is already changing the name of the team."

As the new owner, Trump unleashed his media blitz. As Lupica put it in May of 1984, "Steinbrenner is Burt Reynolds. Trump is the new kid, say, Tom Selleck." Says Steiner: "Donald, who watched George do what he did and how he did it, could take it to the next level: *the electronic media*. So he would be on the radio, he would be on television doing sound bites." In a case of what would later be called "synergy" or "integration," using his sports ownership to publicize his real estate business, Trump held Generals press conferences at Trump Tower. The three-and-a-half-foot-tall T's managed to appear prominently in every shot. If the sounds from the piano tinkling and the sixty-foot-high waterfall were suboptimal audio, it was a small price to pay for the exposure.

Trump enlisted his wife, Ivana, to design the cheerleader uniforms. A team vice president sycophantically suggested that the cheer team be nicknamed the Trumpettes. Naturally, the Generals held cheerleading tryouts at Trump Tower. Trump invited the media and stocked the judging panel with "celebrities" — his newest offensive lineman, the artist LeRoy Neiman, the opera singer Beverly Sills, Andy Warhol, and, inevitably, Ivana. The judges gave scores as the hopefuls danced to the Michael Jackson hit "Billie Jean."

Early in his ownership, Trump began talking up the Galaxy Bowl. The *what*? He was quick to point out that he had conceived of the name and the idea itself. The game would pit the Super Bowl winner against the winner of the USFL's championship game. It would take place when the NFL's TV deal was up for renewal and — of course — was contingent on the USFL moving to a fall schedule.

As for the team itself, Trump constructed the roster much the same way he built his buildings: he set his sights on the best amenities money could buy. He attempted to woo Don Shula, the iconic coach of the Miami Dolphins. According to Trump, negotiations broke down when Shula asked for an apartment in Trump Tower. "That's something more valuable than money," Trump said. "That's something I really consider gold." (Shula later told *GQ* that no such negotiation occurred. "All I did was listen to what he had to say. They approached me. I didn't approach them.") When that failed, Trump interviewed Walt Michaels, something of a local name brand, who had coached the Jets for six seasons. Trump had asked Steiner, the radioman, for input. Steiner recalls that he said it seemed an odd match: the flamboyant, media-hungry owner and a terse coach who was the son of a coal miner. Trump hired Michaels anyway.

Trump spent lavishly on players, committing $5 million to payroll, twice the league average, distorting the labor market. The players loved it. The other owners hated it. The Generals signed Brian Sipe, longtime Cleveland Browns quarterback and the NFL's MVP in 1980. He re-signed Herschel Walker to a deal totaling $4 million. Perhaps most significantly, Trump signed Lawrence Taylor, the fearsome New York Giants linebacker, to a contract that would begin as soon as his NFL contract lapsed in 1987. The publicity alone was inestimable, this upstart reaching an agreement to sign the NFL's premier defensive player. When Taylor eventually re-signed with the Giants, his agent first had to pay Trump $750,000.

And, as expected, Trump pushed to move the USFL to the fall. The league had been founded on the principle of spring football. But Trump had other ideas. Within a week of becoming an owner, he deployed his media strategy. "Trump Would Like to Take on NFL," read a *New York Times* headline.

A few weeks after that — and, as usual, furnishing no concrete evidence—he told reporters that the USFL was "heading very rapidly downhill." (As for why he would buy a depreciating asset, that question was neither asked nor answered.) Trump repeated his claim that the USFL would be well served to move its schedule to the fall, and if it did so, Trump, personally, would deliver a lucrative contract. For the 1984 season, each team made less than $2 million in television rights; Trump pointed to Major League Baseball's $1.2 billion contract as evidence of the USFL leaders' financial incompetence. "I guarantee you folks in this room that I will produce CBS and I will produce NBC and that I will produce ABC, guaranteed, and for a hell of a lot more money than the horseshit you're getting right now."

It was also around this time that Trump began issuing what became a catchphrase: "If God wanted football to be played in the spring, he wouldn't have created baseball."

Other USFL owners held conference calls and met in private, discussing what to do about this bully, this nouveau owner, equally noxious and obnoxious. Some dismissed him as a vain but harmless showman who, if nothing else, was bringing unwanted attention to the league. Others worried that, by putting his personal interests and ambitions ahead of the league, he would bring ruin to the entire enterprise. "He was not an honorable man," Jerry Argovitz, owner of the Houston Gamblers, told the author Jeff Pearlman. "The truth wasn't his thing. But I've always said one thing about Donald Trump. You don't ever underestimate Donald. He can charm you out of your pants."

On April 15, 1984, Trump was at it again. Another story ran in *The New York Times* quoting two "prominent USFL executives" asserting that after the current season concluded in June, the league would play two more spring seasons and then wait more than a year before resuming play in September 1987. The two sources for the story were widely believed to be Trump and Trump.

When the season began, the Generals were a pleasant surprise. With a new coach, new quarterback, new defense, and, yes, new owner, they were unrecognizable from the 1983 vintage. They won their first four games in 1984, including a defeat of the Birmingham Stallions in front of the largest crowd in league history.

The Generals' newfound success doubled as an opportunity to tweak the NFL. A radio ad — dripping, of course, with Trumpian superlatives — compared the Generals with what Trump viewed as the competition:

> Which professional football team in the metropolitan area has the best head coach?
>
> The Generals with Walt Michaels.
>
> The best running back?
>
> The Generals with Herschel Walker.
>
> The best quarterback?
>
> The Generals with Brian Sipe.
>
> The best defensive back?
>
> The Generals with Gary Barbaro.
>
> The Generals have signed on the best, and now they're looking for you, the best football fan in the world . . . It's time you joined the ranks of the best.

The Generals players had great affection for Trump, mostly for two reasons. First, he paid them well. Second, he may have been a football hobbyist, but his appetite for attention meant that they could spend less time talking to the media. On Wednesdays, in particular, the team held media days at Giants Stadium. Steiner recalls: "The players don't want to talk to radio people or newspaper people, because they just don't. Then Trump walks in and all the writers and reporters gravitate towards him. And the players say, 'This is great! He is doing all the shit we don't want to do!' And he, on the other hand, loved it!"

If the players embraced the owner, he hugged back. Trump was a regular in the locker room, especially after wins, glad-handing and giving occasional addresses. Not surprisingly, he developed a special affinity for Walker, his star player, bringing him to business dinners and meetings in Manhattan. Walker recalls that Trump was especially insistent that he learn the names of everyone he met. He also told Walker the importance of interest rates. Soon the running back was telling his teammates how lucky they were to play for such an extraordinary man. He recalls saying, "Donald Trump loves his country and he's a great leader. He could be president one day."

Gary Croke, the team's assistant public relations man, recalled to *Sports Illustrated* that after one Generals home win, he was approached by a Trump assistant. "Listen," the assistant whispered, "I need you to take Donald Jr. and his classmates into the locker room to meet Herschel Walker." Croke thought it was a joke. When he realized it wasn't, he was outraged. The locker room was a cramped space and a sacred space. After the game, the players were getting changed and fulfilling their media obligations. This wasn't the place for a class trip or a meet-and-greet. "That's a direct order from Donald," the assistant said.

Steiner, the play-by-play man, has a similar memory. Early in the 1984 season, the Generals played a road game against the Jacksonville Bulls. It was an oppressively hot and humid Sunday. Steiner was doing his pregame prep work when he scanned the field and saw an unusual figure standing near the 30-yard line. "I see this young boy and he's got a blazer on, a little blue bow tie pressed onto his blazer, short pants, high socks. He looked like a JFK Jr. knockoff at the funeral. And I am thinking to myself: How would it feel to be five years old, or whatever it was then, to be on the field watching a team get warmed up, and then I am dressed like this? Wearing a bow tie? When it's hot as hell? He should have looked happy and he didn't. I felt sorry for the kid. And that kid was Donald Trump Jr."

On June 10, 1984, New Jersey beat the New Orleans Breakers 31–21 and in so doing clinched the Generals' first spot in the USFL playoffs. A league TV crew filmed the owner as he made a triumphant trip into the locker room.

"Congratulations, Donald," said a well-wisher.

"O.K., beautiful, beautiful—beautiful," Trump responded. "Beautiful," he said again to himself as he kept moving through the room.

He came upon a group of players at their lockers. "How's it feel? Champs. Good to be champs, huh? Way to go." He shook one player's hand and shook a fist at another and kept going. He then came upon another group at their lockers. "Way to go, fellas, way to go." He shook his fist again. "Now we've got to go a little further, right?"

They did not. The Philadelphia Stars defeated the Generals in the first round of the playoffs. Still, New Jersey finished 14-4, a hell of a turnaround from the previous season. It should have satisfied the team's new owner. It did not.

On the night of July 15, 1984, Tampa Stadium played host to the USFL Championship Game, six months after it hosted Super Bowl XVIII. The game did not feature a local team. It did not feature the New Jersey Generals or the Los Angeles Express, teams from the league's two largest markets and the employers of the USFL's two biggest (and best-paid) stars, Walker and quarterback Steve Young, respectively.

Instead, the Philadelphia Stars beat the Arizona Wranglers in a tension-free 23–3 slog. The crowd was reported at 52,622, a highly suspect figure, given the vast oceans of empty seats. Television ratings for the game on ABC were down significantly from the previous year, in keeping with a dispiriting season-long trend. For an upstart league hoping to continue building, momentum was suddenly a sparse commodity.

If the game, and the whimpering end to the season, triggered dread at league headquarters, the league's most notorious owner was considerably less dejected. To Donald Trump, this was only more evidence that spring-summer football was a mistake and the USFL would be better off competing directly with the NFL in the fall.

A month after the championship game, the league's executives and owners gathered at the Hyatt Regency in Chicago. One of the highlights of the session: the results from a study that the league had commissioned by a team of consultants from McKinsey, assessing the USFL's long-term future. On the eve of the meeting, *The New York Times* ran a story headlined "USFL Set for Fall Play in '86."

There was no question which owner had planted the story. Never mind that the actual report—prepared by experts for $600,000, no small fee for a league hemorrhaging money—had yet to be presented.

One owner already knew better. "Donald Trump, the flamboyant and innovative New York real-estate developer who owns the New Jersey Generals, said yesterday, 'We're going to ask for the switch to the fall and I think we'll get it.'"

When the report was presented, a partner from McKinsey spoke for more than an hour, relying on research and data. She noted that most start-up leagues lost money initially and the USFL's trajectory was sound. She pointed to a public opinion survey revealing that the USFL was well regarded and drew favorable impressions; but that public feuds among the owners undermined public faith in the league's long-term survival. The McKinsey team concluded that the USFL needed to remain a spring league, at least for the near future.

When the researchers left the room, leaving the USFL owners and executives alone to digest and discuss the findings, Donald Trump was, naturally, the first to speak. "Bullshit," he declared.

Again he pointed to the hundreds of millions he'd been promised by unidentified television executives — but only if the league competed in the fall. Again he challenged the manliness of the dissidents, wondering why they were showing no balls. Again he threatened to desert the league if he didn't get his way.

A Canadian industrialist, John F. Bassett, owned the Tampa Bay Breakers. But in the summer of 1984, especially in the Republic of Sports, he was better known for his offspring. His daughter Carling, then 16, was a tennis sensation, an ascending player encroaching on the top 10, with personality and looks to match her game. At the 1984 French Open, Carling Bassett would reach the quarterfinals and take a set off the great Chris Evert Lloyd; at the 1984 U.S. Open, she would reach the semifinals, again losing to Evert Lloyd.

John Bassett, though, had had it with Donald Trump. The leaks. The anonymous quotes. The duplicity. The bullying. The inattention to detail. The bald lying. All in service of the folly of competing against the NFL. Bassett saw Trump as a malignancy on the league. On August 16, 1984, he fired off a letter to Trump. It read in part:

> While others may have been able to let your insensitive and denigrating comments pass, I no longer will. You are bigger, younger and stronger than I, which means I'll have no regrets whatsoever punching you right in the mouth the next time an instance occurs where you personally scorn me, or anyone else, who does not happen to salute and dance to your tune.*

To the best of anyone's knowledge, Trump never responded to Bassett's letter. He corralled the necessary votes among fellow owners and steamrolled a plan to move the USFL to the fall and, as part of the strategy, sue the NFL on antitrust grounds, seeking more than $16 billion in damages. The USFL played the 1985 season, but with an eye toward its move to the fall. It suspended operations entirely for the 1986 season, awaiting its judgment in court.

On May 15, 1986, John Bassett passed away. Later that summer, at a U.S. district court in Manhattan, a jury returned its verdict. The NFL had indeed operated a pro football monopoly "to control prices or exclude competition" in the "relevant market" of professional football in the United States. However, as a league that had expanded too quickly, was losing money, and wasn't even playing games at the time, the USFL could not prove damages. The jury awarded the USFL $1, which got tripled to $3 under antitrust laws.

The USFL was, effectively, issued its last rites that day. Soon it would officially fold, its losses totaling more than $150 million. Players scattered. Some retired, their football dreams spritzed with embalming fluid. But, testament to the caliber of the USFL, a good many—Reggie White, Jim Kelly, Steve Young, and, not least, Herschel Walker—decamped to the NFL.

As for Trump, he did not recoup millions from litigation. The Generals were not absorbed by the NFL, as he had hoped. He did not ingratiate

---

* As Bassett took this stance, multiple tumors were growing in his brain. In an eerie foreshadowing of John McCain three decades later, here was an older, more accomplished, more dignified, and more respected colleague taking a stand against Trump. And doing so as an inoperable cancer was metastasizing.

himself to the fraternity of NFL owners. Far from it: his bitter feud with the league would only grow more intense.

A quarter century after this peculiar chapter in pro football history, Chet Simmons's old network, ESPN, commissioned a documentary as part of its *30 for 30* series. The director was Mike Tollin, once the USFL's head of production. The film was titled "Small Potatoes: Who Killed the USFL?"

All evidence pointed to one man. And he was just getting started.

6

LARRY VERSUS MAGIC

Standing atop a floor tiled with parquet, they positioned themselves off to the side of the foul line, facing each other like dance partners. Which, in effect, they were. Though they represented one of the great sports studies in contrast, at least they were the same height. Both standing six-nine, they stared at each other eye-to-eye.

Rivalry is the great effervescent of sport, the ingredient that puts fizz in competition. And here was a rivalry within a rivalry, two players pitted against each other for years, representing two teams pitted against each other for decades. It was early in Game 1 of the 1984 NBA Finals, the first of a seven-episode serial that would mark an inflection point — perhaps *the* inflection point — in the history of an entire sport.

Starting when they were college players, Larry Bird and Earvin "Magic" Johnson had been, at once, paired against each other and also yoked together. The whole basketball ecosystem flourished with the Magic-Bird symbiosis. And every fan played the compare-and-contrast game. Less a clash than a collision, they encompassed Black versus white. Urban versus rural. Point guard versus small forward. Magic was the polished, joyous player with "a smile that lights up a television screen from [L.A.] to Bangor, Maine," Brent Musburger enthused on a CBS broadcast. Bird, who once labored on an actual road crew in his Indiana hometown, was the earnest workman, defiant about his refusal to plane his rough edges. Two different approaches to the sport, both appealing and both effective.

Johnson and Bird first intersected as college players when they were teammates on a U.S. amateur team that played in the World Invitational Tournament in the summer of 1978. They were also teammates that summer at a college All-Star game against a Cuban team, both somehow kept out of the starting lineup by the coach, Kentucky's Joe B. Hall.

They faced each other in the 1979 NCAA Championship Game, when Michigan State was pitted against Indiana State for the national title. On account of the two stars, it was the highest-rated title game in NCAA history. Magic and Bird both entered the NBA in 1979. The transfer of their rivalry to the professional stage was so highly anticipated that—to the disgruntlement of established players—the two untested rookies graced the cover of the league's media guide that year.

As was so often the case with sports rivals, for all the crass contrasts, the two athletes exhibited more similarities than differences. In addition to being known by a single name, both Magic and Bird competed with honor. Both made their teammates better, devoted, as each was, to that underrated basketball gerund: passing. Both were authoritative yet unselfish. Both were control freaks, in their way. Both were spindles on which their teams were wound. And both teams won routinely, almost as a matter of ritual.

And like most rivals, they exposed the shortcomings and oversimplifications of the comparisons. Bird may have been nicknamed the Hick from French Lick, a nod to his Indiana hometown. But his game came with plenty of urban flavor, from his spin-laced, no-look passes to his heroic blasts of trash talk. Johnson had plenty of substance to go with his style. One example among many: each summer he returned to his (decidedly unglamorous) home of Lansing, Michigan, and worked assiduously on a new dimension of his game. One summer it would be his three-point shot, another his hook shot. Just as Bird possessed plenty of flair, Magic betrayed plenty of toughness.

Their personal rivalry was fueled by the teams they represented. Magic was chosen by the Lakers with the top pick in the 1979 NBA Draft; thanks to the sleight of hand of the Celtics' front office, Bird had been selected by Boston the previous year, when he still had a season of college eligibility left, a loophole that closed after that. Two seminal players drafted by the NBA's two seminal teams. In the first year, Bird beat out Magic to win Rookie of the Year honors. But Magic — again with the deceptive toughness — led the Lakers to the 1980 NBA title.

Bird's Celtics and Magic's Lakers not only took on the characteristics of their teams' respective stars, but also those of their teams' respective markets. Nicknamed "Showtime," the Lakers were a team of glamour, who, mirroring Magic, didn't so much *play* basketball as they *performed* it, happy to improvise and project a Hollywood ethos. Inasmuch as the Celtics had a style, it was one befitting a Massachusetts longshoreman: tough and sharp-elbowed and proudly inelegant. In keeping with Bird, they didn't so much *play* basketball as they *worked* it.

The Lakers were owned by Jerry Buss, a lounge lizard who only sometimes buttoned his shirt and — to the embarrassment of his twenty-something daughter, Jeanie — was known to light his chest hair on fire as a party trick. The Celtics were owned, principally, by Arnold "Red" Auerbach, a bald Jewish basketball lifer, seldom seen without a cigar in his mouth.

Even the team's sixtysomething *announcers* limned the difference between the teams. Francis Dayle "Chick" Hearn was a Lakers institution, a smooth and affable man-about-town who, around the time of the 1984 Finals, had filmed a cameo in the movie *Fletch*. Chick gave the basketball lexicon such terms as *slam dunk, air ball, no-look pass,* and *finger roll.* The Celtics' games were called by Johnny Most, the epitome of a homer — "Big Ralph Sampson picking on the little people! I'm Ralph Sampson and I've got the right to break your head!" — whose raspy voice sounded as though he'd just eaten a pack of Marlboros for breakfast.

Yet for all these delicious clashes and contrasts, for their first five seasons in the league, Magic's Lakers and Bird's Celtics were two ships (no-look) passing in the night. In 1981, the year after Magic's heroics, Bird led the Celtics to the title, defeating Houston in the Finals. The following year, Magic and the Lakers beat the Sixers, before losing to them in 1983. By 1984, Magic and Bird were, incontestably, the two best players in the NBA. But they had never faced each other in the postseason.

Early in their careers, sports journalists are taught the adage "No cheering in the press box." Rooting for a team on the job is seen as a breach of professionalism, a puncture of the veil of neutrality. Likewise, in league offices, employees are instructed not to root openly for one team, for fear it will give rise to institutional favoritism and conspiracy theories. But in the summer of 1984, when the Celtics beat the Milwaukee Bucks in the Eastern Conference Finals and the Lakers beat the Phoenix Suns in the West, there was an open giddiness in press boxes and at the league headquarters in Midtown Manhattan.

David Stern, the league's newly anointed commissioner, was among those smiling broadly. Even in the years before he took office, he had been stressing the critical importance of television and the metric of ratings. Want to spread the gospel of basketball? Beam it up to satellites and, like a crisp bounce pass, send it into as many living rooms and bars and hotel rooms as possible. Now, for his first NBA Finals as commissioner, he had potential television gold.

It wasn't just that Bird and Magic were both in full blossom. Yes, Bird would win the MVP award that season — the first of three straight, only to see his run ended by Johnson, who would go on to win three himself. But if the series had its two leading men, it also had a rich cast of all-star supporting actors. Even at age 37, Kareem Abdul-Jabbar, the Lakers' begoggled center, was a formidable player. A few weeks earlier, he had surpassed Wilt Chamberlain as the most prolific scorer in NBA history. (Said Chamberlain: "If this [record] is so great, well, it's only one of about ninety I held. I must be in a world by myself.") Four other Lakers stars — James Worthy, Byron Scott, Michael Cooper, and Bob McAdoo — could each have been the best player on most other teams in the league. The Celtics' long-armed forward Kevin McHale was a future Hall of Fame player; so were center Robert Parish and point guard Dennis Johnson.

Like any Hollywood blockbuster, the series also provided a rich dramatis personae of secondary characters. The Los Angeles crowd was energized by the Laker Girls, a troupe of young and shapely aspiring starlets, basketball's answer to the Dallas Cowboys cheerleaders. The Celtics had reserve player M. L. Carr, a towel-waving provocateur; Carr was equally adored by Celtics fans and abhorred by Lakers fans. Same for Cedric Maxwell, who gleefully called the Lakers "the Fakers," and Magic Johnson "Tragic Johnson" and "Cheesy Johnson." Wearing his black horn-rimmed glasses, Kurt Rambis, the Lakers' forward, looked like one of the Hanson brothers from the movie *Slap Shot,* and played with similar intensity.

Jack Nicholson was then among the most well-known actors in Hollywood, but he was perhaps better known for his Lakers fandom. He sat courtside, his feet resting on the parquet — decades later, prime seats at sporting events would still be called the "Nicholson Seats." But that was for home games. On the road, he would sit in the stands among the partisans, willing to accept abuse from opposing fans if it meant getting to watch his team in person. Though the Celtics were coached by K. C. Jones — a Hall of Fame player in his own right, and one of the few African American bench bosses — it was Auerbach who was the team's ultimate authority, something akin to both godfather and consigliere.

The Lakers, meanwhile, were coached by Pat Riley, who may have come from upstate New York but by this point was the paradigm of L.A. mid-eighties slick. Then in his late thirties — just two years older than Kareem — Riley thrived in the position, a master motivator who connected with the players and who looked the part, from the natty attire on his body to the abundant product in his hair.

By 1984, there was also abundant history between the two franchises.

The Celtics and Lakers were not merely the NBA's two marquee teams; theirs was already a rich and textured rivalry. The Celtics were angling for the 15th championship in franchise history. The Lakers were going for their ninth. Seven times the two teams had met in the Finals; Boston had won each time.

Race figured heavily in the dynamic as well. In the mid-eighties, Boston was still in the throes of a school desegregation and busing crisis. Representing a city known, rightly or wrongly, as being inhospitable to African Americans (athletes included), the Celtics featured three white players in its starting lineup. The Lakers had only one white player, Rambis, in their regular rotation.

The terms used to describe the teams were often shabbily coded. The Lakers were "athletic" and "flamboyant" and played with "flair." The Celtics "hustled" and played with "heart and savvy." The Lakers were "high-flying" and the Celtics were "landlocked." (In Boston's case, there was often an overlay of ethnic pride. That the team was named the Celtics and wore green and bore a shamrock as a logo — for a sizable cohort of Boston fans, it was like rooting for the Irish Olympic team.)

Above all, this matchup had the ultimate rivalry accelerant: mutual antipathy. Neither team liked the other; they actively *disliked* each other. The Lakers perceived the Celtics as arrogant bullies who played in a provincial market, before boorish (and maybe racist) fans. The Celtics perceived the Lakers as soft and precious drama queens, whose fans were poseurs and whose entire ethos smacked of Hollywood schmaltz and fraudulence.

This dislike extended to Bird and Magic. At the time, Bird considered his counterpart inauthentic and, as he would later put it, in a wonderful mixed metaphor, "more razzle-dazzle than steak." Magic thought his adversary was unnecessarily surly and wondered to friends whether Bird wasn't being graded on a curve as the Great White Hope in a Black league.

When Magic and Bird were asked about the other, as they inevitably were, they tended to duck the question and minimize the role of rivalry.

It's a team game. We're not guarding each other. I'm just focused on winning. Not everyone was buying it. "Naturally they want to be at their best," the esteemed coach Pete Newell told *Sports Illustrated* in the summer of 1984. "If you were Raquel Welch and you lived across the street from Marilyn Monroe, you'd make damn sure you looked good every time you went out the front door."

Lakers beat writers knew that there was no better way to shut down Magic, otherwise so outgoing and quick with a smile, than to ask him about Bird. Gritting his teeth behind a smile, Magic inevitably spoke blandly about their "competitive nature." Bird was, not surprisingly, less diplomatic. As he later told fellow Hoosier David Letterman, "My thing was when you compete, you're really not friends. You wanna keep an edge . . . Earvin is an outgoing guy. He loves everybody, he wants to high-five. And he's got that big smile. My goal was to try and take three of them teeth home with me."

This animosity trickled down to fans. Even outside of the two markets, you picked your side, and it said plenty about your values and personality. Boston versus L.A. . . . or L.A. versus Boston. At the time, dividing lines were as stark as Reagan versus Mondale, Mustang versus Camaro, Coke versus Pepsi.

If David Stern and his minions were thrilled by this matchup, so were the suits at CBS. Through the years, the network had wavered in its commitment to — and fondness for — professional basketball. But CBS realized the importance of this series.

Brent Musburger, then age 45 and the voice of the network, hosted the NBA Finals broadcast. The games were covered by the team of Dick Stockton and Tom Heinsohn. The former was a measured play-by-play voice, already known in Boston both for calling Celtics games on radio and then for calling Red Sox games on the local station, WSBK. When the Sox reached the World Series, NBC supplemented its team with local broadcasters. So it was that Stockton called Carlton Fisk's iconic game-winning home run in the 1975 World Series.

His partner, Heinsohn, was an authoritative analyst but, like Johnny

Most, not exactly a model of tempered neutrality. He had not only played for the Celtics — beating out teammate Bill Russell to win Rookie of the Year honors in 1957 — but coached the team from 1969 to 1978 before turning to broadcasting. Rounding out CBS's team, Lesley Visser, a former *Boston Globe* scribe who was transitioning from print to video (and, the year before, had married Stockton), reported on the Celtics, while Pat O'Brien, a golden-lunged announcer who could match Riley for clothes and hair product, was assigned to the Lakers.

In their 1984 collective bargaining agreement, the NBA and the players' union fashioned policy on travel. Teams would travel to games on the first morning flight, commandeering as many first-class seats as possible, which would usually be distributed on the basis of seniority — rookies in the back. Connecting flights were to be avoided whenever possible.

For the players, this was considered a win at the time. Private flights were for the Rolling Stones and CEOs, not for employees in a league trying to break even. Fewer layovers: that was a welcome change. And the first-class stipulation meant that at least some of the tallest men on the planet had the benefit of the extra legroom. Still, flying commercial was becoming increasingly problematic as NBA players — thanks to television and the fact that they performed in shorts and T-shirts, unobscured by helmets — became increasingly recognizable.

For the Lakers, there was a mob scene throughout LAX as they left for Boston. Far worse, when they arrived in Boston, they had to do the equivalent of a perp walk through Logan Airport. When they got to the baggage carousel, they waited 45 minutes, and when their bags arrived, some were unzipped.

When the Lakers checked into the team hotel, employees were decked out in Celtics paraphernalia. When players asked to have no calls put through to their rooms, the requests went unheeded. Half of Boston not only knew that the team was staying at the Marriott Copley Place but knew the room numbers of the players. Not surprisingly, at three in the morning, the hotel's alarms were triggered. Riley discouraged his players from ordering room service and drinking water from the tap, including at the Boston Garden.

Initially, anyway, the Lakers were seemingly unbothered by the inhospitable conditions. In Game 1, they outplayed the Celtics from start to finish. In Game 2, Los Angeles led 113–111 with 18 seconds remaining. And they had the ball after McHale missed two free throws, causing Nicholson, sitting in the stands and not courtside, to smile and offer the universal sign for "choke." But there was a slight glitch: Riley had instructed the Lakers to call a timeout if—and only if—McHale made the free throws. When McHale missed, Johnson called a timeout anyway.

The Lakers played the last few seconds as if the outcome was no longer in doubt. James Worthy casually inbounded the ball to Magic Johnson, who passed it back to Worthy, who casually wafted a crosscourt pass toward Byron Scott. The ball fluttered in the air like a balloon. On the Lakers sideline, Riley swore he could see the seams of the ball "spinning in slow motion." Celtics guard Gerald Henderson charged forward, intercepted the pass, took one dribble, and scored a layup. From his courtside seat where he was broadcasting the game, Heinsohn smiled. "The Leprechaun," he told the CBS audience in his rolling bass of a voice, "is at work here at Boston Garden."

The game was now tied and, more important, the Lakers were an alloy of frustrated, scared, and nervous. In the waning seconds, Johnson spent so much time dribbling that the clock expired before the Lakers could offer a shot. The game went to overtime. By then it was clear that the Basketball Fates had already written the script. The Celtics again stole a critical pass and, with it, the game, 124–121.

In the Lakers' despondent locker room, players filed in wearing masks of disappointment.

In the Celtics' locker room, a jubilant M. L. Carr slapped each teammate with his ubiquitous white towel. Henderson, the game's hero, entered clutching the game ball. It wasn't simply that the Lakers lost and the Celtics won. It was that the game conformed both to history and to stereotype. The lax Lakers folded. The resourceful, never-give-up Celtics somehow prevailed.

Bird conceded that if the Celtics had gone down 0–2, "we probably would've been swept." Now they were back.

Though less overt, the glee in the Boston Garden was shared by the NBA and CBS executives. Here they had their dream matchup. The Lakers had been within seconds of standing halfway to a series sweep. Instead, thanks to what became known simply as the Henderson Steal, the series was tied 1–1, and the plot thickened considerably.

Stern's directive to "grow the league" included courting the media. "All these newspaper columnists who love baseball and football, we need to get them to migrate to basketball," he told his minions. When those columnists and other media heavyweights took an interest in this blockbuster NBA Finals, the league responded in kind. In both Boston and Los Angeles, Brian McIntyre, the NBA's head of PR, set up a "hospitality room" where writers, television reporters, and the players themselves could mingle. Which is to say, eat free food and drink free beer. (And, at least in one case, sleep there — one writer canceled his room but then put in for a night's lodging on his expense report.)

At the hospitality room at the Marriott, some of the writers came up with the (alcohol-fueled) idea to fill an ice bucket with water and place it over the door. When unsuspecting guests arrived, they would be doused. As luck would have it, Pat Riley was among those to arrive. Accompanied by a beat writer from *The Orange County Register,* Riley figured he'd stop by the hospitality room for a beer. When he saw a cluster of grinning writers, he stopped. His companion, though, entered. The bucket not only soaked him but landed on his head, slicing his nose, which would require stitches.

The following morning, the caravan headed to Logan Airport for the early flight to Los Angeles. The NBA personnel shared an American Airlines flight with the Lakers. Brian McIntyre, the PR man, took his seat in the last row of the plane. Before he could fall asleep, he felt a hand on his shoulder. It was Pat Riley, who leaned in, brought his face inches from McIntyre's, and said, "We're never staying at your hotel again."

When the Celtics landed in Los Angeles, it was their turn to absorb the wrath of fans. They were heckled as they walked through the terminal at LAX. When the Celtics checked in at the Airport Marriott, some of their rooms were not yet ready. Fans wearing Lakers jerseys clustered in the lobby, including a group dressed in tribute to Kurt Rambis, complete with horn-rimmed glasses.

If this made for an inconvenience, it also helped cement bonds between the fans and the players. McHale thought to himself, *At least this many people care.* It wasn't just that thousands of fans were invested in the outcome of the Finals. Somehow these personal interactions with players they would watch on television — in airports, at bars, in hotels — deepened their passion and connection.

Another striking difference between the Celtics and the Lakers: their respective venues. Hilariously named, the Boston Garden was more hothouse than garden. A sweatbox of a downtown arena, it was inelegance in architectural form. Rodents boldly scampered around the concourses and tunnels. It lacked air-conditioning. (More on this later.) At the time, there were no rules requiring patrons to wear shirts.

The Lakers played in the anti-Garden, "the Fabulous Forum," which, as the grandiose name suggested, was a palace where Hollywood grandees came more to be seen than to watch basketball. An arena surrounded by acres of parking lot, it often seemed like a Sunset Strip lounge, with a basketball court grafted on. Celebrities and high rollers would have their cars parked by valet and enter through the Forum Club. Often they would drink their champagne and eat their canapés until well into the first quarter before finally, and conspicuously, taking their courtside seats. Seats that, Brent Musburger breathlessly enthused on the CBS broadcast, "will cost you *one hundred dollars* a game."

For Game 3, the latecomers missed a vintage display of Showtime basketball. Magic Johnson orchestrated a series of weaving fast breaks — these braids of beauties — and handed out 21 assists, a record for the Finals. The Lakers scored 47 points in one quarter, also a Finals record. The Celtics offered little resistance, least of all Dennis Johnson, whom even Heinsohn referred to as "a dog." The final score was worthy of a December blowout of a lousy team, not a critical NBA Finals game: Lakers 137, Celtics 104.

After the game, reporters waited for the Lakers to emerge from the locker room. When *Los Angeles Times* columnist Scott Ostler asked what was taking so long, someone quipped, "They're handing out rings." In his column Ostler wrote, "This series isn't over. The Celtics might bounce back. The Lakers might slow down. It might snow tomorrow in Laguna Beach."

In the other locker room, Bird was fuming. "We played like a buncha women!" he said, with the kind of casual misogyny that didn't invite much condemnation in 1984. "We have a bunch of great players on this team, but we don't have players with the hearts sometimes we need. You see Magic slappin' high-five and guys goin' behind their back, guys shootin' layups all day long, you'd think someone would put a stop to it. . . . We're supposed to be a physical team, they're supposed to be a finesse team. We stood around and let them push us around and do what they wanted." McHale added, "Every man in this room ought to be embarrassed."

Transcribing Bird's rant, the press — either saving a star athlete from himself or shortchanging accuracy — changed "women" to the more benign (at least by 1984 standards) "sissies." Regardless, Bird's message was clear. He was resorting to the oldest of motivational ploys in sports and challenging his team's collective manhood. Game 4 continued the clash of styles. The Lakers ran at every opportunity, Magic distributing the ball as he saw fit. When the Lakers couldn't run, they dumped the ball to Abdul-Jabbar and let him deploy his tricks, including another shot christened by Chick Hearn: the skyhook. The Celtics, more methodically, often ran their offense without a true point guard and craftily moved off of screens and picks, often so Bird could unfurl his jump shot.

Game 4 was physical and, unlike Game 3, competitive. But the Lakers led consistently as they tried to build an all but insurmountable 3–1 lead. Midway through the third quarter, the Celtics missed a shot, catalyzing another Lakers fast break. Abdul-Jabbar grabbed the ball and threw it to Worthy, who passed it to Rambis, who took one dribble before going in for—

A few feet from the basket, McHale intercepted Rambis like a hockey player checking an opponent into the boards. Only more violently. McHale extended his left arm and, making no attempt to block the shot, clotheslined Rambis. Already in midair, Rambis absorbed so much force that his leg flew up, nearly touching the net. He landed on the yellow court with an audible thump. "It's part of the game, ya know," Heinsohn, the Boston-loyal CBS announcer, said, laughing.

But the play was so jarringly violent that Bird, of all people, ran toward Rambis to try to help him up. Rambis was having no part of that. He popped up, Hanson brother style, seeking to fight McHale. Instinctively, James Worthy tried to play peacemaker, a move he would instantly regret. Attempting to restrain an off-balance (and crazed) Rambis, Worthy inadvertently pushed his teammate into the photographers' row. Again Bird offered to help him up, and this time Rambis accepted.

After the ensuing chaos, Rambis went to the line to shoot two free throws. That's all. No technical fouls were called. No flagrant fouls. No offsetting technical. No leave-the-bench technical. And, though today such a foul would likely earn a player a suspension for the rest of the series, there was no talk of ejecting McHale. Just two free throws for a foul while in the act of shooting.

The Lakers were leading 76–70, and the entire complexion of the series had just changed. What had been a merely chippy game now turned violent. Kareem swung an elbow near Bird's head when fighting for a rebound. When Bird protested, Abdul-Jabbar yelled, "White boy, I'll kick your ass." Tired of being insulted, Magic Johnson, departing from character, headed to the Celtics bench and challenged M. L. Carr to a fight. James Worthy nearly ripped the shirt off Celtics guard and irritant Danny Ainge.

All this aggression, though, took the Lakers out of their game. As Bird rightly noted, Los Angeles was a finesse team, not a brute squad. As the Lakers mishandled passes and missed shots, the Celtics warmed to this style of play. Bird made shot after shot, each with a higher degree of difficulty than the previous one.

With the score tied and a few seconds left, Magic Johnson again dribbled too long, before throwing an errant pass that Parish intercepted. With 35 seconds left in overtime, Johnson had a chance for redemption but missed two free throws. When Boston took possession, Bird — who had 21 *rebounds* in the game — demanded the ball and flicked a fallaway jump shot over Magic, which proved to be the critical shot. Final score: Celtics 129–125 in overtime.

The series was tied 2–2. The country was officially captivated.

After the game, Stern sat with Red Auerbach at the Marriott restaurant. "David, this is killing me," Auerbach told the commissioner. "All the back-and-forth, back-and-forth."

"Me, too, Arnold," Stern responded, assuming that Auerbach was talking about the heart-stopping drama and swaying momentum of the series.

Auerbach, though, meant *literally* the back-and-forth. The cross-country trips. On commercial flights. Often in coach class. Sometimes on red-eyes. The Finals format of home games — 2-2-1-1-1 — meant that a seven-game series would entail as many as four cross-country flights for the home team and *six* for the road team.

Stern agreed, though for an additional reason. Thinking, as always, about boosting the league's profile and publicity, the commissioner added, "It's bad for newspapers."

Auerbach flashed him a look that said, unambiguously, *Newspapers?*

Who gives a shit about newspapers? But Stern reasoned that with all that travel, it was prohibitively expensive for newspapers to send reporters to cover each game. And West Coast deadlines only added to the hassle. And so it was established. Going forward, the NBA Finals would be a 2-3-2 series: two home games for the team with home-court advantage, three for the opposition, and the final two, if necessary, for the home-court team.

Stern, though, had a more immediate issue. Captivating as the Series was, the violence of Game 4 was threatening to eclipse all the Bird-Magic Celtics-Lakers storylines. Stern and the NBA sent word to both teams warning them about exceedingly physical play. Stern would later joke, "I'm not sure either team actually conveyed this message to the players."

Again the Lakers received something other than a warm welcome when they landed at Logan Airport. There was construction at the airport. When a team bus failed to show up at the appointed time at Terminal C, Magic and Kareem shrugged and jumped into the back of the same cab.

Riley, still seething about the Celtics' play in Game 4, held an impromptu press conference. "I think what Boston did was the equivalent of two gang warlords meeting the night before a rumble and deciding on the weapons. They both say 'bare fists,' and one of them shows up with zip guns. We now know what the weapons are. It's a shame that it has to be this way."

The reporters ran to the Celtics for comment. Not one to back down, Auerbach, then 66 years old, shot back, "He's just saying that because he got beat."

Boston weather reports from Friday, June 8, 1984, indicate that it was "hazy and humid in the low 90s." Hot, but not oppressively so. That dispatch clearly did not come from inside Boston Garden that night. There, it was 97 degrees, with stifling humidity. And, of course, no air-conditioning. Naturally, the Turkish prison that doubled as the visitors' locker room was the hottest area in the building. The idea of wearing sweatpants was so preposterous that both teams warmed up in their game shorts and jerseys. Dozens of fans, even in the seats ringing the court, watched the game shirtless.

As *Boston Globe* columnist Larry Whiteside wrote, "Years from now, nobody will remember the score. Only the heat that made your clothes cling like they do on those dead-of-August days at Hampton Beach. Only the heat. The ferocious heat that reached 97 degrees and made sweat drop like raindrops." His colleague Bob Ryan described it as "the most unusual night in the Boston Garden in the history of the Boston Celtics." Abdul-Jabbar used different imagery. How hot was it? "I suggest you go to the local steam bath with all your clothes on. First, try to do a hundred push-ups. Then run back and forth for 48 minutes."

In the first half, veteran referee Hue Hollins became dehydrated, fainted, and was replaced for the rest of the game. ("We've got to get him in better shape," Riley quipped.) The Lakers didn't fare much better. As predicted — or as planned, the conspiracy theorists would say — the conditions revealed the character of both teams. The team of glamour boys from Los Angeles sucked oxygen. Literally. Fifteen-year veteran Abdul-Jabbar came to the bench and strapped on the kind of mask that falls from overhead in an airplane.

The Celtics relished the atmosphere. The fans went crazy. Instead of waving his towel to fire up the crowd, M. L. Carr jokingly whipped it around players' faces in the manner of a fan. Bird recalls that to him it felt fine. If anything, it was cooler than playing an outdoor game in August Indiana humidity. He played 42 minutes, scoring 34 points and accumulating 17 rebounds. He took 20 shots; he made 15.

The Celtics won, 121–103. Abdul-Jabbar lamented, "I just didn't have that certain *je ne sais quoi.*" This was a subtle dig: he was still smarter and more worldly than the sweaty, grubby, benighted Celtics fans. Other Lakers took a less cerebral approach. Though armed with no evidence, they were convinced that Boston had played dirty again. Only this time, instead of clotheslining a player, they had manipulated the conditions.

McHale responded, "After a hot June day, you put 15,000 fans in a building without air-conditioning and what do you expect?"

Riley tried to improve the morale of his troops. "We're going home," he said. "The temperature will be 75, the humidity will be 30, and the usual 17,505 will be for us."

It was and they were. By this point, it was clear that the basketball gods had ordained that this transformative series — which had gripped America by the lapels and eclipsed everything from the presidential race to midseason baseball in the public consciousness — would go the full seven games. How could it not?

In addition to another coast-to-coast flight, the Lakers faced another challenge before Game 6. Kareem Abdul-Jabbar woke up the night before feeling as though a large animal were sitting on his skull. It was his sixth migraine of the series. He didn't even attend a pregame warm-up.

But then he played what was perhaps his best game of the series. Unfurling his skyhook — the shot he developed as a five-foot-eight nine-year-old when his conventional offerings were blocked by opponents on his playground — he scored a game-high 30 points and played all but six minutes. The Lakers made a furious second-half comeback and won 119–108. For good measure, Worthy shoved Cedric Maxwell in the back, sending him into the basket stanchion, an indication the Lakers could play dirty, too. And as M. L. Carr left the floor, a Lakers fan threw a beer at him and drenched him.*

Riding an elevator after the game, Stern allegedly told a colleague he was happy to see the series go to a Game 7. (While consistent with the league's best interest, decades later Stern professed no recollection of this comment.) When word got to Bird, he was livid. "He's the commissioner and he shouldn't be saying anything like that. The NBA wanted a seventh game because they wanted to make more money, and they got their wish. . . . Maybe he said it in jest, but I am trying to make a living and

---

* Recounting this in 2019, David Stern raised a fair point. When it came to concessions at sporting events, "beer was much less expensive . . . than it is now."

win a championship." (The NBA rejected Bird's comments as "ridiculous.")

More problematic for Boston was the return flight. Because the team wanted to get back home as soon as possible, they booked a red-eye. The only problem: there were no seats on the flight to Boston. So they flew overnight to New York and changed planes. Let's repeat that: flying home to Game 7 of the NBA Finals — the decisive game of the season — the Celtics *did not fly nonstop.*

It was misery for everyone, save one man: Leigh Montville. A wonderfully mordant *Boston Globe* columnist, Montville flew in the smoking section and was seated next to an extraordinarily tall and extraordinarily attractive woman. A Boston television reporter offered Montville a microwave oven if he would switch seats so he could sit next to the ravishing woman. Montville refused. He asked to borrow one of her Pall Malls and they struck up a conversation. She was a model from Australia who had just turned 20. Her name was Elle Macpherson.

By this point, perhaps for the first time ever, the NBA Finals had captivated the entire country. What had typically been of interest to only the two relevant markets and hardcore pro basketball fans, the Finals were now relevant to even the most casual sports fans throughout America.

For this decisive game at the Boston Garden, there were 14,890 fans in attendance. But there were also hundreds of other fans. Electric fans, handheld fans, ceiling fans. This was done at the direction of the NBA. The Celtics couldn't install air-conditioning in their venue. But the most important game in NBA history could not feature a repeat of Game 5, with referees fainting, players taking oxygen, and shirtless yahoos cheering at an indoor sporting event featuring temperatures crowding 100 degrees.

Now the best-of-seven series was reduced to one winner-take-all game, stripped of all bravado and subplot. This was sport distilled to its essence. One team would win. One would lose. And everything else was so much window dressing.

Brent Musburger started the CBS telecast for Game 7 with an introduction that was, as was his wont, both comically over the top and pitch-perfect. Departing from his catchphrase, "You're looking live at [insert venue here]," Musburger instead said, "If you could bottle all emotion released in this basketball game, you'd have enough hatred to start a war. And enough joy to prevent one. Here tonight in the ancient Boston Garden we'll run the entire gamut of emotions."

As tipoff approached, the Showtime Lakers were uncharacteristically quiet and pensive, while the Celtics were uncharacteristically loose. Danny Ainge orbited the locker room wearing a stethoscope, pretending to give his teammates mock "heart checks," and concluded that they had the necessary courage. Cornball? Yes. But the shtick had the desired effect.

Maybe not surprisingly, given the stakes, the game itself was no classic. It was uneven and lacking in rhythm. Neither team made more than half its shots. Bird, the self-styled gunslinger seemingly impervious to pressure, missed 12 of his 18 shots. Magic was comparably inaccurate, shooting 5-for-14. Instead, other players came to the fore. Abdul-Jabbar turned in another strong performance, finally putting to rest any doubt that he was a big-game player. Cedric Maxwell, Most Valuable Player of the 1981 Finals, led the Celtics with 24 points, 14 of them on free throws.

Heading into the fourth quarter — with the entire crowd yelling *"Beat. L. A.!"* on repeat — the Celtics led by 13 points. The Lakers came within three points with less than a minute left, and the ball was in Magic's capable hands. But he committed still another late-game mistake, jumping in the air without committing to a clear plan of action. The Celtics stole the ball, sealing the game, the series, and the season.

Fans, predictably, jubilantly stormed the court, one of them assaulting Kareem Abdul-Jabbar and swiping his goggles. In what was a formality, Bird was named MVP of the series. Multiple teammates recall Bird saying something to the effect of "I finally got him," a reference to exacting personal revenge on Magic for the 1979 NCAA title game, more than five years earlier. Interviewed by Musburger, Bird dismissed any personal rivalry with Magic but then shook the trophy and brayed, "This one's for Terre Haute," the town where Indiana State University is located, not far from French Lick.

For all the raw, hot emotion coursing through the game, the outcome could best be explained in the cold, hard statistics of the box score. The Celtics may have shot dreadfully, but in rebounding—that basketball metric that translates as "hustling"—they held a whopping advantage, 52–33. For the series, the Celtics outrebounded the Lakers in five of the seven games and grabbed 131 offensive rebounds—almost 20 per game—a record for the NBA Finals, outscoring the Lakers 159–90 on second-chance points. Which is to say, the data supported—perhaps even confirmed—the deeper themes of the rivalry. Maybe the Celtics *were* the superior competitors. As the cliché-prone basketball coach might put it, maybe they did "want it more." Playing in all-the-chips-on-the-table seventh games in an NBA championship series, the Celtics were now 7-0 in the franchise's history. The Lakers were 0-5. The head-to-head score in NBA Finals was now Celtics 8, Lakers 0.

After the game, Johnson offered a glimpse of his likable and convivial personality, but also a strange nonchalance. "The ending was not good. I felt like we handed it to them, but I'm still going to party, because I'm a party guy. We didn't get the title, but we came darn close. We deserve a party." (Suffice it to say that if the Celtics had lost Game 7, Larry Bird would not have suggested a party.) It was only later, when Magic was alone in his hotel room, that he allowed himself to cry.

The Celtics' celebration was considerable, both in intensity and length. After guzzling champagne in the locker room and in the halls of the Boston Garden, the players repaired to a downtown bar, Chelsea's. The party then moved to the home of the team's director of marketing. According to one account, "Bird stayed out until the sun came up, did a live interview with a Boston radio station, then went home to Brookline to sleep." By that time, nine Celtics players had gathered at Terminal A of Logan Airport to jump a flight to Washington, D.C., and head to the White House. Bird did not make it. "If the president wants to see me," the best basketball player on the planet famously put it, "he knows where to find me."

If that did not delight the new commissioner, this did: the seventh game delivered the largest audience in NBA history. The game's 19.3 Nielsen rating and 33 share equated to 40 million viewers. A few seasons prior, the NBA Finals weren't even broadcast on live television. By 1984, more than 16 million homes were tuning in. For the new commissioner, who talked about television with an evangelical zeal, this was, in his words, "an epic win."

He didn't mean for the Celtics. He meant for the NBA.

The series was, in effect, an early version of reality television, an unscripted and unchoreographed drama with a seven-episode arc. There were feuds and tensions. There were characters acting out of character, not least Magic's subpar performance. There was a climactic brawl. There was resolution. For those two weeks in June of 1984, a country was captivated by the drama and captured by the rivalry — two very different teams, led by two different players.

And there would be an encore. The following year, the Lakers would face the Celtics in a rematch. This time Los Angeles would win, finally breaking the Celtics' spell. Which only added more heft and texture to the rivalry. And the summer after that, Magic would visit Bird's Indiana hometown and the two would film a Converse commercial. After a week spent together — after Bird's mother, Georgia, hugged Johnson — the rivals became friends.

And with that, the NBA was transformed. After the Celtics-Laker finals in 1984, the league achieved a sort of cruising altitude that it would never lose. Ted Shaker, head of CBS Sports, may have put it best when he reflected on the 1984 Finals: "We all knew something very special was happening here. Some of the problems the NBA had for years before were going away. And all of a sudden the NBA was cool."

And exactly one week later, Michael Jordan would enter the league.

7

HEIR JORDAN

In the spring of 1984, Donald Dell, 45 years old and already a sports titan, was luxuriating on a Saturday morning at his 26-acre estate in Potomac, Maryland, when he received a phone call. Figuring it was a personal call, not business, he picked up. Dell immediately recognized the raspy, tobacco-dipped voice. It was Dean Smith, North Carolina's head basketball coach, on the other end.

Though Dell had played on the Yale basketball team, he was better known in tennis circles. He played at Yale and then on the pro circuit, was close friends with Arthur Ashe, and helped found what is now the ATP, the men's tennis tour. After tennis, Dell had graduated from the University of Virginia Law School and gone on to work as an advance man on Bobby Kennedy's presidential campaign. But he had also become a pioneer in what was still a relatively new field — sports agenting — bringing to bear his polish, his social savvy, his connections, and his navigational tactics.

He and a group of friends and law school classmates had formed the

Washington, D.C., law firm Dell, Craighill, Fentress and Benton and spawned a sports division, ProServ. Dell and his colleagues would negotiate the contracts of professional athletes and help find them business opportunities — endorsements, as they were soon to be called. The firm also promoted sporting events and sold television rights. In exchange for these services, Dell would receive a commission, a few percentage points on playing contracts and prize money, and 15 percent, even 20 percent, on endorsements.

In 1983, the partners divorced. Lee Fentress and Frank Craighill split off and formed a new sports marketing firm they called Advantage International Inc. They walked out the door with a handful of clients. Dell remained at ProServ. As for key employees, they had a decision to make.

Jeff Austin had just finished up a professional tennis career. While he had not replicated the success of his kid sister, Tracy, he did get to No. 52 in the world. In the summer of 1984, he was a fledgling sports agent with a bright future. A year earlier he had married Denise Katnich, a bubbly fitness instructor. Perhaps prescient that Denise Austin would go on to sell more than 25 million fitness videos and DVDs, Jeff Austin took a professional risk and decamped to Advantage.

David Falk, an indefatigable young lawyer in his early thirties, was wearying of his role as Dell's glorified assistant. But for now, anyway, Falk chose to stay with Dell at ProServ.

As with most divorces, friends of the firm felt as though they had to choose sides. But not Dean Smith. He'd known them all. He'd worked with them all. He liked them all. Craighill had been a Morehead Scholar at the University of North Carolina, which had endeared him to Smith. But Smith had also bonded with Dell over their left-of-center politics. Through the years, Smith had directed a steady flow of Tar Heel basketball players to Dell, Craighill, Fentress and Benton. And Smith had been pleased with the services rendered.

In the spring of 1984, after the agency split, Smith came up with a Solomonic solution. But he didn't have to split any babies; he had two babies to distribute. There were two All-American players on his roster who were destined for the NBA, surefire top draft picks. He would "direct" Sam Perkins, a sleepy left-handed big man who played with a sort of lazy grace, to one agency. He would "direct" Michael Jordan to the other.

Left unspoken: while both firms would walk away with a client, Smith was going to use this as a bake-off. "Dean was almost diabolical in the way he advocated for his players," recalls Fentress, laughing. "We saw this as [Smith] setting up a competition. We're looking down the road — remember UNC had Brad Daugherty, Kenny Smith coming — we're thinking we need to prove ourselves."

With Dean Smith present, both firms made presentations to Jordan and Perkins. If the agents weren't totally agnostic, they hardly approached it as though there would be a clear-cut winner and a clear-cut loser. A six-ten forward, Perkins projected as a reliable, long-term NBA forward — a destiny he would fulfill, playing for 17 seasons. Jordan was flashier and more charismatic but didn't have an obvious NBA position; he was higher-reward, no doubt. But he was higher-risk as well.

When Perkins sent word that — with Dean Smith's heavy influence — he was selecting Advantage to represent him, the office erupted with glee. Fentress figured his new firm would go to great lengths to represent Perkins honorably and capably, the pipeline would be tapped, and Dean Smith would continue "recommending" players to agents, and vice versa.

Jeff Austin was especially thrilled. He would be taking the lead representing Perkins, a plum client for a young agent. "This is great," he enthused to a colleague in the early summer of 1984. "We signed the kid coming out of North Carolina! And I'm going to be running point!"

"Michael Jordan?" responded the colleague, only a casual basketball fan. "You just signed Michael Jordan?!"

"No, Sam Perkins!" said Austin.

"Uh, cool," the colleague said softly, before going back to work.

As for Donald Dell, he was more confused than elated when Smith rang him that Saturday morning. If it would rank among the most fateful calls made in the history of sports business, it sure didn't feel like it at the time.

"Donald," Smith said, "I'm here in my office with Mrs. Jordan and Michael. He's coming out as a junior. Would you like to represent him?"

"Sure," said Dell, without hesitation. "I'd love to. Put him on the ph—"

Jordan broke in. "I don't want to come out! I want to stay one more year! And Coach Smith won't let me!"

Deloris Jordan wasn't thrilled with the idea that her son would be leaving college before graduation. When Michael complained, she said nothing.

When the call ended, Dell was . . . perplexed. He had just been asked to represent Michael Jordan, a charismatic kid and an exhilarating player. Or at least he thought he'd been asked to represent Michael Jordan. Dell was confused as to whether he'd be working with Jordan or whether the young man was returning to school for his senior season.

That Jordan was even considering entering the draft marked a minor upset. In the popular retelling, Jordan was a good college player but one restricted and constricted by his coach, able to soar only once he'd been liberated in the NBA. True, he averaged only 17.7 points a game in college—what would later approximate his average for one *half* of a game in the NBA—and scored fewer points as a junior than he did as a sophomore. (The obligatory quip: Dean Smith was the only figure in basketball capable of holding Jordan to fewer than 20 points a night.)

In truth, Jordan's greatness was manifestly obvious while he was in college. For the 1983–84 season he earned a clean sweep of the seven major college player-of-the-year awards. He had been featured multiple times on the cover of *Sports Illustrated.* And he embraced the attention. "The publicity has been fun, I have to admit," he told the local media. "All in all, it's more fun to be noticed."

Still, it was uncommon for even the best players *not* to fulfill their four years of college eligibility, especially players from North Carolina.

In the future, players would spend as little time as possible in college. This change would be less about slouching standards than economics. In 1984, a year of free education versus the NBA league minimum salary of less than $70,000 was a fair fight. Today, when NBA rookies make millions guaranteed and get a one-year head start on a max contract that can exceed $10 million for marginal players and $40 million for stars, it's a considerably different calculus.

Why was Dean Smith so eager for Jordan to decamp to the NBA, so willing to lose a year of service from such an extravagantly talented player? One source of speculation: a few years earlier, when North Carolina was playing Maryland, some fans who were upset by a referee's call had thrown ice on the floor. James Worthy, UNC's best player, slipped on a wet spot, broke his right ankle, missed 14 games, and played his next season with a six-inch rod in his foot. Smith didn't want Jordan to risk an unhappy plot twist in his promising—and so far unpaid—career.

Jordan was so agonized by the decision that on April 26, 1984, he called a press conference and announced . . . that he still wasn't sure. In one breath he said, "I'm planning on staying here and I'm looking forward to my next year here." In another he said, "Coach has always looked out for his players and wants what's best for his team."

Around the same time in Beaverton, Oregon, a group of Nike executives gathered for a strategy session. Technically, Nike was more than 20 years old, founded with $1,200 by an eccentric University of Oregon alum, Phil Knight, and the school's track coach, Bill Bowerman. It had been 13 years since Knight famously paid a graphic design student $35 to come up with the company's insignia, a "swoosh" denoting energy and progress. It had been a full decade since the company's Waffle Trainer shoe was patented.

By the late seventies Nike had, forgive the pun, gained traction for its running shoes. And it was now turning to basketball. It had entered the endorsement game, paying a few marginal NBA players as much as $10,000 to wear its shoes. But given that the NBA's most luminous stars — Larry Bird and Magic Johnson and Julius Erving, d/b/a Doctor J. — were locked up by Converse, space in pro basketball was limited. Nike figured the real inroads were to be made in high school and college basketball.

To help achieve this, Nike turned to Sonny Vaccaro. The son of an immigrant steelworker, Vaccaro was a high school teacher in Trafford, Pennsylvania. But he was also an ambitious and relentlessly outgoing middleman in youth basketball circles. He had persuaded the *Pittsburgh Post-Gazette* to sponsor a national high school basketball showcase, the Dapper Dan Roundball Classic.* Through that event, he'd met not just young players but most of the college players in the country.

Nike quickly hired him for $500 a month to help penetrate youth basketball. Vaccaro seized on the idea, asking college basketball coaches to switch their footwear allegiance and outfit their players in Nike gear. When they asked "Why?" Vaccaro had a response ready. Nike would pay the coaches on the order of $10,000, which represented several months of their salary. By 1984, the quartet of schools that reached the NCAA Final Four were all "Nike schools."

Emboldened by this success, in the spring of 1984, Nike was reconsidering how to reenter the NBA and siphon market share from Converse and Adidas. So it was that a small group of executives gathered at "the Mansion," a house in suburban Portland that the company used for off-site strategy meetings. Rob Strasser, Nike's young director of marketing, was joined by Howard Slusher, an NFL agent and longtime consultant, confidant, and friend of Knight's. Vaccaro flew up — on his own dime, he was quick to point out — from his home in Los Angeles.

On February 15, 1984, Howard Slusher had written to Strasser with recommendations for allocating Nike's marketing money on the 1984 draft class. Slusher, Vacarro recalls, mentioned Kentucky senior Sam

---

* The *Pittsburgh Post-Gazette*'s philanthropic arm was named "Dapper Dan Charities." Yes, newspapers at the time were sufficiently profitable that they had philanthropic arms.

Bowie by name, declaring him "worth it." But Slusher added a list of underclassmen — he had Jordan fourth — and implored, "If the underclassmen come out, spend money!"

They did and they did.

At this summit, Strasser announced that Nike was committing a princely sum of $500,000 to lavish on three promising players in the 1984 draft. One would be the charismatic mold-breaker Charles Barkley — that was a foregone conclusion. Michael Jordan was another name in heavy rotation. The third player might be John Stockton, the young — and, pointedly, white — guard from Gonzaga, who embodied Nike's cult appeal and Pacific Northwest origins. Sam Bowie's name was suggested but then dismissed, as there were concerns about his proneness to injury.

"This is crazy," Vaccaro said, laughing. "Give it all to the Kid."

"What?" Vaccaro recalls Strasser responding, incredulous. By the standards of the 1984 market, this was preposterous. At the time, Lakers forward James Worthy, a young but established star in the Los Angeles market, was believed to have the most generous shoe contract in the NBA. His deal with New Balance paid him $150,000.

"The Kid! Give the whole thing, all five hundred grand, to the Kid. Michael Jordan. Don't split it three ways. Commit the whole thing to Jordan."

Silence descended on the room. Vaccaro happily filled the vacuum. Over the years, he had noticed that, while Converse had paid NBA players well, it wasn't a particularly deep relationship. The players were handed a check and in exchange they filmed a commercial, posed for a promotional poster, and were expected to play basketball in the shoes they were being paid to wear. The end. This had struck Vaccaro as shortsighted.

"Why not build entire marketing campaigns around one player?" Vaccaro recalls saying. "Hell, for $500,000, why not give a player his own shoe? You could have *the* Michael Jordan shoe."

• • •

By early May of his junior year, only weeks before the draft, Michael Jordan had *still* not made up his mind. In the second semester of his junior year, he had dutifully studied for his final exams and even written a final paper for a class on his experience at the Olympic Trials. Reading these tea leaves, Kenny Smith, a North Carolina guard, was convinced that Jordan would return as a senior, to complete his degree in geography and finish out his final season.

On Saturday, May 5, Jordan held another press conference at UNC's Fetzer Gym, a campus rec center. Wearing two gold chains, a golf shirt, and a look of nervous uncertainty, he sat next to Dean Smith on the podium. Smith did most of the speaking for his player, confirming suspicions. In what might qualify as a Freudian slip, Smith said flatly, "At this time we are announcing that Michael will denounce his college eligibility."

Jordan then filled in the timeline and reiterated just how excruciating a decision this had been. "To tell you the truth, I only just decided an hour and a half ago," Jordan said in a voice not exactly saturated with joy. "I was fifty-fifty and I talked to Coach this morning. He helped me. My parents helped me, and everything looks bright for me. I think the future holds—hopefully—the best for me. And I thought it would be better for me to start now."

The indelicate issue of finances bubbled just beneath the surface. Jordan, an unapologetic capitalist, was happy to indulge the topic. "Money played a big part," he said. "Who knows? I may not be around next year, and I've got the opportunity at hand right now."

James Jordan, Michael's father, was happy to joke about his own economic status change. James was, rightfully, proud of his job managing inventory control at General Electric's Wilmington plant. But Michael's departing college was going to change his personal finances. "Once he leaves and goes out on his own," said the elder Jordan, "I'm automatically going to get a raise. I don't have to give him two or three dollars and stuff like that. Michael has turned 21. Once a guy turns 21, he feels like he can make his own decisions."

By May 10, Rob Strasser was on the case. He wrote Dean Smith a note on behalf of Nike. "We're very interested in beginning an endorsement relationship with Michael Jordan." He went on to explain that Nike was shifting its endorsement philosophy and moving from mass exposure to a smaller number of players. Nike's plan to seduce Michael Jordan was officially under way.

8

THERE'S A DRAFT IN HERE

In a fit of self-aggrandizement—and one that deeply discounts the Roman Colosseum, for starters—Madison Square Garden, in New York City, has long billed itself as "the World's Most Famous Arena." Whatever truth that claim may or may not hold, its annex venue surely ranks among the world's *least* famous arenas.

Positioned directly beneath the Madison Square Garden floor, the Felt Forum—at this writing in 2019, it's named the Hulu Theater—is unknown even to some hardened New Yorkers. A low-ceilinged band-box, it seats 5,000 or so and is used for everything from high school graduation ceremonies to off-brand boxing cards and sales conventions.

On the afternoon—*afternoon*—of Tuesday, June 19, 1984, the Felt Forum was the site of the NBA's annual player draft. New York commuters coming in and out of Penn Station that day were forgiven for walking alongside the Felt Forum entrance on Eighth Avenue and having no clue that the theater was even in use. There was no marquee, no signage, and no rabid crowd out front.

This was in keeping with the NBA's reputation as a league lost in the sports hinterlands. Among the "Big Four" North American sports leagues, by most every metric, the NBA was far closer to the NHL than to the NFL and Major League Baseball. Just four years earlier, the Lakers had played the 76ers in the NBA Finals and CBS declined to broadcast Game 6 live. So it was that pro basketball fans on the East Coast were required to stay up until 11:30 p.m. to start to watch a *tape-delayed* broadcast of the decisive game of the NBA Finals. In a self-fulfilling prophecy, the audience was minuscule.

Another devastating blow landed two years later when the *Los Angeles Times* "reported" that 75 percent of the NBA's players were on drugs. And the issue of race bubbled just beneath the surface. Left unsaid—though it hardly needed to be said—these drug-addled athletes were overwhelmingly Black. Both the data and the methodology were laughably suspect. The story also offered no basis for comparison, ignoring the concurrent MLB cocaine scandal and the innumerable NFL players being shot up with painkillers that could paralyze a horse. The "story," though, made a considerable impact. The NBA and the Players Association reached an agreement that players could be drug-tested based on "reasonable cause" for suspicion. And the reputation stuck like a persistent defender: the NBA was a league for degenerates, which, put lightly, was not good for business.

At NBA headquarters in Midtown Manhattan, the league's employees had two jobs. They had their full-time position in broadcasting or legal or accounting. Their other job: convincing the world—starting with potential sponsors—that the league's unsavory reputation was undeserved. Steve Mills, who had played basketball for Princeton and then overseas, started working in the league office in 1984. He recalls, "If you had 30 minutes with a prospective sponsor, your first 20 minutes were spent trying to convince him that the players weren't all on drugs."

Complicating matters, during the 1980–81 season, 17 of the NBA's 23 teams had lost money. In every city that was home to both an NBA and an NHL franchise, it was the hockey team that brought in more fans and more revenue. This was to say nothing of baseball. An average Saturday afternoon *Major League Baseball Game of the Week* on NBC brought in a 4.5 Nielsen rating. Though there were only five regular-season NBA games that aired nationally on CBS, they were lucky to draw a 2.2 rating.

Average NBA attendance barely eclipsed 10,000 fans a game, or 58 percent of arena capacity. The Cleveland Cavaliers lost more than $4 million, selling only 28 percent of their seats. The Boston Celtics were valued at $18 million. A middling franchise like the Indiana Pacers would have fetched half that.* The median NBA player salary in 1984 was $340,000. "We had to come through the worst of the allegations about drugs," said Stern, "and the concern that America wouldn't support a Black sport."

By the summer of 1984, though, the NBA was on a mild, if rare, upswing. A week before the draft, the Celtics and the Lakers had brought the NBA into the national conversation as they finished their tense series featuring the two brightest stars in the basketball cosmos. Maybe just as important, the league had recently come under the leadership of a new, young commissioner, David Stern, a workaholic whose unofficial motto was "a relentless pursuit of perfection."

As a lawyer at the Manhattan white-shoe firm Proskauer Rose, Stern had been mentored by a labor lawyer named Ed Silver.† Very much by chance, Stern handled much of the NBA's legal work. He helped negotiate the Oscar Robertson antitrust settlement. (The suit was filed in 1970; when it was settled, in 1976, it formed the basis for what remains of the NBA's free agency policy.) A management-side lawyer through and through, he helped establish a salary cap, putting a ceiling on player wages and, in effect, saving the owners from themselves. Stern also

---

* In the late 1970s, the Pacers' coach, Bobby "Slick" Leonard, and his wife held a local telethon just to keep the team afloat.

† Because Proskauer had a no-nepotism policy, Silver's son, Adam, began his legal career at another New York firm, Cravath, Swaine & Moore.

played a prominent role in hammering out the merger agreement between the ABA and the NBA, whereby four teams in the former were absorbed by the latter.*

At the time, the NBA's commissioner was the polished, if not particularly effective, Larry O'Brien, who saw talent in the league's rumpled outside lawyer. In 1978, he persuaded Stern — by then a young partner — to leave Proskauer and become the NBA's first in-house general counsel and 24th full-time employee. The other Proskauer partners shook their heads and told him he was crazy. Why would Stern abandon the secure and cosseted life of big-firm practice to work for a second-tier sports league?

David Stern was the son of William Stern, whose deli on Twenty-Third St. and Eighth Avenue in Manhattan, a few blocks from Stern's first boyhood home, was open seven days a week. David Stern stood five-nine. In contrast to Mills, who played at Princeton and then overseas, Stern's basketball pedigree entailed rooting for the Knicks as a kid, paying 50 cents to sit in the blue seats at Madison Square Garden and hoping an usher would let him sneak down.

But Stern possessed a sharp mind, sharper elbows, and an iron ass. When he was in ninth grade, his family moved to New Jersey, where David finished high school and then went to Rutgers. At Columbia Law School, Stern was known as the king of the all-nighter. It didn't take him long to decide he'd rather use his gifts to solve basketball's legal riddles than transact the dry corporate and labor work he might do at Proskauer.

Stern also brought to bear an abundance of confidence and a temper, which often worked in concert. When CBS broadcast the 1983 NBA Playoffs and showed pastures of empty seats during the Knicks-Sixers

---

* In fairness, Stern's fingerprints are also all over the best/worst deal in sports history. In exchange for forfeiting a spot in the NBA, the owners of the ABA's Spirits of St. Louis accepted one-seventh of the television revenue of the Nets, Nuggets, Spurs, and Pacers *in perpetuity.* When the owners mercifully settled with the NBA in 2014, they had earned close to $1 billion from a dysfunctional ABA team that lasted only two seasons.

series, Stern was on the phone haranguing network executives. As Ted Shaker, CBS's executive producer for sports at the time, told *Sport Illustrated,* "I can think of any number of phone conversations where he did all he could to reduce me to the size and stature of an ant. Or at least to leave me with the opinion that my brain is the size of an ant."

The more time Stern spent at the NBA, the clearer it became that he was endowed with still another gift: entrepreneurship. His legal work had been based on cold and clinical analysis, solving problems and reacting to the challenges confronting clients. At the NBA, he could play more offense than defense. After a series of fast promotions, Stern held the vague title of executive vice president, the league's number two behind the commissioner. But he used the ambiguity of his position to his advantage, learning the business, or, less charitably, acquiring territory. The general counsel couldn't sit in a marketing meeting or express opinions about the best broadcast camera angles. But who's to stop the league's executive vice president?

Around the office, Stern was famous for his mantra: *If you're doing the same thing tomorrow that you are doing today, you are falling behind.* Says Brian McIntyre, the league's director of basketball communications in 1984, "David was constantly learning new things and imploring us to do the same. *Why aren't we doing this? . . . We should be doing that.* He was always looking to shake things up."

In the manner of his law school professors at Columbia, Stern was known for peppering employees with questions and challenging them to find creative solutions. *Why not market the league outside the United States—it's a ball and hoop and we have the best players in the world. Wouldn't people in Europe or China or South America appreciate that? The NBA should be a global brand! . . . Why not make the All-Star Game a bigger deal? Why not market the dunk contest, maybe add a shooting contest, and wrap it around an entire weekend? . . . Couldn't the NBA have its own licensing arm? . . . Basketball players are real-life superheroes who perform half-naked. This is a competitive advantage. How do we mint more stars?*

Time and again, NBA employees, exhausted by the barrage of ideas, complained to Stern, "We can't do everything."

"Why not?" he shot back.

"Everything can't be a priority," employees would protest.

"You are wrong," he'd reply. "Everything *is* a priority."

Stern was obsessed with a central, overarching question: How could the NBA become more relevant to sports fans? More relevance meant more growth and more audience, which meant more revenue and value. So often, Stern's answer to this existential riddle reduced to two letters: TV.

In the early eighties, Stern saw a new landscape where sports and entertainment intersected; where broadcasting rights would become more important and valuable than ticket sales; where technology and distribution would improve, opening new markets; where — to borrow a phrase that came later — the world was flat, and global borders would become increasingly porous.

Colleagues recall seeing Stern seated on the commuter train from his home in Scarsdale, his suit somehow already rumpled, reading *The Economist* or the business section of *The New York Times,* and only skimming the sports section. Stern was known to leave the office and attend obscure seminars about cable TV — this at a time before cable was commercially available.

"What," he'd be asked, "is the NBA doing here?"

His response: "We are only the largest provider of reality programming in the world!"

He left convinced that NBA games were perfect fare — *content,* it would later be called — for new networks. He ordered the staff to digitize old videos, reasoning, presciently, that such footage would one day be valuable. He put in place plans for the NBA to build its studio in New Jersey. He encouraged the league's teams to upgrade the quality of their local-game telecasts.

Stern then bought every team a three-quarter-inch Panasonic VCR. For $25, he hired an employee to go to the broadcast truck, make a tape of the contest, put it in a FedEx envelope, and send it to Secaucus, New Jersey. He then hired loggers to annotate individual games. He saw to it that the tapes were preserved in a temperature-controlled building. "And," he said, "suddenly we have a library."*

Stern was quickly outgrowing his role as the league's number two. For all their differences and dissatisfactions, the NBA's 23 franchise owners agreed about this as well. At the 1984 All-Star Game, in Denver, Larry O'Brien was given a grand send-off. The next Monday, Stern assumed the role of commissioner. As a joke, he put his hand on a league guide and took a mock oath of office. At the time, the NBA's annual gross revenues were $118 million.†

Outside of pro basketball circles, Stern's profile was modest. So modest that when he was announced as commissioner, a young CNN sports reporter, Dan Patrick, had the idea to take to the streets for a shticky piece asking New Yorkers if they knew the name of the new NBA commissioner. Howard Stern they knew. Isaac Stern, the violinist, drew a few mentions. David Stern didn't register.

Nor should it have. Stern was only 41 years old. And he cut a much different figure from his predecessor. O'Brien had been a polished bon vivant, once a campaign manager for John F. Kennedy, a member of Lyndon Johnson's cabinet, and the Democratic National Committee chair. Stern was less inclined to attend black-tie Manhattan dinners than to stay late and field calls from executives of West Coast teams. It was an article of faith that when NBA employees arrived on the 15th floor, Stern would already be occupying his office in the southwest corner. When they left, his lights would still be on, his clipped voice echoing through the halls. When *he* left the office, it wasn't for long. And when he left the job for good, in 2014—almost 30 years to the day after he took the oath

---

* In 2019, Stern would joke that, ironically, he was an investor in an Israeli company that used artificial intelligence to create highlight packages. "So my life's work has been overtaken by science."

† By the time Stern left the commissionership, the NBA's gross revenues were . . . $5.5 billion. His successor? Ed Silver's son Adam.

of office — he would do so as the most successful and powerful commissioner in the history of American sports.

In a remarkable bit of foreshadowing, the first real crisis of Stern's commissionership was brought on by Donald Sterling in the summer of 1984. The miserable owner of the Clippers, Sterling had made his fortune by renting out down-at-the-heels apartments in and around Los Angeles — a "Slumlord Billionaire," *The Nation* would later call him. He wasn't any less miserly as a sports team owner. "The checks bounced higher than the basketballs when Donald Sterling took over," Bill Walton, a former Clippers center, complained.

The team played in San Diego, but Sterling lamented the small crowds and the limitations of the market. Sterling and his aides-de-camp — president Alan Rothenberg and general counsel Arn Tellem — watched closely as Al Davis successfully sued the NFL for the right to relocate his football team, the Raiders, from Oakland to Los Angeles. When the courts ruled that, under antitrust law, the NFL could not block the Raiders' move, Sterling was emboldened. In 1984, without seeking league approval, he moved the Clippers to Los Angeles without NBA approval.

Livid, Stern fined Sterling $25 million, double the amount Sterling had paid to buy the team in 1981. Sterling countersued for $100 million. "[The NBA] can't win," said Rothenberg, citing the Davis case.

Stern was uncowed and unbowed. He was convinced that even if case law wasn't on his side, he couldn't allow a rogue owner to undercut the league. He ordered the NBA to fight the suit. Years later, the NBA and the Clippers settled. Sterling could keep his team in Los Angeles but would have to pay a fine of $5.7 million. Thirty years later, Sterling was revealed to be a vile and flagrant racist, which posed the first real crisis for Stern's successor, Adam Silver. The new commissioner forced Sterling to sell the team, which he did. For $2 billion, or 160 times his purchase price.

The 1984 draft, though, marked one of Stern's first major achievements. The commissioner had watched as pro football — with the NFL and the USFL — became a year-round sport and Major League Baseball's "hot stove league" ensured that the sport stayed relevant after the World Series and until spring training. The NBA needed to follow this model. And, as Stern saw it, a splashy draft was a first step. For years, the event had been no event at all. The owners would gather casually on a conference call and then in person, in a hotel ballroom, to select college players for, comically, 10 rounds. After the first few rounds, owners passed around sports magazines, relying on them for their selections. Some owners bypassed the last few rounds entirely to catch earlier flights home.

Stern was intent on changing this. The Draft — he insisted it be capitalized to underscore its importance — marked an opportunity to celebrate and introduce the next class of NBA players. At Stern's behest, the league *paid* for the USA Network to produce the event and broadcast it, not vice versa. For its announcing team, USA paired Al Albert, best known for his work on boxing broadcasts — as well as for being a kid brother of sportscaster Marv Albert — with Lou Carnesecca, the St. John's coach. Albert opened the 1984 draft telecast with the slightly desperate-sounding entreaty "For the next three hours, the USA cable network wishes you to join us."

In what looked more like a bingo parlor than the site of a significant league event, team representatives sat on metal folding chairs in rows behind a small stage adorned with a banner advertising beer, reading MILLER TIME. In front of the stage: lots of empty seats and little energy.

The other glaring deficiency: players. With so many likely draft picks marooned in Indiana for the Olympics camp, Stern and his minions went to great lengths to recruit other players to be on hand. The night before the draft, Stern arranged a dinner for the player likely to be picked first, University of Houston center Akeem Olajuwon — the *H,* reflecting the proper Arabic spelling, wouldn't come until 1991. Olajuwon, his brother, and his parents, who had flown in from Nigeria for the occasion, were there. Stern wanted to welcome the Olajuwon clan to what he called "the NBA family."

When the Olajuwons accepted the invitation, Stern thought it might ease any awkwardness if he invited other prospective draft picks as well.

Few other players were up for it. The NBA finally prevailed on Ohio State forward Tony Campbell, mostly relying on the sales pitch that Campbell and Stern were from the same town, Teaneck, New Jersey, and had gone to the same high school. (When Campbell was selected with the 20th pick the following night, Stern slyly announced the selection by noting that Campbell was a product of Ohio State University *and* Teaneck High School.)

The awkwardness was compounded when the dinner guests arrived at the Italian restaurant on 33rd Street and realized that the ceilings were dangerously low. Olajuwon would later recall that he didn't get up during the meal to go to the bathroom for fear he'd get a concussion.

The Houston Rockets held the first pick in the draft. Which was remarkable, given that the team had held the first pick the previous year as well, using it to choose seven-foot-four Ralph Sampson. While many considered it redundant to select another center, size was the coin of the NBA realm. A big man like Olajuwon, possessing grace and balletic footwork and athleticism, was simply too good *not* to take. The Rockets made no secret of their plans. They would pair Olajuwon and Sampson and brand them, inevitably, the Twin Towers.

On draft night, as Stern took to the podium, many of the seats to the left and right of him were vacant. Presiding over his first draft, the commissioner wore a blue suit, a thick cookie-duster mustache, wire-rimmed glasses, and a look of uncertainty. This marked his first major television appearance as commissioner. He recalled wondering to himself, *How do I go out there and try not to look as nervous as I actually am?*

When Stern, flawlessly, announced Olajuwon as the first pick, the player approached the stage wearing a tuxedo. Albert intoned, "It is official. The well-attired Akeem Olajuwon — who started playing basketball just five years ago in Nigeria — is the number-one pick."*

Stern was thrilled with the selection. For one, he had not botched

---

* As Stern presided over his final NBA Draft in 2014, colleagues surprised him by inviting Olajuwon. Who, again, showed up in a tuxedo.

one of his first big-stage moments as NBA commissioner. He also realized the significance of what had just happened. For years he had been preaching the gospel that the NBA could scale internationally, entering new markets to cultivate fans and, yes, TV audiences. "One day in the future," he enthused to colleagues, "we will have Atlanta playing Barcelona and Detroit playing London." Here was an African player selected with the top pick, a validation that basketball knew no borders.

Olajuwon's selection was also significant in that it accelerated the trend of college players leaving school early. Players conducting their own cost-benefit analysis were increasingly reaching the conclusion that the sooner they entered the NBA workforce and started earning wages, the better. For the fourth time in the past six years, an "early entry" had been taken first. For this draft, there were nine undergraduates who made themselves eligible, including Olajuwon and Jordan, both of whom were 21. Other players—including Georgetown's Patrick Ewing and Oklahoma's Wayman Tisdale—wavered right up until the deadline over whether to turn pro.

The draft's real intrigue revolved around what the Portland Trail Blazers would do with the No. 2 pick. Jordan's NBA-ready game was seductive, but there were some strikes against him, especially for the Blazers. Portland was unconvinced that Jordan could find a position in the NBA, as he was neither a true guard nor a true forward. Besides, the team already had a high-flying swingman in Clyde Drexler (Olajuwon's former teammate at the University of Houston) and a six-six playmaker in Jim Paxson (whose brother, John, ironically, would later be Jordan's longtime teammate).

In Bloomington, Bob Knight heard about Portland's waffling and was baffled. He expressed this to his friend Stu Inman, the Blazers' general manager. "You have to pick Jordan," Knight said. "He's unbelievable."

"We already have a shooting guard and a small forward," Inman explained.

"Shit, pick Jordan and play him at center if you have to," Knight responded. "Just draft him."

By this point, Knight was a full-on Jordan convert. Though Jordan had yet to play an NBA game — and hadn't averaged more than 20 points in a season in college — here was Knight's assessment in the summer of 1984: "If I were going to pick people with the best ability I'd ever seen play the game, he'd be one of them. If I wanted to pick the best competitors I'd ever seen play, he'd be one of them. So in the categories of competitiveness, ability, skill, and then athletic ability, he's the best athlete, he's one of the best competitors, he's one of the most skilled players. And that to me makes him the best basketball player that I've ever seen play."

But what Portland really needed was a big man, and the best center available after Olajuwon was Sam Bowie, from the University of Kentucky. Bowie had missed two full seasons of college with a left leg injury. The Blazers interviewed Bowie's doctors in Lexington and in Memphis, where one of his surgeries had been performed. The team also put Bowie through a battery of physical tests in the spring of 1984. The team's doctors determined that he was healthy. So it was that Stern uttered a sentence that, decades later, still triggers profound distress in the Pacific Northwest: "Portland selects Sam Bowie."

The Chicago Bulls' representatives concealed their smiles. They had always preferred Michael Jordan to Bowie (though not to Olajuwon). When Jordan was still available, the Bulls selected him as reflexively as they might withdraw their hand from a hot stove: less a decision than an instinct. Within a few years, it would become clear that they had just benefited from one of the great spasms of good fortune in sports history.

But that night the Bulls' general manager, Rod Thorn, reacted dispassionately. Whether it was to tamp down fans' expectations, to tamp down Jordan's salary expectations, or *maybe* to express genuine uncertainty about Jordan, Thorn all but apologized for the pick.

"We wish he were seven feet, but he isn't," Thorn forlornly told the Chicago media. "There just wasn't a center available. What can you do?"

Further puncturing optimism, he added, "When you win only 55 games in two years, you don't get well all at once. . . . Jordan isn't going to turn this franchise around. I wouldn't ask him to. I wouldn't put that kind of pressure on him. . . . He's a very good offensive player. But not an overpowering offensive player."

The *Tribune* columnist Bernie Lincicome wasn't buying it. In a column headlined "Apologetic Bulls 'Stuck' with Michael Jordan," Lincicome all but accused Thorn of sandbagging. Jordan was a prized pick, Lincicome asserted. If all went well, he wrote, Jordan might one day even become the next Julius Erving.

Though Jordan was stationed in Bloomington, the NBA not only invited him to attend the draft in New York but offered to foot the bill and fly him from Indiana. Knight rejected the idea out of hand. "No way in hell" was his response. His players weren't missing a day of practice, much less (his phrase) "to get their asses kissed in Manhattan." Only grudgingly did Knight permit the players to be interviewed on draft day on a local television station.

George Raveling, the assistant coach/cool counselor, drove Jordan, as well as Perkins (picked fourth, immediately after Jordan, by the Dallas Mavericks) and Alvin Robertson (who went to the San Antonio Spurs at No. 7), to a small studio in Bloomington. There, they attached an earpiece and took part in a series of "remote" interviews, enduring an awkward delay, taking softball questions, and imparting a few clichés to their markets. Dressed casually in a tan shirt and standing before a backdrop of the exact same shade of tan, Jordan told his interlocutor, "Hopefully, I can go in and contribute and maybe turn it around. I'm looking forward to that."

As Raveling drove the players back to the Indiana gym for practice, he told them that they ought to celebrate this milestone. He was picking up the tab. Where would they like to eat lunch?

"McDonald's," Jordan demanded.

Raveling stressed that the players were now, for all intents, millionaires, and that steak was in order. Jordan persisted. "Coach," he said, "I don't care how much money I make. I'm a McDonald's guy."

So it was that Michael Jordan commemorated his ascendance to the

NBA by scarfing down a Big Mac at a McDonald's in central Indiana. Then it was back to practice.

With the fifth pick, the Philadelphia 76ers chose Charles Barkley, making him the third player among the top five who had left school early. Naturally, the USA broadcast wasted no time mentioning Barkley's weight. As Barkley made his way to the interview, the broadcaster enthused, "Tipping the scales at — the latest — three hundred pounds! He will now be alongside Julius Erving and Moses Malone."

While Jordan had agonized until the last minute over whether to stay at school or turn pro, Barkley easily made his decision to leave Auburn University. Playing at a level high enough to be named Southeastern Conference Player of the Year, Barkley was already considering his draft stock. When he went to Bloomington for the 1984 Olympic Trials and heard that NBA scouts were in the stands, he was more concerned about impressing them — showing that his girth was an asset and not a liability — than about making the Olympic team.

As Barkley saw it, he was simply acting rationally. And he was vocal about this. He was making the school plenty of money. He knew this in part because of the lengths to which the school had gone to make sure he could play. (As he once famously put it: "All I know is, as long as I led the Southeastern Conference in scoring, my grades would be fine.") So long as everyone else was getting paid, why shouldn't he?

During school he took money from three different agents, he later admitted, a violation of NCAA rules that could have made him ineligible. One agent who did not pay Barkley, Lance Luchnick, made a recruiting visit to Barkley's home. As Barkley tells it, in the middle of the presentation, both he and his mother fell asleep on the couch, leaving it to his grandmother to listen to the agent's pitch. In the end, Barkley picked Luchnick, reasoning that he was choosing someone who was incorruptible.

Not quite. Five years later, the NBA Players Association decertified Lance Luchnick after an arbitrator found him guilty of several violations, including overcharging Barkley for services. When Luchnick filed for bankruptcy, Barkley says he was left broke, in tax arrears and unable to recoup money from his bankrupt agent. "I signed with a scumbag," Barkley would later say. "I don't want to mention his name. If I saw him today, I would blow his damn brains out. I hate that SOB."

On draft night in the summer of 1984, Barkley was not especially happy, either. In advance of the draft, Barkley had visited the Philadelphia 76ers. Management informed him that they liked his game but hoped he would slim down to 285 pounds. Barkley complied. Then he learned that the 76ers' two stars, Moses Malone and Julius Erving, ate up most of the team's allotment under the NBA's hard salary cap, leaving only $75,000 for a rookie. ("I didn't leave school to make $75,000," Barkley would later joke. "I could've made that in college.")

Barkley's plan was simple. He went to Denny's in the morning for multiple Grand Slam breakfasts; in the evening, he ate porterhouse steaks for dinner. By the time he showed up in Philadelphia on the way to the draft, he was back over 300 pounds. Undeterred, the 76ers picked Barkley, who smiled through clenched teeth when the camera panned to him. (In the end, the 76ers made some offseason trades to clear cap room, and paid their 300-pound rookie $307,000 for his first season.)

Apart from his play, the team welcomed Barkley's personality, already outsized and already among his selling points. Billy Cunningham, Philadelphia's coach, was dead wrong when he complained, "It's not a very strong draft." But he was dead right when he predicted that Barkley's "reputation for instigating comic relief" would endear him.

Months before the draft, John Stockton had been exploring his options for playing in Europe. He had been a fine point guard at Gonzaga but had no delusions about reaching the NBA, not at six-one, and not after playing for an obscure college in Spokane.

But after Stockton acquitted himself so well at the Olympic Trials, his stock ticked upward. The Utah Jazz selected him with the 16th pick. Stockton was not at the Felt Forum in New York, and he was not in Bloomington. He was home in Spokane, where he had been sleeping in his boyhood bedroom over the summer as he awaited his fate.

Stockton was one of five members of the 1984 draft class to make the Basketball Hall of Fame upon their retirement, alongside Olajuwon, Jordan, and Barkley. The fifth? Oscar Schmidt, a heroic scorer from Brazil who was picked in the sixth round by the New Jersey Nets. Kobe Bryant would have known the correct answer: as a child growing up in Italy in 1984, Bryant was obsessed with Schmidt, the Italian League scoring champ in seven seasons.

Though this was still the era when it was inconceivable that there might be a player who had labored outside of the United States and was capable of holding his own in the NBA, the Nets offered Schmidt a no-cut contract. But it came with a stipulation: he could not play for the Brazilian national team. Schmidt declined. He stayed overseas, where he scored 49,737 points, dropped 46 points in Brazil's memorable upset of the American team at the 1987 Pan Am Games, and is generally considered the best international player of all time. He was also a man whose basketball ego was as prodigious as his scoring. In the run-up to the 1984 NBA Draft, he was asked if he shot too often. "Look," he said, without affect. "Some people are born to carry the piano. Others are born to *play* the piano."

There were also abundant twists and wild cards in that draft. Leon Wood, a free-shooting point guard who beat out Stockton for a roster spot on the Olympic team, was picked 10th. While he would have a forgettable NBA career as a player, he would later rejoin the league as a referee. Rick Carlisle, a guard from Virginia, was the last pick in the third round and made the Boston Celtics roster — in part because Larry Bird liked the way he played cerebrally and, it was rumored, in part because Bird liked the way he played piano on road trips. Carlisle would win an NBA title as a player in 1986; a quarter century later, he would win another as head coach of the Dallas Mavericks.

Nine rounds after selecting Jordan, with their last pick the Bulls chose Carl Lewis, a University of Houston athlete who had never played a minute of college basketball. Still, as the world's fastest man, then prepping for the Olympics, Lewis made for an inspired pick. Not that the Bulls were the only team with this idea. Barely two months earlier, the Dallas Cowboys had used the 334th pick of the 1984 NFL Draft to select Lewis as a wide receiver.

As the reigning NBA champs, the Celtics held the final pick in each round. With their 10th-round selection — the 228th and final pick in the entire draft — they selected Dan Trant, a Massachusetts kid who was a star at Clark College. Trant would never play an NBA game, but he managed a respectable career overseas. On September 11, 2001, he went to his job as a bond trader at Cantor Fitzgerald, on the 104th floor of the World Trade Center's North Tower. He died that day, at age 40.

The "Class of 1984" would rank among the great draft vintages in basketball — if not sports — history. Jordan, Olajuwon, Barkley, and Stockton would all rank among the top 25 NBA players of all time, winning eight titles and making 47 All-Star teams among them.

When the event was over, the NBA held a debriefing session at the league headquarters to discuss what had worked, what hadn't, and what could be improved the following year.

Overall, David Stern was pleased with the event, his first as commissioner. He had concealed his nervousness and botched few names. An international player was picked first, which fit nicely with Stern's organizing principle that the NBA was easily exported. The broadcast was generally smooth. (He did "not for a second" dwell on the fact that Sam Bowie had been picked ahead of Michael Jordan.) David Stern reached this conclusion: "We really ought to keep making a bigger and bigger deal out of this whole draft concept. We can stay relevant in the off-season."

9

JOY IN WRIGLEYVILLE

If the citizenry of Chicago wasn't breaking into spasms of joy over the selection of Michael Jordan, it was not just because they lacked basketball clairvoyance. They also lacked focus, distracted as they were by an unlikely story playing out on the city's North Side.

In the case of the Cubs, the relationship between team and town had long been a temperamental one. Baseball fans in the Wrigleyville neighborhood of Chicago loved their gracious ballpark and its quaint trappings. The ivy-festooned outfield walls. The bleachers and their open seating, which created the feel of an outdoor sports bar — the game itself less important than the beer and the social interactions. The absence of lights, which necessitated day games only and, especially on weekdays, created a shared sense that everyone was in on the same secret, playing hooky while life's suckers were at work and school.

The only problem was the baseball itself. It wasn't just that the Chicago Cubs were bad. It was that they were reliably, consistently, almost devotionally bad. Sometimes they lost in creative ways, blowing late-game leads and committing basic blunders — fielders losing pop-ups in the sun, pitchers treating home plate as if it were terra incognita. Other times the Cubs were routed, allowing opposing hitters to take advantage of the short porches and crush home runs, not simply over the fence but over the bleachers and onto Waveland Avenue, beyond left field, or Sheffield Avenue, beyond right field. In those games, the Cubs lost by football scores: 14–3, 17–7, 13–6.

Still another charming Wrigley touch: a flagpole containing the pennants of National League teams, flying in order of the divisional standings. More often than not, the Cubs flag was positioned at the bottom. The team had reached the World Series in 1945 and, through 1983, hadn't returned to the playoffs.

Cubs fans were often portrayed as the collective personification of patience. "Wait till next year" became their unofficial slogan. This was the franchise of lovable losers, whose fans would endure defeats as fair exchange for a convivial and affordable day at their charming ballpark. This was as much by design as by accident. In the early 1930s, when Philip K. Wrigley inherited the team from his father, the chewing gum tycoon William Wrigley Jr., he decided that resources were better spent on the ballpark's decor than on the product the team put on the field. As Wrigley once put it: "The fun, the game, the sunshine, the relaxation. Our idea is to get the public to see a ball game, win or lose."

Not surprisingly, given those priorities, there was more losing than winning. And even Cubs fans had their limits. On April 29, 1983, tensions surfaced in spectacular fashion. The Cubs slogged through another loss — this one a 4–3 defeat to the Dodgers on account of a wild pitch — putting Chicago's record at 5-14. Though it was only the 19th of 162 games, the season's outcome was, for all intents, already fated. And the 9,391 fans in attendance that day were more than mildly displeased. As the players left the field, they were mercilessly heckled by the crowd, requiring intervention by security guards.

Once he had retreated to his small office, the team's manager, Lee Elia — frustrated by the defeat, the treatment of his players, and the likely reality of another lost season — erupted Vesuvius-style, unleashing a soliloquy diehard Cubs fans would later come to recite verbatim. The money lines: "Eighty-five percent of the people in this country work. The other fifteen percent come here and boo my players. They ought to go out and get a fucking job and find out what it's like to go out and earn a fucking living. Eighty-five percent of the fucking world is working. The other fifteen come out here, a fucking playground for the cocksuckers."

Not surprisingly, Elia did not survive the season as manager. The Cubs closed out 1983 with a record of 71-91, the sixth-straight losing season and fifth-straight year finishing last or next to last in their division. Even with a majestic ballpark, the Cubs drew an average of only 18,268 fans, ranking them in the bottom half of baseball in attendance. For perspective, playing in a much smaller Canadian market and a far less charming stadium, the Montreal Expos outdrew the Cubs by more than 10,000 fans per game that season.

The 1984 season didn't appear to bring an infusion of hope, either. *Sports Illustrated* picked the Cubs to finish last in the National League East yet again. *The Christian Science Monitor* was, perhaps predictably, more charitable in its season preview, stating, "Improvement is the ticket here, but please don't mention pennants." Even *improvement* seemed ambitious, especially when the Cubs ended their 1984 spring training campaign with a record of 3-18.

It wasn't that the 1984 team was bad, so much as it was *strange*. Going into spring training, the roster featured a surfeit of hitting and a deficit of pitching. The outfield featured a converted catcher (Keith Moreland) hidden in right field, a natural right fielder (the eccentric Mel Hall) in center field, and a natural first baseman (the goateed, bespectacled Leon "Bull" Durham) in left field. ESPN would later call it "one of the worst defensive outfields of the last 25 years."

The team, though, had a secret weapon. He was almost 50 years old and moved gingerly. But Dallas Green was among the Cubs' saviors that season. A longtime baseball man, Green had played for the Phillies in the 1960s and managed their 1980 World Series champion team. Standing six-five, with a corona of graying hair and a booming voice, Green commanded a room. But he discovered that his other gifts included assessing talent, finding undiscovered players, and dealmaking. Successful as he was as a manager, he was a born *general* manager.

When the Tribune Company purchased the Cubs from the Wrigley family in 1981, one of its first moves was enticing Green to become the team's top executive. As he surveyed the 1984 Cubs, Green knew he had to upgrade the roster. Operating from what he called a position of "What the fuck do we have to lose?" he went to work.

Green was a baseball lifer who had supreme faith in his intuition. But he also believed in data, or, as it would come to be called years later, *analytics* or *advanced metrics.* He knew, for instance, that in 1983 the Cubs had been a dreadful 13-35 in games played on Astroturf. He made a priority of finding speedy players who could use turf as an asset, and pitchers who performed well on artificial grass.

Green also wasn't shy about using his knowledge of the Phillies organization to his advantage. He had already plucked Ryne Sandberg, then a lightly regarded 22-year-old infielder, as a throw-in in a 1982 trade/steal for shortstops Larry Bowa for Ivan DeJesus. (Sandberg would improve considerably in Chicago.) The week before opening day, Green traded a veteran relief pitcher and a young prospect to the Phillies for left fielder Gary Matthews and speedy center fielder Bob Dernier. With that, the Cubs' outfield was reimagined. So was the team's personality.

Already in his mid-thirties, Matthews cut an outsized figure. He went by the nickname "Sarge," a nod, he explained, to his "take-charge attitude." He also dressed like a man not wanting for confidence. Teammates would debate whether he presented himself more like a mobster or a pimp. But when Matthews entered the clubhouse, clad in an array of velvet suits and matching (and un-matching) hats, armed with a cup of coffee and a newspaper under his arm, he enlivened the room.

The trade with the Phillies enabled Durham to move back to first base. Which made the incumbent first baseman, Bill Buckner, expendable. Wearing shaggy hair and a push-broom mustache, Buckner had been a Cubs stalwart for the past seven seasons, among the few reliable performers who could be counted on to hit over .300. In 1980, he won the National League batting title. But by 1984 Buckner was squarely in his mid-thirties and feuding with the manager, Jim Frey, and the Cubs' front office, which considered him a paranoid malcontent. Durham was seven years younger, less expensive, and thought to be the better defensive first baseman. In May, Green sent Buckner to the Red Sox for pitcher Dennis Eckersley and infielder Mike Brumley.

Green's final chess move came a few weeks later when he traded for pitcher Rick Sutcliffe. A six-foot-seven bearded redhead from Missouri, Sutcliffe was among the more mystifying players in baseball. His talent was undeniable, which was one reason he was making a whopping $900,000 in salary for 1984. But he struggled with consistency. Just as he finished one season with a record of 17-10 and went 3-9 the following year, Sutcliffe would dazzle one game and disappoint the next.

Sutcliffe was widely known for his temper. Left off the Dodgers' 1981 playoff roster, he barged into the office of Los Angeles manager Tommy Lasorda, screaming, "I'll never fucking play for you again!" That, in itself, was a significant breach of baseball protocol. But then, by his own admission, Sutcliffe grabbed Lasorda by the throat and threatened him before picking up his manager's desk and slamming it. Sutcliffe later revealed that it was not the roster omission that angered him; it was his belief that Lasorda had lied to him.

He left the Dodgers but continued in his mercurial ways. Like the Girl with the Curl, when Sutcliffe was good, he was very, very good indeed. But when he was bad, he was horrid. Pitching for the Cleveland Indians, he started 1984 with a record of 4-5 and a bloated 5.15 ERA. On account of a tooth infection, he had lost 17 pounds and, briefly, the hearing in his right ear.

Dallas Green didn't mind this at all. Again mixing intuition and data, Green didn't read much into Sutcliffe's slow start or his perplexing rhythms. He preferred a confrontational style to passive aggression. And, like Sutcliffe, Green himself had been a tall pitcher who struggled with consistency. Chicago's GM saw a potential Cy Young pitcher. But

Sutcliffe didn't come cheap. The Cubs parted with Hall, a relief pitcher, a backup catcher, and the team's top prospect, Joe Carter.

Green had overhauled the Cubs' outfield *and* its pitching staff in the middle of a season. He had also made an unambiguous statement: *We are not the lovable Cubbies playing in the daylight in the cute ballpark. We are here to win, dammit.* By June, Green was thrilled with his team.

The Cubs' status as lovable *winners* was sealed on Saturday, June 23, 1984. Four days after the Chicago Bulls had drafted Michael Jordan, the Cubs hosted the St. Louis Cardinals at Wrigley, and the game was broadcast nationally on NBC. Up to that point in the season, the Cubs had been a pleasantly overachieving team. Given the franchise history, there was justifiable skepticism. Surely, soon enough the Cubs would regress to their mean.

The network's *Game of the Week* telecast was just that — in many parts of the country, an institution that marked the only opportunity to watch live baseball on television. Though only 32, Bob Costas was already a top play-by-play broadcaster. Costas and his partner Tony Kubek called the action from the small Wrigley Field broadcast booth above home plate. Costas recalls that, for those three hours every Saturday afternoon, millions of viewers would put off yardwork to watch the games, which routinely posted ratings on par with the network's prime-time shows.

That Saturday, after two innings, the Cardinals led 7–1, and later 9–3. St. Louis's center fielder, Willie McGee, would bat for the cycle in the game, hitting a single, a double, a triple, and a home run. But the wind was blowing out at Wrigley and the Cubs rallied. Leading off the bottom of the ninth inning, with Chicago trailing 9–8, Ryne Sandberg came to bat. The Cardinals brought in their formidable closer, Bruce Sutter, one of baseball's top relief pitchers.

Sandberg had grown up less than a mile from John Stockton in Spokane, Washington. The son of a mortician, he was a sports omnivore. He nearly attended Washington State on a football scholarship, but chose baseball. A Gold Glove winner in 1983, he had been known chiefly for his defense. But in 1984, at age 25 and wearing uniform number 23,

Sandberg was in full blossom. In a clash of two future Hall of Fame players, Sandberg took two pitches and then smote a Sutter curveball over the left-field fence, over the drunk and topless bleacher bums, and onto the street. "This is a tie ballgame!" yelled Costas over deafening crowd noise.

Yet the Cardinals scored two runs in the 10th inning to lead 11–9. Left unsaid, this was the blessed-yet-cursed Cubs experience writ small. Mount a spirited and dramatic comeback in the bottom of the ninth inning . . . only to lose moments later. *Oh well, at least it was a fun day in the sun at the charming ballpark.*

As the Cardinals' runners crossed the plate in the top of the 10th inning, there was much relief among NBC executives in New York. Immediately after the game, the network was televising a featherweight boxing match at the Centro de Convenciones Atlapa, in Panama City. According to the television contract, the fight would not start until the baseball game ended.

With two outs in the bottom of the 10th, Dernier reached first base on a walk. Sutter again faced Sandberg. In the booth, Costas received word that, immediately after the game ended, he was to throw the broadcast to his colleagues in Panama so the fight could finally begin. To save time, during the bottom of the inning, Costas began concluding. He declared Willie McGee the player of the game. He quickly noted the game's director and producer and the coordinating producer of baseball, Harry Coyle, and was prepared to deliver the standard disclaimer: *Any reproduction, rebroadcast, or retransmission of this game without the express written consent of Major League Baseball is prohibited.* "Literally, once the last out was recorded," recalls Costas, "it would be *ding-ding-ding,* Round 1 from Panama."

But on Sutter's third pitch, with the Cubs down to their final half inning, Sandberg *again* jacked a home run to left field, this one landing in the middle of the delirious bleacher bums. Twice Sandberg had come to bat with the game on the line; twice he had hit a home run to tie the game. Costas enthused, "Do you believe it? It's gone!"

The film *The Natural* had been released a few weeks earlier, on May 11, 1984. Based on the Bernard Malamud book, it told the story of Roy Hobbs, a fictional baseball player endowed with great natural talent. Though the movie was filmed in Buffalo, the climactic scene was staged to take place at Wrigley Field, with Hobbs hitting a game-winning home run. After Sandberg's blast, Costas said, "That's the real Roy Hobbs, because this can't be happening! We're sitting here, and it doesn't make any difference if it's 1984 or '54—just freeze this and don't change a thing!" (Later, Costas kicked himself for not deploying the pun about "reel life" versus "real life.")

As for Costas's counterpart a few doors down in Wrigley Field's radio booth, this marked an instance when Harry Caray's signature call of "Holy cow!" managed to *understate* the occasion. Meanwhile, in Panama, two featherweights remained in their dressing rooms as the crowd of fight fans, indifferent to a manic baseball game on the North Side of Chicago, had grown restless wondering what the hell was taking so long.

By now it was clear: the Fates had written the script for this game and, for a change, had the Cubs winning. In the bottom of the 11th inning, with the bases loaded, Cubs backup infielder Dave Owen knocked a pinch-hit single to right field and the Cubs won 12–11. Now the damn fight in Panama could finally start.

In what immediately became known as "the Sandberg Game," the eponym would finish with five hits, two home runs, and seven RBIs. It was only one game in late June. The Cubs were now 37-31, happily overachieving, but not exactly the 1927 Yankees.

Still, the game had a perpetuating effect. It cemented Sandberg as an MVP candidate. And the game certified the Cubs. In addition to the 38,079 fans at Wrigley—and countless more on the rooftops—the rest of the country bore witness. Not just to the team but to the entire Cubs experience. To the neighborhood, old-timey Wrigley Field, with its manually operated scoreboard and its ancient organ and its susceptibility to the winds coming off Lake Michigan. To the diehards like Bill Murray and the fans in the bleachers, lacking in shirts and sobriety and having a good time. To a fan base and a team celebrating a win in the 68th game as if it were the seventh game of the World Series.

Baseball was very much the national pastime in America that summer. *The Natural*—with its themes of redemption, romance, and the celebration of pastoral America through baseball, bolstered by a winning performance from Robert Redford, then age 47—quickly became a classic film. Bruce Springsteen crooned of "Glory Days," and while he inexplicably called a fastball a "speedball," the song was a reminder that sending a baseball whistling past an opposing batter was a signifier of American manhood. As John Fogerty was recording a song about center field—forever popularizing the phrase "Put me in, coach"—another band, a British one, ironically, called the Outfield (formerly the Baseball Boys) was recording an album titled *Play Deep.*

Though the Detroit Tigers were, by all measures, the best team in the majors, the Chicago Cubs were the national darlings in this Summer of Baseball. Galvanized by this one game, the Cubs kept winning. By early August they were in first place in the NL East. And, like most winning teams, the Cubs had fun along the way. Matthews had a director's chair in front of his locker. To express his authority, he would sit in the chair and, conspicuously, read the business section of the *Chicago Tribune.* A prankster—later revealed to be Sandberg—adjusted the brackets before Matthews entered the room so the chair would collapse when he sat down.

The players became the darlings of Chicago as well. When they went carousing on Rush Street—another advantage of playing day baseball—they never paid for a drink. When they flew to road games, the team's traveling secretary built in extra time, accounting for the crush of autograph seekers mobbing the players as they walked through O'Hare.

Capitalism being what it is, local businesses tried to profit from the appeal of the Cubs; and the players were happy to supplement their income. Jay Johnstone, a famously mischievous veteran outfielder, was the coordinator of many of the side deals.

One day Green caught Johnstone flipping through the Rolodex of the team's marketing director in an attempt to drum up business. Johnstone had already cut a deal whereby a dozen Cubs players would sign autographs at Chicago shoe stores in exchange for two pairs of expensive boots. (That the shoe store advertised the event in the newspaper and used the Cubs' logo without permission was considered a minor detail.)

Green chastised Johnstone for his dealmaking. *You guys are being paid to play baseball and shouldn't be distracted by side ventures.* And there could be hell to pay for using the Cubs' trademark logo without permission.

"Dallas," Johnstone asked, "what size shoe do you wear?"

"12D," Green replied, winking. "How about two pairs?"

Meanwhile, other players, including Jody Davis, Durham, and Sutcliffe, recorded a self-aggrandizing song titled "Men in Blue." It was a precursor to the Chicago Bears' equally regrettable "Super Bowl Shuffle" the following year. Given how many Cubs believed that the franchise was cursed, it seemed especially odd to tempt fate with lyrics like:

As sure as there's ivy on the center-field wall,
The men in blue are gonna win it all!

10

WAX ON, WAX OFF

I didn't want to see this movie. I took one look at the title and figured it was either (a) a sequel to *Toenails of Vengeance,* or (b) an adventure pitting Ricky Schroder against the Megaloth Man. I was completely wrong. *The Karate Kid* was one of the nice surprises of 1984 — an exciting, sweet-tempered, heart-warming story with one of the most interesting friendships in a long time.

— Opening to Roger Ebert's review of *The Karate Kid,* June 1984

On June 1, 1984, John Avildsen and Robert Mark Kamen threw on fancier clothes than they'd otherwise be inclined to wear and sat in the Baronet Theatre, on Third Avenue in Midtown Manhattan. The occasion was a screening of the movie they had, respectively, directed and written.

As its pedestrian name would imply, *The Karate Kid* would tell the story of Daniel LaRusso, a high school transplant from New Jersey who encounters a pack of bullies as soon as he arrives in California. The bullies kick his ass, as bullies do. Help arrives from an unlikely source: the Japanese maintenance man at the down-market apartment complex where Daniel lives with his mother. This mystical figure agrees to teach Daniel karate and, in the process, life skills.

By the time they settled into their seats at the Baronet, Avildsen and Kamen had seen innumerable cuts of the film and had lost all perspective. They figured they probably had something to be proud of. A Bronx-born tough guy who grew up in a housing project, Kamen was not exactly a delicate artiste, but he had cried when he watched the final five-minute scene a few weeks earlier at Avildsen's home theater. Still, the two men were curious to see how an objective, dispassionate test audience would react to the film.

So it was that they were pleased when the mixed group that had gathered in the Manhattan theater yelled during the fight scenes and filled the room with robust applause as the credits rolled. "Hey, they got it!" the two filmmakers said to each other as they left the theater, concealing their grins. When they walked outside, Avildsen stopped and poked Kamen. "Holy shit, check this out."

Kamen turned to see two Wall Street types, wearing suits and carrying attaché cases, facing each other on the sidewalk. They were each standing on one leg and bending their elevated leg. They were mimicking the crane kick, that signature move that Daniel LaRusso (Ralph Macchio) delivers to the face of Johnny Lawrence (William Zabka), the thoroughbred jerk of a villain, in the film's climactic fight scene.

"*That's* when we knew we had a hit," says Kamen. "The studio [Columbia] was always optimistic. But you never know. We thought what we had made was a cute movie that kids would like. When adults—adults holding fucking attaché cases!—were doing the crane kick on the sidewalk, we were like, 'Maybe we have a hit on our hands.'"

To celebrate the successful screening, Avildsen and Kamen smoked a joint on Third Avenue. As they were approached by a New York City policeman, Kamen said to Avildsen, "This is the headline for tomorrow's *Daily News:* 'Writer and Director for Karate Kid Arrested.'"

They were not arrested. The NYPD had more serious crime to address in the summer of 1984. They were simply told to extinguish the joint, which they did. They then repaired to a bar, where they shared tequila shots and continued to marvel over the audience's reaction to their modest film.

After getting his Ph.D. in American history from the University of Pennsylvania, Kamen left Ivy League academia and took up writing screenplays. He sold *Crossings* for $140,000 and, although the film was never made, used the entire windfall to buy a plot of land in Sonoma. He then wrote the screenplays for *Taps* ("a good film," he says flatly) and *Split Image* ("not such a good film"). He was still in his mid-thirties.

For his next film, Kamen adhered to that time-honored rule of the craft: *Write what you know.* After getting jumped by a gang of bullies as a teenager at the 1964 World's Fair in Queens, Kamen had taken up karate. He was instructed at first by a former Marine, who saw martial arts less as a form of combat than as a philosophy. Kamen was hooked on karate, but, seeking a more spiritual experience, he switched to Okinawan-style karate and fell into the thrall of his traditional sensei, a man of few words named Chojun Miyagi.

In the early eighties, Jerry Weintraub, a legendary Hollywood producer (and former promoter of Elvis, Frank Sinatra, and Bob Dylan), had optioned a story about a nine-year-old boy tormented by neighborhood bullies until his single mother took him to the local karate school. Weintraub vaguely recalled that Kamen had a passion for martial arts. Might Kamen be interested in writing a screenplay to wrap around this basic premise? Of course he would.

Kamen banged out the screenplay in four months, starting in June of 1982. He quickly admitted that it wasn't particularly sophisticated. It followed the well-worn sports movie template:

(a) underdog protagonist faces adversity and injustice, compounded by romantic trouble;

(b) underdog protagonist meets unlikely mentor with his own inventory of demons;
(c) underdog protagonist overcomes steep odds to win big contest in the third act. He gets the girl, the mentor is redeemed, justice is dispensed. It's a reminder that sports — and, by extension, humanity — is a meritocracy. Audience leaves the theater inspired, humming along as the lead track of the soundtrack blares.

Beyond the familiar sports tropes, the movie proved to be a slick combination of genres. It took the Bruce Lee martial arts film (popular at the time, but with a niche audience), married it with a sports narrative, and combined that with elements from the coming-of-age teen movie, an emerging genre in the eighties. (John Hughes, the godfather of the category, released his first directed film, *Sixteen Candles,* in May of 1984.)

The Karate Kid turns on the surrogacy relationship between mentor and student, between Mr. Miyagi and Daniel, who, conspicuously, has no father figure. The pivotal moment in the film is not the climactic fight scene but the "epiphany scene," in which Daniel comes to trust Miyagi fully. Frustrated after a day of menial work that seems pointless, Daniel bitches to Miyagi. Calmly, Miyagi demonstrates to Daniel that the same "wax on, wax off" motions he used when applying a layer of sheen to a 1947 Ford Super Deluxe Club Convertible would form the basics (and basis) of karate defense.* Daniel would now be able to assimilate these skills without thinking. (Years later, this would form a central tenet of sports psychology: learning through experience — and developing muscle memory — is more effective than formal instruction.)

When Kamen wrote Miyagi's part, he remembered his own Okinawan sensei, but also channeled two other mystical cinematic figures

* The car is often referred to as a 1948 model. But Macchio is adamant it was a 1947, and we're going with him.

of the time: Yoda and E.T. Kamen recalls that Mr. Miyagi "came from someplace else. He was pure, he had this sort of pure morality and no agenda to him, he had a goodness of heart, he embodied all the things that make you feel good. And he allowed a child to believe and dream and all of that stuff. Mr. Miyagi is the human personification of wisdom and knowledge and goodness and clarity and heart and soul. And he could beat the fuck out of you."

For the director, Columbia tapped Avildsen, who, having directed the Oscar-winning film *Rocky* in 1976, still "had heat," in Hollywood parlance. The two films, in fact, were so similar in arc that even Avildsen referred to the Kamen script as "The Ka-Rocky Kid." The considerable parallels weren't lost on Sylvester Stallone, either. The writer and star of *Rocky* once ran into Kamen and joked, "You ripped off my movie. You have an Italian fighter, and an old man guiding him." (Kamen says he laughed and, with the equanimity of Miyagi, responded, "You're absolutely right. You had one good idea and I ripped it off!")

The movie was given a modest budget of $8 million, which influenced casting decisions. Chuck Norris, a box office star, was targeted to play the role of the sadistic instructor of the Cobra Kai. Jeff Bridges, Christopher Walken, and Kurt Russell were also under consideration. But the part went instead to lesser-known (and cheaper-rated) Martin Kove. For the lead role, Avildsen had considered various teen movie A-listers of the time: Emilio Estevez, Robert Downey Jr., Matt Dillon, Anthony Edwards, Eric Stoltz, a young Johnny Depp. None felt quite right.

Kamen recalls that Avildsen summoned him to his apartment on 89th Street in Manhattan. "He said he was bringing someone over. I open the door and there's Ralph: no musculature, a skinny little string bean of a kid."

Macchio was not a total unknown. He'd had a big part — alongside Dillon and Rob Lowe — the year before in the Francis Ford Coppola film *The Outsiders.* Before that he'd had a role as an adopted nephew on the prime-time ABC television show *Eight Is Enough.*

The scouting report on Macchio: he was a "good kid," serious about his craft and easy to work with. But by no measure was he a box office star, nor had he played a lead. He was not a strapping physical specimen. Though he looked like a teenager, he was already 21.

Says Kamen: "He wasn't particularly coordinated for martial arts. I showed him some simple blocking and punching moves and he couldn't do them at all. I said, 'That's perfect. We have a kid that knows nothing. I wanted a wimp. And Ralph is the paradigmatic wimp.'"

Macchio read the script and shrugged. "It felt a little corny. Maybe a little overly saccharine," he thought. He hated the title, too. "I fought tooth and nail to change this goofy title, only because I knew there was a chance I had to carry it for the rest of my life." But he took the lead part, thrilled with the $60,000 payday.

For Macchio's love interest, the casting directors passed up Demi Moore and Helen Hunt, among others, and chose a fresh-faced Elisabeth Shue. Known to all as "Lisa," Shue had recently left Wellesley College after her sophomore year to pursue acting. She had played the girl behind the counter in a Burger King commercial and filmed a pilot for ABC. The Shue clan was determinedly East Coast blue blood. (Shue's mother descended from Pilgrim leader William Brewster; her father, a lawyer and entrepreneur, was a former captain of the Harvard soccer team.) Yet she pulled off the role of a quintessential Southern California teenage blonde.

For the Cobra Kai bullies, Weintraub, the producer, had the inspired idea to cast the family members of Hollywood royalty—L.A. kids already imbued with a sense of entitlement. John Travolta's nephew and Frankie Avalon's son were awarded roles; Chad McQueen, son of Steve, played the role of Dutch. "It was basically a box of kids," says Kamen. The exception was Billy Zabka, a perfect bad guy, athletic and blond and sneering, who proved a quick study in martial arts maneuvers.

The real sleight of hand, though, came in the casting of the mystical Mr. Miyagi. Originally, the part was written for Toshiro Mifune, among the most famous Japanese actors of all time. Mifune's agent sent photos of his client clad in a martial arts *gi* — the traditional uniform — and wearing the coveralls befitting the role of an apartment maintenance man. He looked the part. But there was one problem: when Jerry Weintraub spoke to Mifune, he realized that it would be hard to give the role of the gnomic sensei to a man who spoke no English.

The film's casting director, Caro Jones, spoke up. "I have a great idea for Miyagi."

"Who is it?" asked Weintraub.

"Pat Morita."

"Pat Morita!" Weintraub, the former promoter, exploded. "I used to work with Pat Morita in the Catskills!" Weintraub recalled that Morita had nicknamed himself the Hip Nip and performed a schlocky, self-mocking act. "He used to wear his eyeglasses upside down! How can you even think that the Hip Nip is good for me?"

Weintraub had a point. To traffic in understatement, Noriyuki Morita was an unlikely figure for the role. For one, he knew virtually nothing about martial arts — and for good reason. The son of California migrant workers, Morita was born in 1932. He was two years old when he broke his back and developed spinal tuberculosis, causing him to spend much of his childhood in an infirmary outside Sacramento run by priests and nuns. There, he was given the anglicized nickname "Pat." When he was released from the infirmary, it was the middle of World War II. He was escorted by a federal agent to the camp where his family was being interned.

Morita graduated from high school at 16 and was admitted to Berkeley, but he had designs on becoming a comedian. Threading the seams of America, he often devoted his act to mocking Asians and took to going onstage drunk. He caught a small break when he was cast as Arnold, the manic diner owner on the hit show *Happy Days.* There were occasional movie parts, but, as his daughter Aly puts it, "they were these ching-chong Chinaman roles that get tiring and demeaning and draining." So he often found himself on the road as a lounge act, sometimes opening for Redd Foxx.

"That guy," Weintraub wondered aloud, "is going to be the *wise sensei*?"

But Macchio had already been hired. Pressured to complete the casting and start shooting, Avildsen brought in Morita for an audition. When Morita and Macchio read together, Avildsen shot the scene on his own camera. He watched the tape that night and was impressed by the chemistry between Macchio and Morita, two actors with considerable humility, who had yet to break through. Macchio had the same thought; he immediately connected with Morita.*

Avildsen then called Morita back and had him act out the scene in which Miyagi gets drunk recalling his late wife. Performing the scene, Morita mined some dark places and summoned his own difficult life—from the tuberculosis to the time in internment to his struggles as a road comic. As Avildsen welled up, he knew that he had his man. Morita agreed to be paid $30,000 for the role. The cast was set.

Cameras first rolled on Halloween night in 1983. *The Karate Kid* shoot spanned roughly seven weeks, mostly in Southern California. For most of the teenage cast, it had the vibe of summer vacation, albeit off-season and paid. They rode dirt bikes and motorcycles, popping wheelies and pulling donuts on the nearby set of *Fantasy Island.* They played pool, went to Golf N' Stuff amusement park, and spent day after day on the beaches around Malibu. Jake Steinfeld—later to be known as "Body by Jake"—was on hand as a personal trainer to Shue; but her catering was a nightly constellation of burgers and pizza. Shue held her own, adrift amid this ocean of testosterone.

It was a fun few weeks. But there was no sense that these weeks were

---

* The casting video would make it to YouTube: "The Karate Kid 1983 First Auditions for Daniel & Mr Miyagi," uploaded by avildsen1221, March 19, 2012, https://www.youtube.com/watch?v=YPFOHCmtEZI.

going to be transformative. Editors and production team members were lining up their next project before shooting had even commenced. The manager of Ron Thomas (the Cobra Kai's Bobby) told his client, "This movie has no audience. It's not going anywhere." Rob Garrison — who played Cobra Kai henchman Tommy — recalled one occasion when the actors were standing around and laughing. Avildsen broke up the fun. "You guys have no idea what you're making here. This is going to be a classic." Which only made the young cast laugh harder. "We all thought, *Yeah, whatever,*" said Garrison.

While the film was set and shot in Southern California, this was not paradisiacal Los Angeles as it was usually portrayed, all palm trees and backyard pools and airbrushed fabulousness. This was a different kind of L.A., the bland, sprawling monoculture. The karate dojo was situated in a charmless section of North Hollywood. Miyagi's home was in Canoga Park. The LaRussos lived in a dive of an apartment complex, with a pool in the center of the courtyard. The pool was drained and then colored a putrid green.

The climactic scene, the All-Valley Karate Championships, was shot at the Cal State Northridge college gym, the Matadome. Rather than cast thousands of extras, Avildsen had the inspired idea to stage the film's tournament in conjunction with an actual karate tournament being held simultaneously. Tight as the script had been written, it also allowed for a fair amount of improvisation. After the film had been fully edited, Avildsen noticed that during the tournament scene, as LaRusso staggers in pain, there was dead air. Avildsen yelled out, "I need a few seconds of . . . something." During the dubbing session in postproduction, Garrison yelled out the first phrase that came into his head. "Get him a body bag. Yeah!" Avildsen smiled. "That's going to be a classic!" Again the cast rolled their eyes at the director's exuberant optimism.

Likewise, Kamen made up the crane kick on the spot. He knew better than anyone that it wasn't just impractical — it would have been grounds for disqualification in a tournament. But this was Hollywood. "How cool would it be if you saw Mr. Miyagi on a log doing this impossible thing?

You have no balance. Your hands aren't in a defensive position. If you stood on one leg and did that to somebody in a match, they'd fucking kill you. But it was just so *cinematic.*"

Macchio recalls that the famous shot in that last scene is low and wide. "We shot it so many different ways, though. Close-ups, slow motion, [with me] on a ladder, shooting a leg out, over Billy's shoulder, over my shoulder, above us." In the end, they filmed it like a straight-up martial arts scene. "I'm proud of myself for the kick, but I'm equally proud of Billy for taking the kick. Like a great passing play in football, it's all about timing."

Both cinephiles and acolytes of martial arts could—and to some extent did—pick apart the film. Did the Cobra Kai have to be quite so Aryan Nation? *Time* magazine dismissed the film as "maddeningly predictable" and guilty of a flavorlessness befitting its PG rating. ("How one longs to spot a few gremlins chuckling malevolently in the corner," the review said, referring to the more sinister *Gremlins,* released two weeks earlier, on June 8, 1984.)

Others took issue with the soundtrack, which, per an otherwise positive *New York Times* review, "blasts annoyingly through the final climactic fight scene." (The Joe Esposito song "You're the Best," which blares during the karate tournament montage setting up the film's climax, was originally written for *Rocky III.* Two years earlier, Sylvester Stallone—who took over for Avildsen and directed *Rocky II, III,* and *IV*—had rejected the song in favor of Survivor's "Eye of the Tiger.")

But these were, finally, minor quibbles. *The Karate Kid* premiered at a theater on Wilshire Boulevard. Much like the test screening before the Manhattan test audience weeks prior, it played out like a live sporting event. The audience cheered and gasped mid-movie. They laughed at lines like "Get him a body bag." When Macchio delivered the crane kick, one viewer in the front row jumped out of his seat and punched his fist in the air.

The Karate Kid opened nationwide on June 22, in 1,000 theaters. It made $5 million in its first week. And another $5 million after that, more than earning back its $8 million budget. Then another $5 million. And on it went, during a summer when the median price for a movie ticket was $2.50. Says Kamen: "Again, if you had told me it would have made $30 million, I would fallen out the fucking window. That would have been a huge hit. It practically did that within a month."

By the end of the summer, *The Karate Kid* was on its way to grossing more than $90 million. A sequel was soon in the works. Macchio and Shue were suddenly in demand. Morita was nominated for a Best Supporting Actor Oscar, among the first Asian Americans to receive an acting nomination. (Perhaps ironically, he lost out to Cambodian doctor turned actor Haing S. Ngor, who played Dith Pran in *The Killing Fields.*) Owing to his breakout as Mr. Miyagi, Morita went on to star in the ABC television show *Ohara,* one of the first dramas to place an Asian American in a lead role.

To Peter Choi, a Harvard graduate who was working on his first film, this was one of the movie's great legacies. "Other than extras or actors who got roles as the waiter or the busboy or the manservant, the Chinese delivery boy, I didn't see a lot of faces like mine in front of the camera. That was the landscape . . . Suddenly I was on a shoot and seeing a face like mine. For an Asian American kid — and I say it without being hokey — I was really inspired by Pat."

The Karate Kid — lines, scenes, names — would become embroidered in the tapestry of pop culture. A punk band would name itself Sweep the Leg Johnny. Decades later, it still echoed. In the hit musical *The Book of Mormon,* the lead character does the crane stance. The son of Martin Kove, who played the Cobra Kai leader, would own a vape store and sell a vape juice called Sweep the Leg, made by Banzai Vapors. Infamous Brewing Company, in Austin, makes a peanut butter stout called Sweep the Leg. Kamen owns a T-shirt advertising a (fake) car wax called Miyagi's Wax On, Wax Off. (He owns another shirt that reads WAX ON, FUCK OFF.)

In the summer of 2018 — 35 years after he had finished the original script — Kamen was writing lines for a *Karate Kid* Broadway show. He was preparing to make an appearance at an annual *Karate Kid* festival in Southern California. Macchio and Zabka had finished the first season of *Cobra Kai,* a reboot series for YouTube Red channel.*

Maybe most significantly, the movie triggered a martial arts boom. It wasn't just that every kid spent the summer of 1984 mimicking the crane kick. It was that an entire sport had been demystified and made cool. Who didn't want what *The Karate Kid* espoused? Under the tutelage of a wise mentor, with some car-polishing discipline and metaphorical appreciation of a bonsai tree, you, too, could win the grudging respect of the bullies, get a black belt—and perhaps pull a pretty girl in the process? Yes, please.

The "karate boom" was just that. After *The Karate Kid,* thousands of dojos opened throughout the United States. In California strip malls. In urban storefronts. In business districts throughout the Midwest. YMCAs and gyms offered karate instruction. So did after-school programs. That seventies standby the racquetball court was retrofitted into the hallmark of the eighties: a dojo. To lure the next generation of Daniel LaRussos, studios accelerated the progression, in some cases advertising that black belts could be earned within a year.

Despite—maybe because of—this commercialization and black belt inflation, the new "McDojos," as they were called dismissively, would struggle to retain their clientele. Some immutable truths were laid bare. For one, karate is *hard* and requires dedication. The notion of a newcomer to the sport learning a few wax-on, wax-off motions and winning his first tournament? That is Hollywood at its finest. Also, karate seldom involves full-contact sparring. The kids hoping to land crane kicks in weekly sparring sessions were deeply disappointed—just as students in the seventies, drawn to martial arts by Bruce Lee, had been disappointed when they weren't taught to catch swords or jump over rooftops.

---

* At this writing, seasons one and two of *Cobra Kai* have more than 200 million combined views on YouTube.

But if karate would eventually decline, combat fighting would not. Mixed martial arts (MMA) initially pitted fighting systems against one another, an attempt to answer the barroom questions thought to be unanswerable: Would a kickboxer beat a sumo wrestler? Would a jujitsu black belt beat a taekwondo black belt? Suddenly all those products of dojos (and McDojos), endowed with martial arts training and a desire for full-contact fighting—some equivalent of the All-Valley Karate Championships—had a new option.

Buoyed by the Ultimate Fighting Championship (UFC)—the most prominent promotion, which debuted in 1993, pitting fighters against each other in an octagonal cage—mixed martial arts would become a multidisciplined sport unto itself. Soon the UFC, once dismissed as barbaric "human cock-fighting," would penetrate the defenses of the mainstream. So much so that, in 2016, the UFC would sell to a media-management company for $4 billion and would air regularly on ESPN. More than 30 years after Ralph Macchio become a hero to bullied kids everywhere, Dana White, the UFC's longtime president, would say, "There's no question that when you tell the story of the UFC, you have to mention *The Karate Kid.*"

Another enduring legacy of *The Karate Kid:* it contributed mightily to the sports movie canon. When other studios saw that this movie made for $8 million was crowding $100 million in box office returns, suddenly more scripts for sports films were being green-lit. By the end of the decade, Hollywood would serve up *Hoosiers, Major League, Bull Durham, Field of Dreams, Eight Men Out, Wildcats, Over the Top* . . . and, inevitably *The Karate Kid Part II.*

11

THE SHAM OF AMATEURISM

On June 27, 1984, Andy Coats was enduring a foul day at the office inside city hall. The mayor of Oklahoma City, Coats had been disappointed when a sales tax proposal he put forth had been voted down by the city council. His day brightened in the afternoon, though, when he got a call from a former colleague at his law firm. "The Supreme Court decision on your NCAA case is out. And it's wonderful."

A few years earlier, Coats had been an Oklahoma City lawyer in his mid-forties, mulling whether to stay in his job, enjoying the cozy life of firm practice in a small city, or enter politics. His reverie was interrupted when a senior partner at his firm asked him a question.

"How would you like to help sue the NCAA?"

"Well," Coats said instinctively, "what kind of a case is it?"

"Antitrust."

While Coats didn't specialize in antitrust — "I didn't know if it was hyphenated or one word" — he was a nimble lawyer, known for breaking down complex cases so that juries could comprehend and sympathize. Figuring good fortune had fallen into his lap, he agreed to take the case.

The case centered around the NCAA's control of football broadcasts. And in this case, the aggrieved party was Coats's beloved University of Oklahoma.

On September 26, 1981, the Oklahoma Sooners had traveled to Los Angeles to play the USC Trojans. The game pitted two of the top teams in the country against each other and featured the season's Heisman Trophy winner, Marcus Allen. This clash of college football titans was televised nationally. Except in North Carolina and South Carolina, where viewers watched . . . the Citadel beat Appalachian State 34–30.

Yet, that afternoon, all four schools received the same payout in television revenue.

At the time, college football was televised within one Saturday window, on one national network, ABC. There were rules limiting teams from getting too bloated, including a prohibition against appearing on more than six telecasts within a two-year window. Regardless of the ratings the games drew or which program brought the most viewership, all schools received the same payment. In some cases, schools shared in television revenue despite never actually playing a televised game.

The reason: the NCAA controlled broadcast contracts for all of its member schools. Behind its executive director, Walter Byers — who managed to be both a socialist and an autocrat at once — the association believed that controlling the market made for the best television policy. The NCAA's certainty in its righteousness was such that it never bothered to file for an antitrust exemption. The ties to education, its thinking went, would insulate it from any legal claims of unfair trade restraint.

By the early eighties, schools were starting to grow antsy. Some glimpsed the future and the expansion of the television universe, and the money it would bring in. Others simply bristled at how the NCAA set parameters for what schools could and couldn't do to profit from their sports programs. Why did powerhouses like Texas and Oklahoma need to seek the permission of the NCAA — permission that was often denied — for even a regional broadcast of their rivalry game? Why were games between top teams, which would have drawn millions of viewers, not televised when networks would have happily aired them?

Another lawyer in town, Dee Replogle, was a regent for the University of Oklahoma and had spoken recently with Donnie Duncan, Oklahoma's athletic director. They'd been in touch with Chuck Neinas, head of the College Football Association, which had been trying to wrest control away from the NCAA. Everyone came to the consensus that the time was right to challenge the NCAA's monopoly.

Coats assumed that this was a class action suit. And he was right. A class action, though, implied an actual *class* of plaintiffs willing to sign on.

Every member school stood to benefit if the NCAA's monopoly power was broken up. And there was no shortage of schools that had wearied of the overbearing NCAA and, in particular, Byers's iron fist.

Oklahoma looked for other plaintiffs. Coats likened it to finding a friend to accompany him to the haunted house on Halloween — someone there for support when spooky, menacing Walter Byers suddenly jumped out. But, when asked to join the case, school after school declined, scared off by Byers and his vindictive streak. A school joining the case was begging to be put on NCAA probation for some minor violation. "The NCAA is like the IRS," Coats was told. "If they want to get you, they'll get you."

Over a period of months, Coats attended NCAA member-school conventions and felt "like the illegitimate child at a family reunion." The other attendees said all the right things but didn't want to be seen in public with the Oklahoma delegation. DeLoss Dodds, titan of University of Texas athletics, sidled up to Coats and whispered in his ear, "I sure hope you win this case. We'll send you some money and help you out."

Coats thanked Dodds and added, "What I really need is a co-plaintiff."

Dodds smiled. "You can't use our name. I'm sure you understand."

In the end, only one other school signed on: the University of Georgia. No matter. *Board of Regents of the University of Oklahoma and the University of Georgia Athletic Association v. National Collegiate Athletic Association* was filed in district court in Oklahoma on September 15, 1982.

The suit was unusual for a number of reasons. For one, in most instances the government—via the Department of Justice—brings an antitrust case. Here was a suit being filed directly by the group claiming to suffer. And the schools didn't seek monetary damages; they simply wanted a free market, a world in which the NCAA could no longer dictate how schools broadcast football games. The schools stressed that broadcasts of their games were those schools' intellectual property—and not the intellectual property of the NCAA.

Simply finding a judge proved difficult, given the Oklahoma graduates and Sooners football fans who felt duty bound to recuse themselves. The case was moved to New Mexico, where it was heard by Judge Juan Guerrero Burciaga, a West Point grad and former Air Force pilot appointed by President Carter.

Coats referenced both Section 1 of the Sherman Act (he claimed that the NCAA and its many member schools and conferences had unlawfully conspired in ways harmful to Oklahoma and Georgia) and Section 2 of the Sherman Act (he claimed that the NCAA was an illegal monopoly). Coats called one economics expert, who likened the NCAA to OPEC, the oil cartel, with a key difference: "The NCAA had better enforcement mechanisms."

The NCAA warned, direly, that if Oklahoma won, it would trigger a "parade of horribles." If there were a slate of televised college football games, fans would stop going to games in person. And consumers, overfed games on television, would grow tired of watching, which would torpedo ratings and, in turn, the rates advertisers would be willing to pay for 30-second commercials. In short, football supply would outpace football demand, and colleges and students would suffer in the marketplace if the all-knowing NCAA lost control of college football broadcasts.

The NCAA relied largely on Byers to make its case. In the 1960s, Byers had slyly come up with the term *student-athlete,* to ensure that colleges didn't have to provide workers' comp to injured athletes. And now, when he took the stand, he pontificated about the virtues of college sports and predicted direly that there would be chaos if the NCAA lost control. "Hully gully" was his choice phrase this time.

When Coats asked Byers a question, it didn't generate a response so much as a speech. "It was like trying to take a sip of water from a fire hydrant," says Coats. At one point Burciaga told Coats, "You don't need to ask Mr. Byers that question again. He's obviously not going to answer, but I know the answer."

Coats grinned. "In that case, that's all, Your Honor. Thank you very much."

In a firmly written opinion, Burciaga sided with Oklahoma and ruled that the NCAA had indeed engaged in illegal price fixing and limiting production of games. This was cartel behavior that interfered with a school's ability to compete, the judge ruled, and it was thus prohibited by antitrust law. (He also rejected the idea that the NCAA was exempt from antitrust scrutiny.)

Coats figured it was time to negotiate. Not so fast. "I learned," says Coats, "that the NCAA stands for 'Never compromise anything anytime.'"

The NCAA appealed, but the U.S. Court of Appeals for the Tenth Circuit upheld Burciaga's ruling by a 2–1 decision. The association pressed on, though, and appealed to the Supreme Court, which, in a mild upset, agreed to hear the case.

By this point Coats had been voted Oklahoma City's 32nd mayor. When he took the case, he'd never imagined that it would lead to his arguing before the Supreme Court. And he'd never imagined preparing for oral arguments after tending to the business of a major American city. But there he was on March 20, 1984, putting his mayoral duties aside for the week and arguing before the highest court in the United States.

He had been advised by a partner that appearing before the Supreme

Court was a businesslike affair. This was not a time for courtroom theatrics or witty asides. But when he received his first question from the bench, Coats couldn't resist. He was asked, "How come you want Oklahoma to be on television every weekend?" Coats responded, "Well, we lost four games last year, and if we don't do better than that, no one is going to want us on television."

The NCAA was represented by Frank Easterbrook, who would go on to become a prominent federal judge. The NCAA's position was simple: the "exclusive" broadcast windows made for greater viewership and drove up the market for the fees the NCAA could charge the networks. Plus, if every school could cut its own TV deal, not only would the market be saturated, but attendance would suffer. This wasn't antitrust; this was one negotiator benefiting all of its constituents. In a four-year contract that ran through the 1985 season, CBS and ABC were each paying the NCAA roughly $35 million per year, which it would distribute among member schools. How could anyone complain about that?

As the session neared its end, Justice Byron White glanced at Coats and flashed a look that projected not so much contempt as resignation. White had been an All-American halfback at the University of Colorado and finished second in the 1937 Heisman Trophy voting before becoming the fourth pick in the 1938 NFL Draft. (He led the league in rushing as a 21-year-old rookie on the Pittsburgh Pirates and was the NFL's highest-paid player, having deferred his admission to Yale Law School.)

"You may win this case," White said. "But you're going to grow to regret it one day."

Yes and no.

In July of 1984, the Supreme Court issued its decision, ruling for Oklahoma 7–2, largely relying on the decision Burciaga had rendered in New Mexico. The decision ended — or at least eroded — the NCAA's 31-year-old monopoly over college football TV contracts. Justice John Paul Stevens delivered the majority opinion. Stevens agreed that "a plan that places the NCAA in complete control of the broadcasts that reach this market creates the type of monopoly that the Sherman Act was meant to prevent. By limiting the number of live broadcasts, the Court found that the NCAA was attempting to artificially increase the value of live tickets, in the same way that a monopolist seeks to manipulate the market by limiting output."

Justice Stevens went on to write that, while the NCAA had no right to restrict competition on TV deals, the NCAA implicitly held the right to restrict competition in other ways. In a bit of self-indulgence that wasn't central to the overall decision — dicta, in legal-speak — Stevens considered the great role of the NCAA and college sports. Little did he know that his throwaway passage would turn a short-term loss for the NCAA into a long-term victory. He wrote:

> In order to preserve the character and quality of the "product," athletes must not be paid, must be required to attend class, and the like. . . . The NCAA plays a critical role in the maintenance of a revered tradition of amateurism in college sports. . . . The preservation of the student-athlete in higher education adds richness and diversity to intercollegiate athletics and is entirely consistent with the goals of the Sherman Act.

That week — to the amusement of the partners in his firm and his colleagues at city hall — Coats was referenced alongside John McEnroe and Michael Jordan in the sports sections of major American newspapers. *Who knew you could sit behind a desk all day and still make the sports pages all over the country?* Coats was pictured smiling — and not simply because the decision meant that the NCAA would finally have to pay his legal fees. "I think you will see a big increase in revenues for all conference schools," Coats told the Associated Press. "The ruling is a victory for free enterprise."

Still, the Supreme Court decision didn't merit much attention. It didn't make the national newscasts and drew scant mention on ESPN, the growing all-sports network. Certainly there was no sense that, fundamentally, it was going to change college sports beyond recognition.

And if this was a victory, it sure didn't play out like one. At least not at first. With schools free to negotiate their own television contracts, the sudden sharp increase in supply led to a sudden sharp decrease in demand. A 30-second commercial during a football game aired under the NCAA deal had been priced at $60,000; after the Supreme Court decision, that same commercial suddenly sold for $15,000.

"Colleges May Find TV's Golden Egg Is Tarnished," read the headline of an August 26, 1984, *New York Times* article focused on how the impact of the Supreme Court decision was a shrinking of college sports revenues. Sam Jankovich, athletic director of the University of Miami, the reigning national champion football program, moaned, "I figure we left about $42 million on the table."

But within a year it would be clear: the Supreme Court's decree, had, in football terms, sent television contracts breaking through the line and into the open field. Byron White's doomsday free-market scenario — "unbridled competition in the economic sphere" — was becoming reality.

With ESPN fattening its balance sheets with all that bounty from subscription fees and looking for more games to televise — live content — and other cable networks joining the bidding, the market expanded. It grew still more when other networks arrived and then realized they could expand that Saturday afternoon television window. Virtually every conference would start its own sports network for the spillover games it couldn't sell to the bigger networks.

Conferences negotiated with networks. Schools defected from one conference to another, prospecting for TV cash. Notre Dame went directly to the networks to cut its own deals. Eventually schools, starting with the University of Texas — ironic, given DeLoss Dodds's reluctance to join the Oklahoma Board of Regents lawsuit — made perhaps the ultimate move and created their own television *networks* to address the national market for football. As CBS Sports later put it, "June 27, 1984, allowed college football to eventually become America's second-most popular sport behind the NFL."

Within a few years, most *conferences* were making more from television than the value of the nationwide NCAA contract prior to the *NCAA v. Board of Regents* decision. Eventually, individual *schools* were making more than the value of the entire contract. By 2014, 30 years after the decision, the University of Oklahoma would make $134 million in football revenue, the majority of it from television payouts.

The impact of this television money, negotiated in the free market? As rivulets of revenue turned to rivers, college sports—and, within college sports, football programs in particular—became its own industry, increasingly divorced from the rest of the university.

Schools began engaging in arms races for the supreme talent and facilities. In most states, the head football coach of the state's biggest school—sometimes calling himself "the CEO of the program"—is the highest-paid public employee in the state, earning more than both the university president and the governor. Games air six nights a week. Conferences are forever realigning. (The Big Ten Conference currently includes 14 schools from Nebraska to New Jersey—this manifest destiny designed around expanding the conference's television footprint across multiple time zones.)

Now the dean emeritus of the University of Oklahoma College of Law, Coats admits to some ambivalence. Arguing before the Supreme Court marked a career highlight. At the same time, he recognizes that, as a direct result of the decision he won, college football has "become a monster that goes way beyond any sort of rational relationship with the university. No one saw this coming. Now college football is the tail wagging the dog, something that's gotten so big it towers over the actual university."

Despite all the television money sloshing through big-time college sports, one party doesn't share in the windfall: the athletes themselves. Even as programs can make more than $100 million, *assistant* football coaches can earn more than $1 million in annual salary, teams fly on private jets, and players train in facilities festooned with indoor waterfalls and play in 100,000-seat football palaces, flush with luxury suites with leather-bound seats and scoreboards the size of a cornfield . . . the labor is free. Athletes receive room and board and full tuition; they do not receive paychecks, despite the vast revenue they generate. No matter how much money is minted from their labor, their names, and their images, college athletes remain amateurs.

When athletes have tried to mount a legal challenge to the NCAA and demand compensation or the right to bargain collectively, they have leaned on the *NCAA v. Board of Regents* decision. In the summer of 1984, the Supreme Court made it perfectly clear: the NCAA is not entitled to operate as an illegal cartel and is not above the law when it restrains competition.

Here's the twist: time and again, when the NCAA has defended the "revered tradition" of amateurism, it has leaned on . . . the *NCAA v. Board of Regents* decision. Buried deep in the dicta of Stevens's majority opinion, that one pesky sentence: *In order to preserve the character and quality of the "product," athletes must not be paid, must be required to attend class, and the like . . .*"

From the NCAA's perspective, the Supreme Court made it perfectly clear. The restraint on trade — "athletes must not be paid" — is justified because amateurism is a sacred principle, necessary for the advancement of education.

As for the notion that televising games would hurt college football attendance — the NCAA's fear from 1984 — well, that never materialized. All the media coverage has increased interest. Which has made a ticket to see games in person all the more coveted. Most top programs play to sold-out crowds, even when the games are broadcast. That includes Oklahoma.

So it was that, in the fall of 2018, Andy Coats, now in his eighties, was lucky enough to take his seat at an Oklahoma football game. The enthusiasm of the crowd was considerable, but dulled by the game's start time, 11:00 a.m. Morning football? It was a concession, still another sacrifice to appease the television gods. Sheepishly, Coats looked around his section and felt a stab of guilt, thinking back to the unlikely Supreme Court case he won in the summer of 1984. He suppressed the urge to turn to everyone in his section and apologize.

12

STROKES OF GENIUS

In the summer of 1984, John McEnroe conjured a level of tennis—equally athletic and aesthetic—so sublime that it overshadowed his antics. Or at least caused authorities to look away. At the time, McEnroe had effectively chased off one rival, Bjorn Borg. Another, Jimmy Connors, was in his mid-thirties, then the athletic equivalent of dotage. A third, Ivan Lendl, had just achieved his awaited breakthrough at the French Open—coming back from the brink of defeat to beat McEnroe in the final, a loss that haunts McEnroe to this day. But that was on clay; on the barbered lawns of Wimbledon, Lendl professed an allergy to grass.

With so few challengers, McEnroe treated the All England Club as his personal performance space, the guys on the other side of the net not so much opponents as accompanists. McEnroe's lyrical flourishes were in full effect. He unspooled his sidewinding lefty serve to great effect. He attacked the net, executing angles no other players would even conceive of, much less conjure. He deployed pointillist volleys.

How well did he play?

So well that his extravagant tennis stifled his volcanic temper — a volcanic temper that never would have been tolerated in a female player.

Facing little resistance, McEnroe won Wimbledon and, in the process, won over the British crowds that before had been so ambivalent — attracted as they were by his tennis and repulsed by his outbursts. This two-week cadenza on the grass would mark the highlight of his gilded 1984, a year in which McEnroe would go 82-3 and win 13 titles.

At the time, McEnroe was only the *second* most dominant force in the sport.

As the tennis circuit left Paris and wended its way to Wimbledon in the summer of 1984, Martina Navratilova had won 31 straight matches and, almost comically, 85 of her last 86. She had won the two previous Wimbledon titles and four overall.

While Chris Evert Lloyd was Navratilova's greatest challenger at the time, their rivalry approximated the rivalry between a lawn mower and a swath of grass, a hammer and a nail, Mozart and Salieri. Navratilova had won each of their previous 10 matches. Almost as an afterthought, Navratilova paired with Pam Shriver to win the doubles titles at all four majors in 1984 as well, an achievement that no other player in tennis had ever pulled off.

At the time, the annual event in Eastbourne, a Wimbledon tune-up tournament played in England and on grass, doubled as the site of the WTA's player revue, something akin to a summer camp talent show. At one point in the evening, a group of players performed a spoof to the tune of Michael Jackson's hit "Beat It," from the previous year.

Martina you're too good, just give us a break
You're beating us too bad, it's getting hard to take
Quit eating that food, and lift no more weights
So stop it! Just stop it!
Have some more sex, have some more booze
It doesn't matter if you win or lose.

Reporters asked Don Candy, Shriver's coach, how the great Martina Navratilova could possibly be beaten. Candy paused, contemplated, and finally responded, "Drive over her foot in the car park."

No one did.

While McEnroe dropped only one set in winning the 1984 Wimbledon singles title, Martina Navratilova dropped none. While McEnroe left the All England Club with a match record of 47-1 on the year, Navratilova left having won 92 of her last 93 matches. While McEnroe would win two majors that year, Navratilova would take three. She would win $2,173,556 in prize money in 1984, more than any player — male or female — ever had in a single year.

Wimbledon 1984 marked peak Navratilova. In every sense. She came to Wimbledon, her personal grass playground, as the top seed. She also came with a new entourage. Renée Richards had returned to her Park Avenue practice, so Navratilova turned to a new coach, Mike Estep, a former player on the men's circuit. Navratilova had split with Lieberman and had a new love interest — Judy Nelson, a Dallas society housewife and mother of two who had never been with a woman but had met Navratilova and "instantly felt a bond."

The day before Wimbledon, Nelson filed for divorce from her husband, a Dallas physician. The media, especially London's Fleet Street tabloids, dined out on Navratilova's personnel and romantic roster moves. There were the usual mocking references to her entourage, which included a dog walker and a dumpling maker. ("Never mind that it was the same person," says Navratilova. "A friend who happened to be a good cook.")

For the tournament, Navratilova had rented a Georgian house in Wimbledon Village, a few minutes' walk from the All England Club. Tabloid paparazzi camped out on the lawns, hoping to capture the scandalous image of a champion and her blond girlfriend. Reporters rang her doorbell early in the morning and late at night.

Navratilova being Navratilova, she did not exactly retreat. From her townhouse, she would taunt the paparazzi, calling them "scum." After she won an early-round match, Nelson blew her kisses from the stands. The click of shutters from the courtside photographers' pit was louder and more sustained than the applause of the crowd. Navratilova smiled at the men in the pit, shook her head, and muttered, "You guys are pathetic."

She began her post-match press conference by declaring that she would be taking all British events other than Wimbledon off her touring schedule. "I love the people here and I love playing here," she said. "But I have decided that the harassment I have been getting here is not worth it, and I should not subject myself to it."

It all made for a dissonant tableau. Here was Wimbledon, the emblem of elegance, this decorous affair for the landed gentry, with its whites-only dress code and white tennis balls and breaks for tea and strawberries. And it was being confronted by the outspoken, muscular, lesbian star, her flamboyant lover in the stands, and paparazzi attempting to capture it all. This was a skunk at what was, quite literally, a garden party. The conventional wisdom: loathsome as the tabloids might be, Navratilova bore some responsibility as well. Even sober *Time* magazine scoldingly noted that she possessed "a certain careless openness about her private life."

During the tournament, London's *Daily Express* ran a masthead editorial headlined "Don't Turn Martina into an Oscar Wilde." What was, notionally, a defense contained lines like this: "She's every man's anti-heroine. Her muscles are too big. She doesn't bounce around like two cute little tennis balls, making pretty pictures for the newspaper. . . . Navratilova's almost pathetic attempts to disguise her discontent with her own looks ('the best you can say is that I have a strong face') haven't helped her."

The editorial then urged sympathy. "I object to the Oscar Wildean witch-hunt of this unusual and lonely figure, who doesn't please men. If male reporters want to be nasty, let them lob their insults at the silly celebrity-smitten Texan blonde housewife who has filed for divorce and at least temporarily left two very young children to follow Navratilova."

In response to the twittering and titillation over Navratilova, the Women's Tennis Association called an emergency mid-tournament meeting at the All England Club, condemning the press's treatment of Navratilova as "horrendous." Wimbledon officials issued a statement permitting players to walk out of press conferences when the questions departed from tennis and became "provocative."

Other forms of rejection came with more subtlety. Navratilova was not assigned to play on the showcase, cathedral-like Centre Court as often as a player of her stature normally would be. NBC, the network holding American television rights, went to strenuous lengths to avoid covering Navratilova until the latter rounds, when it was absolutely necessary. (The network defended this by noting that Chris Evert's matches drew higher ratings.) Behind the scenes, officials wrung their hands, concerned that Navratilova-as-figurehead would foreclose sponsorship revenue.

Navratilova was, of course, ahead of her time. Uncannily so. Following her lead, other gay athletes would come out during their careers. (When, in 2013, NBA player Jason Collins told the world that he was gay — the first active American athlete from a major team sport to do so — he cited Navratilova specifically as his inspiration.)

In time, athletes would realize that the powerful megaphone they own as cultural forces makes them effective voices for political and social causes. The veins and muscles that earned Navratilova sideways glances and snark? They became de rigueur for athletic girls, who now proudly post #myfirstvein photos. Navratilova's "entourage" and "royal cortege," so roundly mocked, became commonplace in tennis and in all individual sports; it's just been rebranded as a "team." The "computer data" Navratilova consulted to devise strategy grew into the cottage industry of sports analytics.

But at the time, at Wimbledon 1984? A new love with a new woman? A romance being picked apart by the tabloids? The public scorn about her muscles, her entourage, the boldness to believe she was entitled to voice opinions on matters that went beyond sports? The pressure of playing Wimbledon, the crown jewel of the tennis season, knowing that she was expected to win, to hold court, as it were, that any result short of taking the trophy would constitute a considerable upset? Disgust inside and outside the locker room with her rippled, "unladylike" body? Any one of those factors could crush a player.

Yet Navratilova brushed it all off like so much lint on her tennis whites. At her Martina-est, she won with power and guile and athleticism. She won from the backcourt and from the net. She served better than the other 127 players in the field; she returned better as well. Her matches bore little tension; the drama instead resided in how Navratilova's talent and shot-making manifested themselves.

And, at odds with the mechanical intensity with which she was too often portrayed, Navratilova went about her business wearing a carefree smile. "It looks like she's having fun playing tennis," said the American player Peanut Louie, "[so] even if you get murdered, you don't feel so bad."

She won her first matches without so much as dropping a set. In the final, Navratilova won the title — her third-straight at Wimbledon — by beating Evert for the 11th-straight time, 7–6, 6–2. That Evert had played well, and taken a full eight games, made for a moral victory.

The great Frank Deford took the measure of Navratilova and put it this way: "To have achieved so much, triumphed so magnificently, yet always to have been the other, the odd one, alone; left-hander in a right-handed universe, gay in a straight world; defector, immigrant; the (last?) gallant volleyer among all those duplicate baseline bytes . . . Can't she ever get it right?"

Success emboldened her to speak up and use her platform for causes and concerns having little to do with tennis. It was somehow fitting that less than a week after Navratilova won Wimbledon, Democratic presidential nominee Walter Mondale chose as his running mate Geraldine Ferraro, the first woman on a major-party ticket.

Basking in her 1984 Wimbledon title, Navratilova was reminded that, just a year earlier, she had stated that in sports — with the constant competition, the steady flow of motivated newcomers, the small margins of defeat and victory — total domination was an impossibility. What did Navratilova now make of this assertion?

"Well," she said. "I lied."

13

SWOOSHING IN TO WOO JORDAN

During the Olympic Trials, Jordan had grown close to University of Iowa head coach George Raveling, who was in Bloomington as one of Bobby Knight's assistants. An African American in his mid-forties, Raveling was a charismatic presence and a first-rate storyteller. Orphaned as a child in Washington, D.C., Raveling persisted and played college basketball for Villanova.

In 1963, Raveling, then a strapping man in his mid-twenties, agreed to be a volunteer security guard when Martin Luther King came to Washington. He was steps from the podium when King delivered his "I Have a Dream" speech. Afterwards, Raveling asked King if he could have a copy. *Sure,* the reverend said, and absently handed Raveling his copy. Years later, Raveling would turn down offer after offer — some well into seven figures — and still holds the original copy. Jordan would sit enthralled as he listened to Raveling's stories.

As an assistant coach at Villanova and then Maryland in the late 1960s, Raveling had crossed paths with Sonny Vaccaro at the Pittsburgh high school basketball showcase Vaccaro ran. After Vaccaro left for Nike

— convinced that a footwear company could sell millions of basketball shoes if it aligned with the right players at an early age — Vaccaro and Raveling had stayed friends through the years.

In the summer of 1984, Vaccaro asked Raveling if he could put in a good word "with the Jordan kid." Raveling was happy to help an old friend.

When Raveling broached the subject of footwear with Jordan, he didn't get far.

"Nike's getting bigger and bigger," Raveling said. "I have a friend there you should meet."

"Nah," Jordan responded. He then explained that, while he wore Converse in college, his choice brand was Adidas. Gary Stokan worked as the Adidas rep in the Southeast. He had a relationship with North Carolina State and had recently signed Herschel Walker, the University of Georgia football star. Occasionally he'd come to Chapel Hill, meet Michael Jordan for Cokes on Franklin Street, and hand him a pair of shoes. Jordan liked Stokan and he liked his wares; he was partial to the Adidas look and feel. Once out of Dean Smith's sights, Jordan would wear the shoes from the competing brand.*

"I'm telling you," Raveling said, "Nike is coming on strong, and they approach things differently."

"I'm an Adidas guy," Jordan responded.

Meanwhile, Rob Strasser was hard to miss as he walked around the manicured grounds of Wimbledon. Bearded, burly, and in his mid-thirties, Strasser weighed upwards of 300 pounds and had an outsized personality to match.

A recovering lawyer, Strasser had started working for Nike in the early seventies as a marketing whiz. When the company went public

---

* Basketball lore: Once, before practice, Walter Davis, a UNC player, put on his uniform and a pair of shoes he had in his locker. The shoes were not Converse. "Put on your uniform, Walter," coach Dean Smith snapped. "Huh?" Davis responded, confused. Smith: "If you're not wearing Converse, you might as well be barefoot."

on December 2, 1980, he became a millionaire overnight at age 33. He quickly became a favorite of Nike's eccentric CEO, Phil Knight, in part because of his fearless charisma and in part because of his fierce defiance of convention.

Strasser didn't just veer across lines; he swerved over the median entirely. And he knew how to cut deals. Knight nicknamed him "Rolling Thunder" and would later say, "I was sending [Rob] into every negotiation with total confidence, as if I were sending in the Eighty-Second Airborne."

"Rolling Thunder" had rolled into Wimbledon to talk with the tournament executives about a potential sponsorship arrangement with Nike. It was a counterintuitive marriage: the stodgy British tennis tournament known for its lusty embrace of tradition and this maverick shoe company from Oregon. But so counterintuitive it just might work. And then the meeting started.

Strasser had always grasped the power of aesthetics and worked closely with a Nike designer, Peter Moore, whom he had taken with him to Wimbledon. At the start of the meeting, Strasser stood up and smiled mischievously. His belly slumping over his belt, Strasser handed out some large printouts that Moore had created. They contained black-and-white photos of Wimbledon after it had been bombed by the Germans in 1940, piercing the Centre Court roof. The tagline read "Brought to you by the people who wear three stripes."

It was a reference to the German-based shoe company Adidas — the company Nike was trying to unseat as the leading sports footwear brand. And it was meant as an icebreaker. *Surely you're not going to give a contract to the company that bombed you!*

It did not play well in the room. Moore would remember that Wimbledon officials ended the meeting by declaring that thereafter "Nike" was to be added to the list of four-letter words never to be uttered at the club.

But that was okay, because Strasser — and Moore — had another daring project to undertake. On an oppressively hot Saturday morning a few weeks later, in July of 1984, they arrived in D.C. Strasser, as usual, was saturated in sweat. They were headed to the office of ProServ, the management company.

Strasser had always believed in the force of personality—both for himself and for athletes. In 1983, he wrote in a company memo, "Individual athletes, even more than teams, will be the heroes; symbols more and more of what real people can't do anymore—risk and win."

In 1984, Nike, for the first time, tripped over a hurdle. Its growth trajectory had suddenly tailed off. It was coming off the first losing quarter in its history. Reebok, an up-and-coming company based in Massachusetts, was a darling among analysts, largely because it was dominating the women's aerobic shoe market. But here was a chance for Nike to risk and win.

The day he left for ProServ, Strasser told colleagues, "We're going to Washington today to negotiate for Michael Jordan. We're going to create shoes, advertising, and whatever else goes with him. If Jordan does what we think he can, and if we can execute, this can be big."

Though it was ProServ's cofounder Donald Dell who had traded on his relationship with Dean Smith and signed Jordan out of UNC, Dell was often too busy for his new client—off to cut a deal for a client in Europe or broadcast a tennis tournament. In Dell's absence, a relationship was growing between Jordan and Dell's young and hard-charging acolyte David Falk. When ProServ recruited Jordan and presented its marketing plan, Falk had been present but hadn't said much. He met Jordan again when the U.S. Olympic team played an exhibition game in Greensboro, North Carolina. Again the interaction was brief.

But Falk was cultivating a relationship with Jordan's parents, James and Deloris. He kept them informed of business opportunities and deals but also paid them social calls. They conveyed to Michael their fondness for Falk. Soon it was not Dell but Falk who was filling the role of Jordan's principal agent.

After Strasser cooled off in the air-conditioning in Dell's office, he made himself at home and sat on the floor. Strasser knew Dell, but he had gotten to know Falk, who was closer in age, and they had developed a rapport and trust. Strasser would phone Falk and ask about prospects, "Off the record: is this kid any good?" Falk would sometimes call for Strasser's offhand advice when dealing with other sports brands.

On this day, before Strasser could pitch ProServ on Nike, ProServ pitched Nike on Jordan. Having cut their teeth as tennis agents, Dell and Falk saw how players could transcend the sport and become their own — that word again — brands. John McEnroe had a singular image that marketers could sell. Stan Smith, even in retirement, had his own line of signature shoes within the Adidas brand.

They didn't just want to slap Jordan's name on a product in exchange for cash. They wanted their client to align with a company that would be — and wanted to be — in the Michael Jordan business. Jordan would need his own signature line. He would need a marketing-and-advertising budget of at least $1 million. He would need a royalty deal on sales.

Falk knew that Adidas and Converse wouldn't go for such an arrangement. But this was precisely the kind of break-the-mold campaign that comported with Nike, the company predicated on break-the-mold thinking.

Though he was in complete agreement with Falk about how to market an ascending athlete — and about the potential value of a signature Jordan line — Strasser ribbed the agent.

"You're trying to turn Michael Jordan into a *tennis player,*" Strasser said.

"Exactly," Falk smiled.

Asked what this new rollout should be called, Falk had an answer at the ready. "The Michael Jordan line."

Strasser and Moore made faces as though they'd smelled rotten cheese and furiously shook their heads. This was supposed to be fun and dynamic, an athlete appealing to kids, not a fashion model appealing to middle-aged women.

"What should it be called, then?" Falk asked.

"That's the trick," Strasser said.

"What about Jordan Air?" Falk suggested.*

"Nah. Sounds too much like the national airline for the country of Jordan."

Falk took another shot attempt.

"Air Jordan?"

Not bad.

Moore jotted the term in the sketchbook that was all but surgically attached to his hands.

On the flight home, he took out his omnipresent notepad and began doodling. He asked a flight attendant for the set of wings that usually get distributed to kids on board. The pin became the inspiration for the original Air Jordan logo, two unfurled wings bracketed by a basketball.

* From the "success has many fathers" department . . . Different parties — with different agendas — offer different, often competing recollections of some of the details.

14

DOWN GOES TYSON

The right hand landed squarely, a punch delivered perfectly, sourced as much from the legs as from the arms. Then came an overhand left that started with the torquing of the upper body and was executed with precision and force.

It was the kind of one-two combination, served up with wounding precision, that the boxer had rehearsed and rehearsed in the gym, an act of muscle memory that had become as natural to him as swallowing food or tying his shoes. Within just a couple of years, he would be channeling this violent fury in an attempt to divorce challengers from their consciousness as he scored knockout after devastating knockout and cleaned out his division.

But on this day, July 6, Mike Tyson was raining blows with wounding precision not against the face and body of a pitiable opponent, but against the trunk of a cedar tree. He was slicing his hands, but that was no deterrent. As Tyson threw punch after punch, he howled in pain, tears streaking his face.

In a soft, high-pitched voice—jarringly at odds with his chiseled physique and hard ways — Tyson berated himself with a withering self-assessment flecked with words like *coward.* As Tyson whaled away on the tree that stood alongside a Las Vegas freeway on-ramp, the man who served as his trainer, manager, and legal guardian stood back passively.

Cus D'Amato, then 76, may have been an unlikely mentor for a teenager; but like a boxer who knew, instinctively, when to maneuver inside and when to create space, D'Amato kept his distance. Tyson had just turned 18, and he had just lost his shot at competing in the 1984 Olympics.

In the first round of the Olympic boxing trials, in Fort Worth, Texas, Mike Tyson fought — and beat — Henry Milligan, a civil engineering major in Princeton's class of 1981. It was an all-time mismatch, at least in terms of pedigree. A hell-raiser from the Brownsville section of Brooklyn, Tyson was first arrested at age 10. By the time he was 13, he was living at the Tryon School for Boys, his fourth New York State reform school.

A former fighter named Bobby Stewart worked as a counselor at the school. He saw Tyson's aggression and physique, but also his native intelligence, and, figuring formal boxing training might do him good, introduced Tyson to his own former trainer, Cus D'Amato.

Decades earlier, D'Amato had made his bones in boxing as a trainer, guiding Floyd Patterson to a heavyweight championship. But D'Amato had repaired to the Catskills, in upstate New York, to live a life of repose. That changed when he watched Tyson spar in his gym and immediately saw the kid's aggression, his compactly built physique, his limitless potential. Glimpsing Tyson, D'Amato turned to his associate Jimmy Jacobs, a noted fight-film collector and boxing authority.

Not one given to hyperbole, D'Amato said, more as a statement than a prediction, "Mike Tyson is going to be the heavyweight champion of the world." When he went home, D'Amato told his companion, an elegant Ukrainian named Camille Ewald, "This is the one I've been waiting for all my life."

By 14, Tyson was a national Golden Gloves champion, his fights invariably ending by knockout. Barely a year later, he was expelled from Catskill High School for a series of transgressions, so the notion that "boxing was his salvation" is too tidy. Still, it's impossible to exaggerate D'Amato's influence. Early in 1984, D'Amato and Ewald had officially become Tyson's legal guardians. Tyson lived with his adopted parents, as well as other fighters, in a nine-bedroom Victorian mansion on the banks of the Hudson River.

D'Amato also became Tyson's manager and trainer. Tyson became D'Amato's reason for living. "If he weren't here, I probably wouldn't be alive today," D'Amato said in the summer of 1984. "Seeing him improve gives me the motivation to stay alive."

Tyson presented a tangle of contradictions. Hard and soft. Wild and docile. He often lacked impulse control but also could be deeply contemplative. He was capable of startling cruelty — and startling sensitivity. He was, by conventional measures, poorly educated, yet he could lose himself for hours in books about boxing history. As a fighter, Tyson was feared and fearless, ferocious but also still learning how to *box*. His fury was a virtue, but it was also in need of governance.

Short for a heavyweight, he stood under six feet tall and inevitably surrendered a reach advantage. But he was built thick like a fire hydrant, and he, reliably, dictated the action.

Reflecting boxing's place in the sports hierarchy at the time, the Olympic Trials were not only broadcast but broadcast nationally, on ABC. And the network dispatched Howard Cosell, then the most prominent broadcaster in the country, to call the action from ringside.

In the second round, Tyson nailed Milligan twice, causing the Princeton boy to wobble and take two eight counts from the ref. A final barrage sent Milligan down, and the ref waved off the contest at 2:19. Ringside, in his inimitable — but ceaselessly imitated — voice and cadence, Cosell declared, self-referentially, "SUD-denly. From NO-where. ALL of the power I told you about!"

The following day, Tyson faced Henry Tillman in the final. Tillman was, like Tyson, no Princeton graduate. The Tillman backstory traced a familiar arc in boxing: a troubled boy delivered via boxing. Growing up in a rough patch of South-Central L.A., Tillman had, as a teenager, served time for drug use, grand theft and battery, and then armed robbery. For the last conviction, Tillman was placed at a California Youth Authority facility in Chino. There he met a diminutive boxing coach, five-foot-three Mercer "Smitty" Smith, who taught the kid the sport and gave him an outlet for off-loading his aggression.

Tillman was six-four — while Tyson was, generously, listed at five-eleven — and he had a six-inch reach advantage to go with it. But the critical difference was this: Henry Tillman was 24, no teenager. Tyson may have been a superior physical specimen, armed with superior power and with superior potential in the sport. But Tillman, seven years Tyson's senior, had more maturity, more poise, more reach, and, above all, more grasp of the Olympic points scoring system. He knew Olympic scoring was about quantity over quality; a whoomphing haymaker counted for no more than an innocuous jab.

That afternoon in Fort Worth, Tillman danced and flicked off jabs that technically landed but never came close to hurting Tyson. In the first round, Tyson knocked Tillman down with a flurry of body punches. But Tillman arose and went back to tossing off glancing — but scoring — jabs, that counted just as much as Tyson's power punches. The *L.A. Times* likened Tillman to a matador, manipulating Tyson and his bull-like charges. Tillman then fought a smarter fight and won a 5–0 decision, scoring one-point margins on the cards of each of the five judges.

The qualifying process for the U.S. team — convoluted even by boxing's limbo bar standards for confusion — required that a "box-off" be held a month later, in which each division's winner from the Trials would face a designated "most worthy opponent."

This format was designed to safeguard against upsets and ensure that the most deserving fighters earned the Olympic berths. Tyson was deemed "most worthy" for heavyweights, which meant a rematch with

Tillman. If Tyson knocked out Tillman or won by referee stoppage, he would go to the Olympics and represent the U.S. team in Los Angeles. If Tyson won by decision, he and Tillman would fight a *third* time, and the winner of the rubber match would make the team. If Tillman won this second fight, he would get the spot.

The event was held at the Caesars Palace Sports Pavilion, a tin shed adjacent to the casino. There were four weeks between the first Tillman fight and the Vegas rematch, and the Tyson camp used the time judiciously. D'Amato had set up Tyson's camp at the Olympic Training Center, in Colorado Springs, and arranged to have superheavyweight Tyrell Biggs serve as a sparring partner, a stand-in for Tillman who could simulate his moves and replicate his height advantage. But Biggs failed to show up. Still, Tyson and D'Amato watched film for hours and devised a strategy based on geometry. The plan was for Tyson to cut off the ring when Tillman tried to run.

Again ABC would televise these bouts, part of the network's plan to popularize the fighters before the Olympic Games. And again Howard Cosell would be ringside. His summation of young Mike Tyson: "Just extraordinary punching power. The upper-body strength evident as you merely look at him. The upper arms enormous. The boxing skills? Perhaps developing but certainly relatively minimal at this point in time."

Before his bout, Tyson noticed a strange sight in a Caesars banquet room. Pernell Whitaker, a 132-pound southpaw from Norfolk, Virginia, was pacing angrily while his manager, Lou Duva, was rearranging tables and chairs in the otherwise vacant room.

Much like Tyson, Whitaker had lost his previous bout not because he was an inferior fighter but because he was undone by the amateur points system. He had charged directly at this opponent, Joey Belinc. Whitaker was a three-time world amateur boxing champion, but when he charged in at Belinc, the opponent caught him with counterpunches and scored points, no matter how feeble the blows. If he had designs on making the Olympic team, Whitaker would have to beat Belinc in their rematch.

When Duva had moved enough furniture to create a makeshift ring, he began teaching. "Come at me," said Duva, who was 62 years old and weighed 100 pounds more than Whitaker. "I want you sliding off to the sides . . . If you come straight I'll punch you in the nose." A 22-year-old whose amiable disposition earned him the nickname Sweet Pea, Whitaker wasn't about to hit a fleshy man three times his age; but neither was he going to let the old man hit him.

Whitaker dutifully went through the drill with Duva. When he again faced Belinc, Whitaker fought an entirely different fight, attacking from angles. If his punches weren't as crisp as those launched from a straight attack, they scored points with the judges. This time, three of the five judges sided with Whitaker. By virtue of his 3–2 win and a tiebreaking third match, he was headed to Los Angeles — and from there to a Hall of Fame professional career.

As Tyson watched Whitaker go through his paces with Duva, the parallels to his own predicament were unmistakable. He, too, had lost to an inferior opponent. And he, too, had fashioned a new strategy with an older sparring partner. Now, like Whitaker, Tyson simply needed to put the plan into practice.

Tillman emerged from the locker room wearing a lavender tank top and white trunks. Tyson wore tight trunks that hugged his protective cup and were decorated with the Stars and Stripes (not unlike the signature attire of Apollo Creed from the *Rocky* movies, the fourth installment of which would be released the following year). Tyson was already basted in sweat as he bounded out from the locker room.

In the first round, Tyson betrayed nothing resembling a strategy, circumnavigating the ring seemingly with no determined purpose. He would later admit that he might have been overcome by the occasion, the pulsing lights both in the Caesars arena and the city itself. But he either waited too long to squeeze off punches or flailed and missed. Tillman, on the other hand, abided by a time-tested fight plan: stick and move. "If you stand there and let a guy hit you . . . put an X on your jaw . . . of course he gonna knock you out," Tillman told Cosell beforehand. Tillman's jabs may have been more irritating than damaging, but they scored points.

With eight seconds to go in the round, Tyson stepped into the center of the ring and waved Tillman in to follow him. The gesture encapsulated Tyson's frustration, and was so damn obvious to everyone, most especially to Mike himself: *He* had the great fund of talent and power. *He* was the true heavyweight. The wunderkind who should already be king. Of every rank of fighting — amateur, professional, bareknuckle, all of it.

Tillman, feeling, not wrongly, no need to prove his machismo, ignored Tyson's exhortations.

After two rounds of (in)action, Tyson was reduced to sticking out his tongue at Tillman. Inexplicably, Tyson remained pegged to the center of the ring, never even coming close to cutting off angles, let alone confining Tillman to a corner. Between rounds, Tyson's corner minced no words; they implored him to throw his big right hand.

Which he did in the third round. Four times he made harder contact than Tillman had yet mustered at any point in the bout. Tyson couldn't pull off the knockout, but at the final bell he raised his arms, authentically believing that his aggressive fighting would be rewarded and that he had done enough to win favor with the judges. As the two men came to the center of the ring to await the decision, Tyson, having removed his headgear, wore a look of hope.

The public address announcer intoned: "Ladies and gentlemen, the winner in the heavyweight division . . . and an established —"

With that adjective, Tyson knew they were referring to the other fighter. He wriggled free of the referee and tried to leave the ring, only to be restrained.

". . . member of the 1984 Olympic team, from Los Angeles, California, in the red corner: Henry Tillman!"

Two judges favored Tillman 60–57 and two favored him 58–57. One preferred Tyson 58–57. "Mike was robbed," said Tyson. "That's my official statement." Tyson may have been a bit young to be referring to himself in the third person, but most of the crowd of 3,089 shared his displeasure with the decision. Boos competed with the smoke to fill the air.

Howard Cosell didn't miss the chance both to explain the decision and to self-aggrandize: "So they gave it to Henry Tillman, obviously on the basis of more apparent style and class. The aggressor was Mike Tyson, but, as I explained, aggressiveness in amateur boxing is not rewarded with points."

When the announcement of the official decision was completed, Tillman attempted to console Tyson. Young Mike Tyson, though, was beyond consolation. He began inhaling deeply, holding back tears. He then removed his boxing gloves and prepared to leave the ring. By then his emotions — a cocktail of rage and disappointment and embarrassment and self-pity — roiled, and he kept walking. Out of the ring. Past the locker room. Out of the arena. Beyond the parking lot. He kept walking for hundreds of yards, until he found that tree to pound.

After unloading his last punch, hand to timber, Tyson would calm down and bury his head in D'Amato's embrace, his face lashed with tears. The sting of defeat, of failing to make the Olympic team, would lodge itself deep in the rafters of his consciousness. This moment, this humiliation, would become one of his motivating forces.

As Tyson's biographer William F. McNeil would later write, "The two losses to Henry Tillman may have been more important to the advancement of Mike Tyson than any of his spectacular victories . . . His string of easy knockouts in the amateurs made him arrogant and difficult to control. He felt invincible and viewed his opponents with utter disdain . . . The two losses to Tillman helped snap Tyson out of his sloppy training habits."

Beyond that, Tyson had learned a stark and stinging lesson about subjectivity and bias and unfairness. He learned that a slick and polished adversary can juke and jive around a fighter endowed with superior talent and merit. That judges' decisions are just that: cloudy and personal determinations. That, once again, an institution had failed him. Mike

Tyson got still more reinforcement that day. Screw nuance — he would need the unambiguity of the knockout.

And he wouldn't lose another fight for more than five years. By that time, Mike Tyson was 37-0. And only three of those fights were by judges' decisions. The rest were knockouts, each one more sensationally brutal than the last.

15

THE DREAM TEAM

In Indianapolis, a popular 1984 parlor game entailed coming up with the best comparison for the Hoosier Dome, the white monstrosity that had sprouted to blight the city's skyline. *It's like a giant biscuit made from scratch. No, it looks more like a giant pile of white deer crap.* The indoor venue was built with the intent of enticing a professional football team to relocate to town — and on those grounds, it was stunningly successful. On March 28, 1984, the Colts organization had loaded up a fleet of moving vans, left Baltimore under cover of darkness, and decamped to Indianapolis.

But with the 1984 NFL season still weeks away, the first event held inside the Hoosier Dome was, appropriately, a basketball game. As Bob Knight, the unofficial emcee, told the crowd that night, July 9, 1984, "I heard today that basketball was invented in Springfield, Massachusetts, and that is true." (*Pause for effect.*) "God had it invented there so we could import it to Indiana." Deafening applause followed.

Knight and his minions had come to Indianapolis as part of a pre-Olympic summer barnstorming tour. In order to help the team coalesce into a unit, in order to simulate real competition under international rules — and in order to get them the hell out of southern Indiana in the summer — USA Basketball had arranged for a series of games against makeshift teams of NBA players. Like a summer concert tour, the circuit threaded its way through an assortment of cities, some (Minneapolis) more logical than others (Iowa City?)*.

Apart from offering an entertaining summer basketball exhibition, the games doubled as an exercise in patriotism. Knight had already stressed this aspect with his players. Time and again, he reminded them that they were playing as representatives of America, which, as the coach put it, was *one of the great civilizations in world history.* Knight also constantly reminded them of recent Olympic basketball history. Though 12 years had elapsed, Knight often invoked the gold-medal game in the 1972 Olympics, when the Russians "won" an atrociously officiated contest 51–50, the outcome so dubious and controversial that the American players never accepted their silver medals.

With the Soviet boycott of the 1984 Games, there would be no Cold War flashpoint or baked-in rival this time. Still, these were our boys — the same age as soldiers — going off to do battle in an international theater, representing their country and wearing uniforms emblazoned in red, white, and blue.

This patriotic strain was especially vivid in Indianapolis on this night. It was the Monday after Fourth of July weekend. And the unit was led by Knight, a man nicknamed the General, who had started his coaching tour of duty at West Point and fancied himself a military historian. The ragtag mix of NBA players forming the opposition were coaxed into interrupting their summer on the grounds that they were fulfilling a patriotic duty, serving as sparring partners for the American unit.

At the entrance to the Hoosier Dome, local Girl Scout troops handed

---

* This likely was a nod to the Olympic assistant coach George Raveling, whose day job was head coach at the University of Iowa. Raveling not only got to go home for a few days, but brought some revenue to his school.

out miniature American flags to the 67,596 fans who attended, at the time the largest crowd ever to watch a basketball game indoors. During the pregame ceremonies, Knight welcomed the crowd and then handed the stage over to none other than Ronald Reagan. The president had taped a message that played on the video board, declaring that Knight's collection of players was "not just a team. They're the *American* team."

Amid all this patriotic (jingoistic?) fervor, few fans noticed a small interlude on the court. During the pregame warm-up, Michael Jordan, shod now in the Fastbreak model by Converse, the sponsor of the Olympic team, unspooled a series of jump shots. After one errant attempt, his ball squirted away from him, crossed the DMZ of half-court, and bounded into enemy territory, the opponent's side of the floor.

It found its way into the hands of Larry Bird. Fresh from winning the NBA title a few weeks earlier, Bird had, somewhat grudgingly, paused his off-season ritual — consisting mostly of beer drinking and fishing — to take part in this exhibition, a few hours' drive from his famed hometown of French Lick, Indiana.

For Bird, though, there were no exhibition games. Only competitions. Jordan wore a sheepish, congenial *My bad, Larry,* smile as he came to retrieve his ball. Bird, the NBA's reigning MVP, was less congenial. Sneering dismissively, he kicked the ball over Jordan's head and back to the other end of the court, the indoor equivalent of *Get off my lawn, kid.* Jordan walked back, shaking his head, interpreting it as a bit of validation. He was already worthy of Larry Bird's mind games. *See you in the NBA, pal.*

That night, the U.S. women's basketball team served as something of a warm-up act. Led by Cheryl Miller — whose kid brother Reggie would be drafted by the Indiana Pacers three summers later and leave as the franchise's most decorated pro basketball player — the U.S. women cruised to a 97–54 win over a patchwork team of former college players. "Not much to complain about," said the coach, Pat Summitt, who had turned 32 a few weeks before.

As for the main event, the men's game, Bird tricked Jordan into a pair of quick fouls and the NBA All-Stars — featuring most of Bird's Celtics teammates as well as the Detroit Pistons' star guard Isiah Thomas, who had played for Knight at Indiana — took a 16–10 lead. But then the Olympians took over, benefiting from superior depth, cohesion, and ambition. They pulled away in the second half and won 97–82. Bird had 14 points. Jordan had 12. Seven months later, when Jordan next appeared at the Hoosier Dome, he and Bird would be on the same side of the court, teammates representing the Eastern Conference at the NBA All-Star Game.

Apart from simulating battle, the barnstorming tour gave rise to a certain esprit de corps, a chemistry among the unit. Knight experimented with lineups and was intentionally vague and erratic about his rotation.

Players also experienced Knight's brutal, military-style authority. Within a few years, autocrats like Knight would be subject to the equivalent of court-martial — "You can't handle the truth!" we might have later said — for breaches of basic human decency. But in 1984, Knight's M.O. was still acceptable, perhaps especially heading into an international competition.

For Knight, basketball was never about missed shots or made shots. It was about manifestations of character. Were you tough and durable and courageous and unswerving in your convictions? Or did you play with what Knight perceived to be the twin curses of softness and indecision?

Some players recoiled from Knight's style. (That included Larry Bird, who, recruited by Knight in the mid-seventies, had gone home after a homesick month on campus in Bloomington and then transferred to Indiana State.) Others responded to it. Jordan was not merely unbothered by Knight; he warmed to his discipline and his combustible personality and saw value in both. It was all in service of winning. And what's wrong with the alpha acting like the alpha?

Patrick Ewing would later tell the story that one night he and Jordan began play-wrestling in the living quarters. Nothing malicious, just two bored and athletic kids fooling around. Though Jordan spotted Ewing six inches and perhaps 50 pounds, he got his man in a headlock. Ewing capitulated. Neither thought much of it, but the next day Ewing couldn't move his neck.

Worse, he had to tell Knight what had happened and that Jordan had been the culprit. "Coach Knight was *mad,*" Ewing recalled to the writer Jack McCallum in his excellent book *Dream Team.* "But only at me. Michael? Nothing happened to him. Nothing *ever* happened to Michael."

Which wasn't entirely true. Knight went after Jordan plenty. But sometimes it was to test Jordan's resolve. Other times it was to send a message: *No one is above the law.* (On these occasions, Knight would sometimes warn Jordan what was coming.)

Jordan's college coach, Dean Smith, was a strong authority figure who brooked no bullshit. But this was at an entirely different level. Which was fine by Jordan. Asked—as he invariably was throughout the tour—to compare coaches, Jordan smiled and offered a winning line: "The only different thing is the vocabulary. From Coach Smith I learned the four-corner offense. From Coach Knight I learned the four-letter word." (Wait for laughter.) "I've heard some of the words before that he's used, but never from a coach."

Referring to Knight by his first name, he continued, "Bobby doesn't scare me. I'm taller than him." (Wait for more laughter.) "But I see what gets him mad, and I make sure I don't do it. He's taught us all a lot, and his way of getting a point across doesn't take the fun out of this. Now, if you ask me whether I'd want to play for him for four years, I'd have to think about it."

Jordan was more amused than anything else by Knight's eruptions. He often confided in Raveling—who had known Knight since the late 1960s and counted him as a friend—jokingly referring to Knight as "your boy." As in: *You're never going to believe what your boy did today.* Or: *Check out what your boy called me this morning.*

All bullies, though, need a target, and Wayman Tisdale, a silky lefty forward from Oklahoma, was a particular victim of Knight's. Confidants of Knight's explain that he didn't hold Tisdale's college coach, Billy Tubbs, in especially high esteem. Tubbs's teams played a high-scoring, defense-free style, absent of structure. (By received wisdom, Tubbs played comparably fast and loose with the NCAA rule book.) Knight was going to impose discipline and, by proxy, repudiate Tubbs and his slapdash approach to basketball.

During a practice before an exhibition in Greensboro, Knight stopped the session and demanded a black Magic Marker. He then bent down, wrote an X on the floor, and added a date. As Knight knelt on the court for this art project, the players exchanged quizzical looks. When the coach finished, he declared, "I just wanted to mark the time and place that I first saw Wayman Tisdale take a charge." More than once, the General kicked Tisdale out of the gym, leaving the player in tears. Asked what he thought of Knight's methods, Tisdale would say, "When I get back to Oklahoma, I'm going to hug every mean person I used to think was mean."

While it wasn't quite the Harlem Globetrotters vs. the Washington Generals, with scripted outcomes and storylines, everyone knew the rules of engagement for these exhibition games. The NBA players were expected to try hard, but not their *hardest,* and keep the games close. They were not supposed to win. So they didn't. But the games were often competitive, sometimes intensely so.

On July 12, the Olympians played an exhibition game in Milwaukee. Before the game, Tim Hallam, a young staffer in the Bulls' public relations office, drove up from Chicago with a photographer. His task: get Michael Jordan to pose for a portrait photo in a Bulls uniform. Hallam introduced himself to Jordan for the first time and was impressed when the kid smiled, looked him in the eye, and seemed to grasp the exercise. *Hey, a team needs to sell tickets. I'm the new draft pick. This comes with the territory.*

But with tip-off looming, there was no time to set up proper lighting. So there, in the middle of the locker room in Milwaukee, surrounded by teammates, Jordan changed out of the Olympic uniform and into the Bulls uniform and sat for the damn photo. While he would later razz Hallam about this imposition on his time — this, the very first of countless requests the Bulls' public relations staff would make over the years — on this night, Jordan could not have been more accommodating.

While Jordan was posing for the photo shoot, Knight was in the other locker room, encouraging two of the NBA stars, Mike Dunleavy and Doc Rivers, to knock his players around a lot. They obliged. So did their teammate, Mickey Johnson, of the Golden State Warriors, who took advantage of the tour's unlimited fouls policy, committing 13 infractions. But when the game turned from physical to violent, Knight reconsidered, screaming at the referees to get control of the game: "Too much is at stake."

In the second half, Jordan went in for a breakaway dunk. Dunleavy swooped in, extended his right hand, and raked Jordan across the face. After thudding to the ground, Jordan popped up like a jack-in-the-box, glowering and looking to fight Dunleavy. By the time he was restrained by teammates, he was already cocking a fist. "I didn't come out here to not play hard," Dunleavy said.*

After the game in Milwaukee, Knight was still hot. He declared Charley Vacca, a college official, "the most incompetent sonofabitch I've seen referee. . . . What do you want me to do, sit on my ass and let a million-dollar player's career be ruined by some asshole with a whistle?"

Apart from assholes with whistles, the tour was a smashing success that achieved its goal. Some games were blowouts, the team playing in harmony. Other games were close, and the Olympians were forced to show some mettle, scoring baskets and making critical stops on defense.

---

* Seven summers later, Jordan would get his revenge, winning his first NBA title in 1991 as the Chicago Bulls defeated the Los Angeles Lakers, a team coached by . . . Mike Dunleavy.

But the Olympians played against the best and brightest in the NBA (Bird in Indianapolis; Magic Johnson in Minneapolis; Clyde Drexler in Iowa City; Alex English and Kiki Vandeweghe in Phoenix). In the end, the Olympians won all eight games; roles and responsibilities became more clear; collectively and individually, confidence swelled.

But the tour also did something else: it highlighted the lavish skills of Michael Jordan. The games foreshadowed just how seamlessly Jordan's game, his explosive athleticism, his position — for that matter, his *disposition* — would translate to the NBA.

Jay Bilas had finished his sophomore year at Duke and played sporadically on the basketball team. He'd harbored interests beyond basketball and that summer served as a production assistant for ABC for Olympic basketball telecasts. While most of his work came at the L.A. Games, Bilas was also assigned to work some of the exhibition games between the Olympians and the NBA players.

Having played against Jordan at the rival school less than half an hour away, Bilas had seen Jordan average 20 points in the Atlantic Coast Conference. He was unsurprised when he attended a pregame practice in Minneapolis and it was abundantly obvious that Jordan was the best player on the team.

But then the game started. Jordan was competing against the likes of Magic Johnson, Kevin McHale, Isiah Thomas, and Mark Aguirre. "He was still the best player — by far," says Bilas. "It was pretty clear that there wasn't anybody in the NBA or internationally that could hang with him. Jordan did stuff where it was like *Are you kidding me?* And I saw him do it in college a little bit, but this was a different level. I remembered, as a kid, people used to say that when Mickey Mantle made contact, his bat made a different sound from everyone else's. It was like that. He was making moves and you were like *It's just different. No one else is doing that.*"

Toward the end of the tour, the U.S. team played a collection of All-Stars in Phoenix. After Jordan dropped 27 points and the Olympians won their eighth-straight game, 84–72, the opposing coach was visibly slack-jawed. How good was Jordan? "He's as gifted a player as any I've ever seen play ball," responded Pat Riley, the Lakers' coach — who was, bear in mind, just a few weeks removed from watching Larry Bird, Kevin McHale, Magic Johnson, James Worthy, and Kareem Abdul-Jabbar duel for seven games in a classic series. "What happened here and then through the Olympics will only make him better. I don't think he realizes how good he really is."

16

THE VICTORY TOUR

Michael Jackson became known as the King of Pop in 1989, when Elizabeth Taylor conferred the nickname upon him at the Soul Train Music Awards show. And the characterization stuck. But Jackson was truly at the peak of his regal powers five years earlier, in 1984. That year, characterizing Jackson as the king would have understated his supremacy and sold short the sweep, scope, and scale of his popularity.

The 1950s had Elvis, the hip-shaking troubadour. The sixties had the Beatles, the transformative British quartet. The seventies had the heavier and more subversive energy of Led Zeppelin and Pink Floyd, as well as the goofy disco era. By 1984 it was already clear that the defining star of the entire decade was a compulsively entertaining, racially and sexually ambiguous singer/dancer/weirdo possessing a sweet, high voice and shrouding himself in mystery. At the 1984 Grammys, Jackson won a record-breaking eight awards. Largely because of his presence, it was the highest-rated Grammys broadcast in history.

If you wanted to create a star entertainer ideally suited for the times, that figure would have looked a lot like Jackson. He was, firstly, a singer, delivering ridiculously catchy pop songs in a striking voice, at once soft and authoritative. He was still relatively young — he turned 26 in 1984 — but was already well known, having pierced the public consciousness as a young boy, the showstopping junior member of the Jackson 5.

Jackson was an incandescently talented dancer, showing off footwork, both smooth and sharp, as he belted out songs. He quickly mastered the new art of the medium, the music video, telling the story of his songs in a visual form that often played out as compellingly — and sometimes cost as much to produce — as full-length feature films. Like a presidential candidate who crossed demographics, Jackson was both a towering figure and a relatable everyman. His reflection — the man in the mirror, you might say — was open to interpretation. Fans could see him as whatever they wanted him to be.

He was the product of soot-filled Gary, Indiana, but lived the glamorous life of a Los Angeles superstar. He danced suggestively and exuded sexual energy, but he also projected the wholesomeness of an avowed virgin who still lived with his overbearing parents and sisters, and went door-to-door several times a week (sometimes incognito and sometimes not), trying to convert Southern Californians to the Jehovah's Witness faith.

Jackson was handsome, if unconventionally so, with rings of Jheri curls framing a boyish face and shy smile. For a man in his twenties who was considered a sex symbol, Jackson seldom showed much skin. (Good luck finding, say, a shirtless photo of him.) He was known for what he wore — his red leather jacket, an array of hats, the ubiquitous single glove. His sexual identity and, later, his racial identity were up for debate. And Jackson, elusive in the extreme, wasn't inclined to help settle those arguments. He was, at once, ubiquitous and unknowable.

But even in 1984, it was clear that Jackson was, objectively, odd. At the time, it was benign weirdness and did not suggest anything more predatory. He was sometimes flanked by two close friends, Brooke Shields and Emmanuel Lewis — the former a child star and, at the time, a Princeton undergrad whose career had stalled, the latter the diminutive sitcom star of *Webster,* who was 13 in 1984, half Jackson's age, and stood three-foot-four.

In May of 1984, Jackson visited the White House, but he hid in a bathroom off the presidential library because the crush of strangers overwhelmed him. When Jackson finally emerged, Ronald Reagan said, cringingly, that if all Americans followed Jackson's example of an alcohol-free and drug-free lifestyle, "we can, in Michael's words, beat it." Yet Jackson's introversion and elusiveness and what was then charitably characterized as "quirk" only fed his popularity.

The scale of this popularity is almost impossible to exaggerate. In 1984, more than a year after Jackson's album *Thriller* was released, it was *still* No. 1 on the charts. *Rolling Stone* magazine, the pop culture bible at the time, determined that *Thriller* had sold more copies than the contemporary albums *Let's Dance* (David Bowie), *Synchronicity* (the Police), *Colour by Numbers* (Culture Club), *Metal Health* (Quiet Riot), and *Seven and the Ragged Tiger* (Duran Duran) combined — and then *doubled.*

Jackson negotiated the highest royalty in music, earning $2.10 on every album, twice the rate of other artists. (Midway through 1984, *Thriller* had sold more than 30 million copies.) Gift shops in the most nondescript malls sold Michael Jackson dolls and posters and jackets and attire. School boards held meetings to determine whether students were permitted to wear a single glove to class, in the manner of Jackson. The most slapdash, unauthorized biographies of Jackson rocketed up the bestseller list. Rights to his autobiography were purchased by Doubleday for seven figures and immediately assigned to one of the house's top editors, Jacqueline Onassis.

Then there was the appetite to see Jackson perform live. The New York promoter Ron Delsener told *Rolling Stone* that Jackson could sell out 60,000-seat Shea Stadium for an entire week and still not exhaust ticket demand. With satellite technology improving, one promoter pitched the idea of simulcasting Jackson's concerts to movie theaters around the globe and selling tickets to the broadcasts.

All the runaway popularity was to be captured in the Victory Tour.

Here was Jackson, this unrivaled worldwide celebrity at the peak of his powers. And yet he launched this tour for the most mundane reason imaginable: his parents told him to.

The idea was simple. All six Jackson brothers would come together to release an album on Epic Records and then tour as a group. Michael would serve as frontman and get his showcase. The other five Jacksons — Jermaine, Tito, Randy, Jackie, and Marlon — would back him up, perform, and be lavished with generational wealth in the process. Michael was reluctant but was talked into the idea by his mother, who hoped her other sons would emerge from the tour set up for life.

Don King, the notorious boxing promoter — known as much for his vertically stationed hair, his mistreatment of the English language, and his outrageousness as for his savvy — caught wind of the Victory Tour. Possessing a bloodhound's nose for opportunity, he insinuated himself. He offered the Jacksons $3 million in upfront advances to become the tour manager, in exchange for 7.5 percent of the back end. Michael had his reservations about King. "I think he's creepy," he told a friend. The other brothers, happy to take their $500,000 share of King's offer, outvoted him. King figured — correctly, it would turn out — that he could make millions by attaching himself to the Jacksons. Plus, he could always go back to promoting boxers.

At a pre-tour press conference, the Jackson brothers explained the basic concept of the tour. This was to be the Super Bowl of rock concerts. It would feature a phalanx of dancers, an army of roadies, and stagecraft so elaborate it would require more than 25 trucks just to haul the gear — including 64,000 pounds of lighting and sound equipment — from one venue to the next. The tour was about "enrapturement," the flamboyant manager explained. Even applying the Don King Hyperbole Discount, the man outdid himself with this statement: "Anybody who sees this show will be a better person for years to come."

King devised an idea that resided somewhere between evil and genius. Because of the astronomical demand, tickets would be sold in blocks of four seats for $120. (At $30 a seat, this was nearly double the price of other arena rock concerts that summer.) What's more, fans would have to enter a lottery, sending in their $120 well in advance. Meanwhile, the Jacksons would invest the money and keep the interest.

King also believed that, just as the Super Bowl thrived on corporate ties, the Super Bowl of rock concerts needed a corporate backer as well. Soon Pepsi came along, offering $6 million to sponsor the Victory Tour. Michael didn't drink Pepsi and opposed this. Again he was outvoted by his brothers, who were happy to divvy up more of what amounted to free money.

So it was set, this over-the-top, once-in-a-generation event, less a concert than, as its name implied, an extravaganza. The King of Pop was the headliner. The Victory Tour had its corporate backer. It had its grandiose trappings. There was just one overarching question: Who the hell would bankroll this?

Billy Sullivan was an unlikely pro football patriarch. The son of a Massachusetts sportswriter, Sullivan found work in the late 1930s as the public relations director for Boston College. There, he became fast friends with the school's football coach, the estimable Frank Leahy.

In 1941, Leahy moved on to coach Notre Dame, and by the late 1950s he was helping Barron Hilton, the hotel magnate, buy the San Diego Chargers, in the fledgling American Football League. Leahy became the Chargers' first general manager for the inaugural season of 1960. Sullivan was by this point the president of a Massachusetts fuel delivery company. Leahy called his old buddy. Might Sullivan be interested in ponying up $250,000 to launch the league's eighth franchise in Boston?

Sullivan had a wife and six children and a burning desire to become involved in pro football. What he did not have was money. But he put down the $8,300 he had in his life savings, borrowed $16,700, and found nine partners to put up $25,000 each. Presto: Sullivan, the affable striver, had 10 percent ownership and the title of president for a pro football team, the Boston Patriots.

In 1970, Billy helped negotiate the merger between the AFL and the

NFL and represented both leagues in getting an antitrust exemption from Congress that allowed for the merger. The NFL was happy to have a franchise in Boston, but it issued an ultimatum: if the Patriots did not find a permanent home, the league might force a sale.

Sullivan and his partners scrambled, spending $6.7 million—later the per-season price of one decent NFL wide receiver—to buy a swath of land in rural Foxborough, Massachusetts. They found a corporate partner in Schaefer Beer ("the one beer to have when you're having more than one"). The Patriots began playing in Schaefer Stadium and changed their name to the New England Patriots. Sullivan was lionized as the man who had kept the NFL in greater Boston.

Throughout the 1970s, though, the Patriots struggled to fill seats. The teams were generally lousy. And the stadium was worse. Though games seldom sold out, fans were forced to endure miles of traffic on Route 1. When they arrived, they sat on cold benches. On more than one occasion, the stadium's toilets overflowed—confirmation that Patriots fans were, indeed, having more than one Schaefer.

As fans were growing impatient with the Patriots, other owners were growing impatient with Sullivan. In 1981, a group of shareholders attempted to replace him with the son of one of the original partners. To fend off this coup, the Sullivan family went deep into the playbook.

Billy's son Charles ("Chuck" to everyone) had graduated from law school and gone to work in a white-shoe Boston firm. He used his legal expertise to help stave off this takeover attempt. Equally adept at finding loopholes in the ownership charter and tracking down sources of financing, Chuck eventually arranged for the Sullivans to buy out the very partners who had chosen to oust them.* The maneuver put the Sullivan family into considerable debt, both financial and political. But Billy

---

* An ascending Massachusetts state representative named Barney Frank was helpful in pushing a bill through the state legislature amending takeover laws to require only a majority, not a two-thirds vote, for shareholder approval.

now owned the New England Patriots. And Chuck owned what became known as Sullivan Stadium, in Billy's honor.

In addition to owning the venue, Chuck became the heir apparent to take over the team from Billy. And he played the part. "The team had become terribly important to him," Camille Sarrouf, a lawyer and former Patriots shareholder, recounted to *Sports Illustrated.* "He once said to me, 'There are 100 U.S. senators but only 28 owners of an NFL team.'"

But soon Chuck Sullivan grew restless and began looking to expand beyond football. The family had a team and it had a large stadium. Why couldn't it find more revenue streams? So it was that in the spring of 1984, Chuck headed to Los Angeles to meet with Don King and try to persuade the Jacksons to play concerts at Sullivan Stadium when the Victory Tour threaded its way through Boston.

Charles was surprised when an executive from Epic Records explained that talks with the original financier had broken off. Never mind holding the Jacksons' Boston concert in Foxborough; Sullivan could finance the *whole damn Victory Tour.*

Chuck had promoted concerts as an undergraduate at Boston College, bringing Duke Ellington to campus, among others. Stationed in Thailand during the Vietnam War, he had served as the Army's coordinator for the Bob Hope 1968 Christmas Tour. And Sullivan Stadium had hosted various concerts through the years. *Entertainment Weekly* would later describe Chuck as "a national-tour greenhorn." But Chuck didn't see it that way. Concerts are concerts — how hard could this be?

Sullivan returned to Boston seduced by the idea of being the moneyman behind this transformative concert tour headlined by Michael Jackson, the biggest performer on the planet. As one associate recalls, "Chuck wanted to be the money. But he didn't have the money to be the money."

So Sullivan took meetings with Boston banks, lining up the financing to back the tour. He tried to encourage other NFL owners to join him as partners. Eddie DeBartolo, owner of the San Francisco 49ers and a man not known for caution, nearly joined, before determining that the deal was too risky. While no other fellow owners made an investment, they were given a sort of favored-nations status. In the end, 26 of the Victory Tour's 55 dates would be played in stadiums that were home to NFL teams.

The terms requested by the Jacksons were, at best, aggressive. Chuck agreed to give the Jackson family $41 million — 75 percent of gross revenues from ticket sales. He also pledged to cover the travel and expenses of Jackson's not insignificant entourage. Sullivan did not have close to that much money. So he borrowed it from various Boston banks. And he put up Sullivan Stadium as collateral by taking out a mortgage.

Well before the shows began, it was clear that if this was truly a Victory Tour, any *victory* would be hard-earned. In January of 1984, Jackson performed onstage at the Shrine Auditorium, in Los Angeles. The occasion was not a concert, but the taping of a Pepsi commercial, per the sponsorship contract. From the start, Michael had declared that he would not drink Pepsi as part of the ad campaign. So instead he performed his hit "Billie Jean" to corporatized lyrics. ("Wouldn't you rather just drink the damn cola?" Don King, not unreasonably, asked repeatedly.)

Midway through the filming, Jackson moved too close to a fireworks display that had detonated behind him. The pomade in his hair caught fire. Jackson continued dancing until he realized that his head was in flames. "Tito! Tito!" Jackson cried to his brother. The fire was tamped out and Jackson was rushed to a hospital, having suffered second- and third-degree burns on his head. (A quarter century later, it would be asserted in court that the incident triggered both Jackson's interest in plastic surgery and his interest in the powerful sedatives that would kill him.)

When the tour kicked off, a theme of "family dysfunction" began echoing. The gulf between Michael and his brothers was vast and could not be bridged. The most famous entertainer (human being?) on the planet, Michael didn't need the money, much less the exposure. For the other five brothers, it was a windfall. While the *Victory* album dropped on July 2, 1984, the same week the tour commenced, the concerts featured no songs from the album. Why? Because Michael, reportedly, refused to rehearse or perform them.

Bad publicity — a rarity for Jackson at the time — accompanied the tour as well. While the tour sold out in record time, the strikingly high price for tickets drew a fierce backlash. African American fans, in particular, were vocal in accusing the Jacksons of greed. Stung by the criticism, Jackson announced that he would donate his cut to a variety of charities, including the United Negro College Fund.

Early in the tour, it became evident that Chuck Sullivan (a) had been badly outnegotiated by King and (b) had badly underestimated the expenses he was obligated to cover. Total overhead exceeded more than $1 million *each week*. The two 175-ton stages required assembly and disassembly after shows. The sheer size of the stages also meant that thousands of seats couldn't be sold. Jackson's entourage didn't travel cheap, demanding premium food and beverages and rooms in luxury hotels. The 250-plus workers on the Victory Tour payroll included an "ambiance director" tasked with providing "homey touches."

As the tour progressed, family tensions deepened. At the hotels, the brothers stayed on different floors. Lawyers and mediators were summoned so the brothers could communicate through third parties. At one point Michael was placed under medical care, citing stress and exhaustion from dealing with his brothers. From the beginning, Jackson, not wrongly, was skeptical of Don King, who sensed this and fomented disagreement, happy to isolate Michael from his brothers.

For Sullivan, perhaps the ultimate indignity came when three scheduled shows at Sullivan Stadium — the venue he *owned*, named for his father — were canceled. "Foxboro Tells Jackson to Beat It," United Press International put it in its wire service headline.

By a 3–0 vote, the town's selectmen denied a permit on the grounds that the concert would bring "an unknown element" to Foxborough. State senator Royal Bolling Sr., the state's senior Black lawmaker, interpreted this, likely quite rightly, as a racial dog whistle. "There seems to be an underlying consideration based on the ethnic composition of the group (black), and that the town might be inundated by minorities."

Midway through the tour, Chuck began seeking relief. He asked Michael Jackson to reduce his take of the gross haul from ticket sales. (To his credit, Jackson agreed, waiving $10 million owed to him.) Still, costs were outpacing revenue. So Chuck made one last desperate gamble. He took out another loan using the stadium as collateral — he was able to do so because it was the only privately financed stadium in the NFL — and offered Michael Jackson $18 million for the licensing rights to certain souvenir merchandise and apparel.

But again, fortune did not smile on Chuck Sullivan. Almost in lockstep with Jackson's signing the deal, Jackson's behavior turned increasingly strange and, eventually, unconscionable. He experimented with plastic surgery. He went into seclusion. He declared that he was taking a break from recording. While Sullivan Stadium was denied a permit to host a Victory Tour concert, it became a repository for all manner of unsold Michael Jackson T-shirts, lunch boxes, and coffee mugs.

In the end, the Victory Tour was, as Don King predicted, the highest-grossing tour in history, selling more than 2.3 million tickets. Each of the brothers received roughly $6 million, including Michael, who donated his fee to charity. Don King made millions. Of course he did.

For Chuck Sullivan and his Stadium Management Corporation, the tour was an abject disaster. Between the concert guarantees and the ill-fated licensing deal, per their own accounting reports, they lost $30 million from Jackson and the tour, more than the Sullivan family's net worth.

Robert Kraft counted himself among the army of long-suffering Patriots fans. In 1971, he was 30 years old. He and his wife had four boys. Kraft decided to splurge and buy season tickets to the Patriots' games. Eight Sundays a year, the Krafts would venture to section 217, row 23, sit on cold metal benches in what was then Schaefer Stadium, and watch their team lose more games than they would win.

As his kids cheered and booed and shivered, Kraft allowed his mind to wander and consider what he would do differently if he ever owned the team. For one, he'd sure as hell improve the stadium experience. He'd also improve the management. And hire a better coach. And make better draft picks by being armed with more information . . .

Kraft was raised in Boston, the son of an observant Jew, a dressmaker in Boston's Chinatown. Harry Kraft wanted his son to become a rabbi. Instead Robert went to Columbia University and then Harvard Business School. In 1963, the year he graduated from Columbia, Kraft married Myra Hiatt, whose father owned a paper-and-packaging company in Worcester, Massachusetts. Jacob Hiatt was president of the Rand-Whitney Group, which manufactured boxes, among other forms of paper products. He offered his new son-in-law a job, convincing him to stay in New England rather than pursue the offers he had received from Wall Street.

After a year and a half, Kraft left to start his own business. Over the course of the next decade, he enjoyed enough success to purchase his father-in-law's business. As he was growing his paper-and-packaging businesses, Kraft diversified and took a particular interest in sports.

In the 1970s, he owned the Boston Lobsters of the World Team Tennis league, sometimes hosting players, including Martina Navratilova, at the family home. The Lobsters folded after the 1978 season, but Kraft set his sights on the Patriots. He had played "sprint football" at Columbia, a version open only to players under 154 pounds.* He figured he had a better shot at the lousy Pats than at the Red Sox or Celtics or Bruins. Still, he joked to friends that he had a better shot at being an NFL quarterback

---

* As testament to the evolution of athletes, the sprint football weight limit for the 2019 season was 178 pounds.

than owning the Pats. There were, after all, more than two dozen NFL teams; there was only one based in Boston.

In 1984, Kraft watched his beloved Patriots descend into insolvency. Will McDonough, a hard-boiled sports reporter at *The Boston Globe,* offered a steady diet of stories detailing the Patriots' financial woes. (McDonough began one story: "Gene Klein was just trying to be funny when he wrote in his autobiography, 'Billy Sullivan is the only guy I ever knew who parlayed his life savings of $8,000 into $100 million of debt.'") It was clear that, absent a miracle, the Sullivans were going to have to sell. And that they were not going to have a lot of leverage in doing so.

Robert Kraft hatched a masterful plan. In 1985, he bought a 10-year option, for $1 million a year, to lease 300 acres surrounding the stadium, allowing him to control nearly all of the parking around the stadium. That investment provided critical operating leverage. Without the necessary parking around the stadium, the team could not get a license to play their games there. Kraft was buying time to put together a bid to buy the franchise, but his early investment provided assurances that the team needed cooperation from him in order to operate.

In 1986, the Patriots reached the Super Bowl, but it didn't put much of a dent in the franchise's debts, which had ballooned to $75 million. They faced stadium foreclosure when they couldn't cover an interest payment to Connecticut Bank and Trust.

The Sullivans scrambled. They appealed to the league for a $4 million loan to help meet payroll. They attempted to take the team public. It didn't work. A conservative, cloak-and-dagger league wasn't about to put itself in a situation where sensitive financial information could be revealed to shareholders and, by extension, the public. The Sullivans finally conceded that the situation was unsustainable and they put the team up for sale.

Paul Fireman, CEO of Boston-based Reebok, made an offer. So did New York real estate magnate Donald J. Trump. Abruptly, Trump backed out, claiming, cryptically, that he feared the NFL would block his efforts to buy the team. He may have been right. A source at the time told *Sports Illustrated* that the NFL commissioner wanted nothing to do with Trump, because of both his casino holdings and his role in the USFL antitrust lawsuit against the NFL. Robert Kraft put in a bid as well, but it gained little traction.

Finally the Sullivans found a buyer in Victor Kiam, owner of Remington Razors — "I liked the shaver so much, I bought the company" — who paid roughly $85 million in 1988.

Meanwhile, with the stadium in bankruptcy, Kraft bought it for $25 million. Kraft's banker told him that he was crazy. He was paying $25 million for a crappy stadium, falling into disrepair, that had been built for barely $6 million. But the lease entitled Kraft to virtually all of the stadium revenues generated by the team, including parking, signage, concessions — essentially everything other than tickets. More important, it came with an operating covenant guaranteeing him that the team would play in the stadium until 2001. This covenant made it practically impossible for the team to leave before its lease expired without the team owner being subject to unlimited financial damages.

Soon Kiam ran into financial trouble himself, compounded by embarrassment when Patriots players harassed a female reporter, whom Kiam allegedly denounced as "a classic bitch."

Unable to guide the team to profitability, Kiam sold the Patriots in 1992 to James Orthwein of St. Louis, a great-grandson of brewing titan Adolphus Busch and a major Anheuser-Busch shareholder. The St. Louis Cardinals had recently decamped to Arizona, and Orthwein had every intention of bringing an NFL team back to eastern Missouri. St. Louis had already committed to building a new domed stadium, financed with public money.

There was one hitch: Robert Kraft held the operating covenant for Sullivan Stadium (which had been renamed Foxboro Stadium), and it contained the provision that the team couldn't move. Orthwein offered Kraft $75 million to get out of the stadium lease. Myra Kraft implored her husband to take the deal. He had paid $25 million for the stadium and was now being offered $75 million just to allow the team to break its lease. Kraft declined.

Exasperated by losing and exasperated that he couldn't move the Patriots to St. Louis — and uninterested in owning a team in Massachusetts — Orthwein put the Patriots up for sale after they finished the 1993 season 5-11.

By that point, Kraft had accumulated significant wealth. He already owned the stadium and the parking lots around it; if he could buy the team, he'd be set. Having spent months trying to insert himself into the sales process, Kraft had to overcome numerous obstacles, one of which was negotiating with Orthwein's lawyer, Walter Metcalfe, who was part of the prospective ownership group if the franchise had moved to St. Louis. Kraft told his wife he was going to fly to St. Louis, meet with Orthwein, and make a bid to buy the Patriots. He could finally realize his dream and try to apply defibrillator paddles to this moribund franchise.

"How much are you going to bid?" Myra Kraft asked her husband.

"It's worth about $115 million," Robert Kraft responded.

"That's not what I asked," Myra Kraft said. "How much are you going to bid?"

"Maybe $120 million," he responded sheepishly. "Or $125?"

Kraft's bid of $125 million was deemed insufficient. But so were the bids of the other suitors, which included the bestselling author Tom Clancy and the movie theater heir Jeffrey Lurie.

Kraft was in his fifties now and realized the opportunity might not come again. He asked what it would take to get the deal done. Orthwein somehow arrived at the number $172 million.

In no rational universe did this make sense. It defied the conventional valuation Kraft's son Jonathan, a recent Harvard Business School grad, had applied. It represented a record sale price for a professional sports franchise. It was far more than the $140 million Jerry Jones had paid for the Dallas Cowboys a few years earlier, a purchase that included the assets of Texas Stadium *and* the Cowboys' Valley Ranch practice facility. (And that was the *Dallas Cowboys*!)

As a business decision, it was barely worth considering. As an emotional decision, it merited Kraft's full attention. Kraft would later recount to *Sports Illustrated*, "Was I scared? Yes, I was scared. But this was my shot. How many times in life do you get your shot to do something you desperately want to do? Logic said no. Instinct said yes. Also, things kept flashing through my mind. The Boston Braves had left, and no team ever replaced them. My sons were getting to an age where smart sons move to take good business opportunities [elsewhere], and I wanted my family to stay intact here. I figured this could be a good family business."

This was, at once, an impulse purchase and one that had been carefully considered for years. Kraft inhaled and submitted his offer: $172 million it was. Which was accepted. He now owned the Patriots. And the stadium. And, after exercising his $18 million option, he owned the land — a rare trifecta that would become de rigueur terms and conditions for sports team owners. His elation was offset by the fact that he had just offered $50 million more than he had anticipated. And he had yet to break the news to his wife. (He softened the blow by promising that this purchase would not come at the expense of the family's charitable contributions.)

It took a few years, but Kraft would deploy his plan. After cycling through Bill Parcells and Pete Carroll, he would override those who counseled against it and hire an unproven head coach, Bill Belichick. The Patriots would mine talent wisely and had the good fortune of selecting Tom Brady in the sixth round of the 2000 NFL Draft. Kraft would construct a new stadium — named, ironically for another razor, Gillette. The team's winning made the traffic to Foxboro worth it.

By 2019 the Patriots had won six Super Bowls under Kraft's ownership, one of the great dynasties in American sports history. The franchise he'd bought for $172 million was valued, conservatively, at $4 billion.

Indirectly, anyway, it had all started with Michael Jackson's ill-fated

Victory Tour in 1984. And Kraft appreciates as much. On the walls of his office, among the photos of triumphant Super Bowls and images of sold-out stadiums, sits a poster from the Victory Tour — perhaps part of the inventory of Chuck Sullivan's merchandising deal gone bad.

Kraft smiles when he sees the image, and it's a conversational kick-starter, a way to launch into the unlikely set of circumstances that led to his owning the team. But he says that it's also a reminder of what befalls a business and a businessman who doesn't control hubris and doesn't control costs.

17

THE ALL-SPORTS, ALL-THE-TIME NETWORK

As 1984 began, America's largest cable network, closing in on 30 million homes, showed nothing but sports. Advertising revenue was improving with each quarter. And while most of the foot soldiers in the Connecticut base didn't even know it was happening, the success of the new subscriber fees — *no, no, no, cable systems: you pay* us *now* — was the proverbial game changer. The going was good.

And then, suddenly, it wasn't. At the beginning of 1984, Texaco bought the network from Getty Oil for $10.1 billion. Texaco had about as much interest in running a money-losing all-sports cable network as it did in building electric cars. The network was labeled "a non-petroleum asset" and quickly put up for sale. Texaco had no loyalty to a particular buyer. It had loyalty to getting the highest possible price.

Even the newsroom employees who had been insulated from the business realities now knew that they were facing a potential crisis. The range of possible outcomes was vast. A young anchor, Bob Ley, was among those who were concerned. He warned his spouse: "There's a real chance I'm either going to lose my job; or keep my job, which will move to Atlanta, and we'll have to decide if we want to go with it."

ESPN wasn't even five years old. And it was facing a life-or-death moment.

The Entertainment and Sports Programming Network was born on Friday, September 7, 1979. For a rookie making a debut on the national stage, the moment was something other than memorable. As the clock struck 7:00 p.m., a producer yelled, "Take one and roll theme," and, with that command, a honeyed voice intoned the following over a video montage of generic cheering crowds:

"If you're a fan — *if you're a fan* — what you'll see in the minutes, hours, and days to follow may convince you you've gone to sports heaven."

Then, with heavy-handed symbolism, the video switched to a tableau of blue sky. The voice continued:

"Beyond that blue horizon there is a limitless world of sports. And right now you're standing on the edge of tomorrow: sports, 24 hours a day, seven days a week, with ESPN, the total sports cable network."

This was followed by a sports jingle as the words "total sports cable network" appeared, in the kind of block graphics that looked futuristic at the time and soon came to look dated.

Pick us up and catch our act, 'cause we're the one worth watchin'.
Total sports entertainment! We're the one worth watchin'.
Come alive without a doubt, you'll see the best, we'll work it out
With total sports and entertainment.
Everything worth seein', everything worth seein'.
Total sports entertainment. We're the newest network:
E . . . S . . . P . . . N
Everything worth seein'!

After the jingle, the camera panned to find a man positioned on a set designed by someone with a deep appreciation for the 1970s. Sitting on a metal chair atop shag carpet, in front of a backdrop of artistic renderings of different generic athletes, the sportscaster wore brown shoes, brown socks, and brown pants pulled up too high.

The sportscaster settled in.

> Hi! I'm Lee Leonard welcoming you to Bristol, Connecticut, 110 miles from New York City. Why Bristol? Because here in Bristol is where all the sports action is, as of right now. And we're just minutes away from the first event on the ESPN schedule. That's the 1979 NCAA college football preview. And then we're going to follow that with a doubleheader of games—two of the professional slow-pitch league softball World Series games will be seen tonight. Now, softball is one of those rare sports that everyone knows something about. Why? Because we all play it on Sunday when we drink a little beer.

And with that, ESPN, the all-sports television network, was officially on the air.

The unlikely nativity of ESPN makes for a sports origin story that ought to take its place alongside that of Dr. James Naismith nailing peach baskets on opposite ends of gym balcony rails and inventing basketball; or Walter Camp taking elements of rugby, doing away with the scrums, placing 11-on-11 teams on opposite sides of a scrimmage line, and birthing football.

The ESPN story in short strokes: In the late 1970s, the Hartford Whalers of the World Hockey League had failed to make the playoffs. Ownership did the only rational thing: they fired the team's . . . communications director. ("It's always the fault of the guy who can't skate," he later quipped.) Bill Rasmussen was in his mid-forties and pondered his next move. He loved sports, he loved media, and he was reluctant to leave Connecticut. And he'd seized on an idea.

What if there were some kind of broadcast television network that aired local Hartford-area college sports games — UConn basketball, Yale hockey, UMass hockey, and the like? And what if the same network aired *nightly sports highlights,* which until then were consigned to the five or so minutes following the weather on the local news each night? Rasmussen knew firsthand that America's collective appetite for sports was growing unchecked. And, while no expert, he knew that satellite technology and cable television were expanding and emerging as well.

It was still early days. But satellites, positioned 23,000 miles above the earth, had recently been used in innovative ways. In 1977, the Red Cross flew a four-foot-wide portable dish to Johnstown, Pennsylvania, and used a satellite hookup to coordinate rescue operations after a catastrophic flood. Hospitals were starting to use similar satellites to link with specialists throughout the United States. In 1978, *The Wall Street Journal* wrote about how the U.S. Postal Service was considering the transfer of "electronic mail" via satellite.

Some experiments and some applications were more successful than others. A joint satellite venture between IBM and Aetna explored whether satellites could be used for videoconferences among workers at different businesses. The demonstration hit a snag when a dog chewed through the rubber coating on the wires, causing the reception to go dead. For every analyst who projected runaway growth for the satellite industry, another analyst preached caution. "Domestic satellites so far have been a disappointing industry," Harry Edelson, of Drexel Burnham Lambert, told *The Wall Street Journal* in 1978.

Satellite technology made for an intriguing proposition in the television universe. For decades, the overwhelming majority of Americans had watched one of four channels — the three major networks and public television. But, increasingly, other networks were able to squeeze into a new ecosystem of "cable networks," often relying on satellite technology to air their programming.

The more Rasmussen poked around and asked around, the less harebrained his idea seemed. The telecom mogul Ted Turner — who was looking to grow a family billboard business he had inherited at age 24, after his father committed suicide — was an early believer in this technology. In 1976, Turner had bought the Atlanta Braves and the Atlanta Hawks, mostly to provide programming for his networks. Next, he was considering launching a cable news network in Atlanta. In 1980, at the launch of his Cable News Network — CNN, in the shorthand — Turner confidently declared, "Barring satellite problems, we won't be signing off until the world ends."

In New York, the Big Three — ABC, CBS, and NBC — were each devising a way to enter this cable landscape, in effect hedging their bets. There were murmurs of a cable network devoted entirely to rock music. Maybe a network devoted entirely to movies. And maybe even one for a particular political bent.

As for the technology, Rasmussen met with RCA to determine the cost. He was told that a five-hour window of channel space would run him $1,250. Offhandedly, Rasmussen asked how much full rental would cost. According to the sales rep's rate card, it was $34,167 a month, or a bit more than $1,000 per day. Why, Rasmussen asked, wouldn't someone simply buy the full 24/7 time, since it was so much more economical? When answers were slow in coming, his proposed network became a full-time operation.

Rasmussen applied for a transponder through the FCC. He gave his start-up the prosaic name the E.S.P. Network — the Entertainment and Sports Programming Network. Friends joked that E.S.P. sounded like a network devoted to New Age fortune-telling and predictions. No matter: a few weeks later, Rasmussen got word that his application to purchase an RCA Satcom I satellite had been approved. He could now transmit these games nationally.

The licenses had essentially been distributed on a first-come, first-served basis, and Rasmussen had submitted his application ahead of other telecommunications giants and media titans. Within hours he was getting calls from the likes of Warner Bros. and Twentieth Century–Fox, promising him great wealth if he would be willing to sell them his slot. This only reinforced his belief that he had stumbled onto something that could be big.

As for the matter of financing . . . Rasmussen was not a man of wealth, nor easy access to capital. After maxing out his credit cards and seeking funding from family and friends, he persuaded a financial institution in Philadelphia to invest $250,000 in his venture. With that having legitimized the operation a bit, Getty Oil then paid $10 million for an 85 percent stake in this full-time sports network.

ESPN, as everyone came to call it, operated on a tight budget. Part of the economizing meant putting the network's headquarters in Bristol, a hard and harsh manufacturing town. (Even that almost didn't happen. A Bristol mayor seeking reelection resisted the move, fearful that ESPN's various satellites could imperil the local bird population.)

The pool of employees came mostly from local markets. Not only did they have to be willing to work in — and live near — Bristol, but they had to flit across the radar of the executives doing the hiring. Producers and directors often came from the local TV stations in New Haven and Hartford and Springfield, Massachusetts. Most of the so-called on-air talent came from New England or metro New York. A few years out of Brown University, Chris Berman was a 24-year-old weekend sports anchor in Hartford when he got the call. Bob Ley was also 24. He had been moonlighting as the public address announcer for the New York Cosmos soccer team and a broadcaster for a small public station in northern New Jersey. He was hired three days before the network launched and appeared on-air five days later. Lee Leonard had worked in New York with network star Bryant Gumbel; Gumbel also referred his older brother, Greg, to ESPN.

Putting the company's roots in Bristol was more pragmatic than strategic. Cheap land and cheap office space were the main motivations. It didn't hurt that northwest Connecticut was beyond the jurisdiction of New York's television labor unions, so the same game that NBC would shell out $80,000 in production costs to air cost ESPN only $40,000.

In a perverse way, Bristol stimulated creative energy and innovation in a way that Manhattan never would have. An army of media consultants and corporate bean counters likely would have argued against, say, a show called *SportsCenter*, devoted entirely to highlights. Or allowing sportscasters to pick their favorite sports to cover. Or permitting a gravel-voiced overnight *SportsCenter* anchor to confer players nicknames, some wittier than others. But when Berman took to calling baseball pitchers "Bert Be Home Blyleven" and 'Frank Tanana Daiquiri," no one in management much cared. Hell, it was 2:00 a.m. On some nights the producer also directed. And it was hard to know who on earth was watching.

Ultimately, ESPN's unlikely setting would become critical to the ESPN culture and, in turn, its success. Though Bristol was indeed — as Lee Leonard told viewers on opening night — 110 or so miles from Manhattan, it might as well have been 1,110 miles away. There was no direct route and no direct transit. Far from the media epicenter and the chattering class, this quirky start-up network could take risks.

Beyond that, with the staff marooned in Bristol, it didn't take long for bonds to harden. There wasn't much nightlife or culture or fine dining. If the choice was leaving work and going to an empty apartment or hanging around the office to watch sports with colleagues, the choice was an easy one for the small workforce, mostly made up of males in their twenties and thirties. They would repair to Hamps bar, nicknamed "Edit Suite H," before, after, and sometimes between shows for a beer and a burger. "Hey," says Ley, "it was the eighties."*

Plenty of nights, two anchors would bet a case of beer on the outcome of a game. After the *SportsCenter* show, the two anchors would invite

* ESPNers became loyal to their company town. So much so that they took offense at digs. On his final broadcast at ESPN in 1984, Sal Marchiano, one of the original *SportsCenter* anchors, remarked, "Happiness is Bristol in my rearview mirror." (It was a takeoff on the Mac Davis country song about Texas.) Marchiano would later claim that, on account of those remarks, ESPN management effectively barred him from ever returning.

the crew and they would split the case in the parking lot, talking until the sun came up. Workers came to know one another's girlfriends and boyfriends and to attend one another's weddings. They played in softball leagues with other late-shift workers at the post office and the fire department.

As for how ESPN was going to make money? That was a question no one could quite answer. Six months after the launch, the network had blown through the $25 million capital investment that was supposed to last until the company broke even in a few years. Alarmed, Getty hired McKinsey consultants to study the network and come up with a long-term strategic plan. Roger Werner, a young associate, was assigned to the project. Werner quickly realized that ESPN had no clear path to break even. And then he quickly came to an irreducible conclusion: if the company didn't come up with multiple streams of revenue, it wouldn't survive. "We had to invert the business model," Werner recalls. "If the business was only going to be advertiser-supported, it was going to be tough sledding."

At the time, ESPN's lone revenue stream was selling commercial time. Anheuser-Busch was an early sponsor of ESPN, ponying up $1.4 million and getting a cut rate of $1,000 for each 30-second spot. This made sense, as the Venn diagram between sports fans and beer drinkers contained a considerable overlap. But even that could be problematic. The first live event to air on ESPN was a slow-pitch World Series game pitting the Milwaukee Schlitz against the Kentucky Bourbons in a game sponsored by . . . Budweiser.

While *SportsCenter* was the flagship show, the network still had to fill hours and hours of programming each day. Occasionally there was coverage of an NHL game or a taped replay of a college football game. But largely it was niche sports: tennis matches from far-flung tournaments, auto races, kickboxing fights, Australian Rules football matches, women's billiards, rodeos, and even tractor pulls.

Soon Roger Werner was hired from McKinsey to become, functionally, ESPN's chief operating officer. He came up with a business plan that included keeping a wide variety of sports on the channel, however bizarre they sometimes were. Werner, presciently, noted that it wasn't about getting the highest ratings; it was about building the widest audience. Tennis fans gravitated to ESPN for their sport. Boxing fans came for the fights. College basketball fans came for hoops. Eventually this breadth would pay off.

Still, for the first few years, ESPN's accounting could be an exercise in creative writing. Charges were carried from one quarter to the next. Losses during the start-up phase exceeded all expectations. Famously, per ESPN lore, one executive allegedly put in an expense report seeking reimbursement for cocaine, on the grounds that it was for entertaining clients. (Hey, it was the eighties.)

In the newsroom, employees were only vaguely aware of — and sometimes willfully oblivious to — the financial challenges. But on occasion, those with more curiosity cornered their colleagues on the business side and asked about the health of the network.

"Don't worry about the finances" was the inevitable response. "We're doing fine."

"Is ESPN profitable?"

"Oh, Lord, no! Not even close."

"Are we gonna make it?"

"Depends on how patient Getty wants to be."

On payday, employees raced to the bank to make sure their checks cleared. Not that the amounts were large. When Berman left his job in Hartford and began working as one of the seven *SportsCenter* anchors, his starting salary was $16,500.

Launching a network — and then maintaining a network — was an expensive proposition. Apart from the technology, there were rights fees and labor and studio construction and production and marketing and the cost of running a 24/7 news-gathering operation.

Beyond that, ESPN paid hundreds of cable operators throughout the country a "carriage fee" to air their programming. It was only a few cents per home, but without this, ESPN had no way of getting on the air. The nine commercial-free pay networks at the time—such as HBO and Showtime—had an effective business model, requiring subscribers to pay fees. The other cable networks, relying on commercials, faced decidedly grimmer math.

It was for this reason that, after wading into this new ocean, the three major networks had effectively given up on cable. In 1982, as losses exceeded $30 million, CBS pulled the plug on its cable venture. The next year, RCA, which owned NBC, gave up on a cable entertainment channel after it lost $17 million. Around the same time, ABC gave up on its Satellite News Channel cable venture. In 1982 and '83 alone, the top 15 cable channels in the United States lost a combined $375 million.

By 1982, ESPN had lost $40 million, and the Getty company chieftains pushed out the founder. Rasmussen was effectively fired, though his dismissal came with millions in severance and his 15 percent stake intact.*

Getty executives were split. Some figured it was time to give up on this quirky sports venture that didn't align with the company. Others, grudgingly, figured the company had already invested so much that it may as well hang on a bit longer. Hedging that cable was a fad quickly coming to an end, employees prepared résumés to send to NBC, ABC, and CBS. Then again, the universe of cable television was expanding. And the immediacy of television—married with highlights—was something no other sports medium would replicate.

Says Berman of the early days hosting *SportsCenter:* "People would wake up and check their local newspaper for West Coast baseball scores and not find it. *Well, I guess the Dodgers-Giants didn't make deadline.*

---

* A thought exercise: If the Hartford Whalers had been a more successful hockey team—and Rasmussen had kept his job with them—would another ESPN have been founded? If so, by whom?

That same morning, they would turn on ESPN, and we didn't just have the score. We had highlights of the game. We figured that had to be worth *something*!"

There was mounting evidence that ESPN was building a loyal audience. When it televised games, staffers would strategically hang banners in the arenas and stadiums. It made for a bit of subliminal (and free) advertising: as cameras panned the action, fans would see the ESPN logo dozens of times each game. On countless occasions, fans would offer to buy the banners, or they simply tried to swipe them.

Accompanied by a cameraman, Bob Ley attended an NCAA Tournament game in Indianapolis. The cameraman absently took an ESPN bumper sticker and put the decal on the side of his camera. Ley was amazed as fan after fan sidled up to the cameraman to express fondness for the network. From the any-publicity-is-good-publicity department, on his late-night show, Johnny Carson made an ESPN/Australian Rules football joke, eliciting spit takes in Bristol. Says Ley, "We were all like *Wait, Johnny Carson knows about ESPN*?"

George Bodenheimer started at ESPN in 1981, shortly after graduating from Denison University, in Ohio. After doing some time in Bristol, working in the mailroom and driving announcers to and from the Hartford airport, he was dispatched to the guts of America — Texas, Chicago, Denver — to try and convince hundreds of cable distributors to carry ESPN. He noticed that in a very short time he went from explaining what ESPN *was* to hearing about games that had aired and fielding unsolicited suggestions for coverage or *SportsCenter* host combinations. "Other networks have viewers" became the ESPN mantra. "We have *fans*."

And the encouraging evidence wasn't just of the anecdotal variety. Each quarter, ESPN brought in more ad revenue. Cable systems weren't just adding more subscribers; they were doing so at an astounding rate of 300,000 *per month*. More homes meant higher ratings, which meant more advertising revenue.

Back in Connecticut, Berman felt as though he was getting a promotion each year. He had sportscaster colleagues who were graduating from the station in Harrisburg to the station in Pittsburgh to the one in Philadelphia. He felt that he was on a similar trajectory, except that he didn't have to move. By the summer of 1984, his duties were expanding and he was making $40,000 a year in salary.

In the fall of 1983, ESPN televised the final of the America's Cup, a quadrennial sailing race that the United States had won for 132 years running. Held in the waters off Newport, Rhode Island, not far from ESPN's campus, the race pitted America against Australia. Improbably, the Aussies were tied with the Americans and their skipper, Dennis Conner, heading to a decisive seventh race.

For the final race, ESPN made a deal with a local Providence station that owned a helicopter. The live feed consisted of a camera dangled from a helicopter trailing two boats in the Atlantic. Cutting-edge television this was not. But the broadcast, televised on a Monday afternoon, averaged a 2.4 rating, a weekday afternoon record for ESPN, and peaked at 4.6. Sailing fans were dispirited by the result as the Aussies and their captain, John Bertrand, pulled off an upset. ESPN executives were ecstatic. Berman articulated what many thought to themselves: *Jeez, if a sailing race drew this kind of an audience—with little marketing, on a Monday afternoon—we must really be breaking through.*

Gradually but steadily, ESPN inched closer to the mainstream in its coverage. Opportunistically, it made television events out of what were once sports afterthoughts. The network may not have had the rights to broadcast NFL games, but, starting in 1980, it broadcast the NFL Draft, upping its quality of coverage and quantity of hours, year after year. (It also began broadcasting USFL games in 1983, trumpeting that this made it the first cable network to carry live professional football.)

It may not have been the chief broadcaster of college basketball, but it was able to pick off the rights to some early-round NCAA Tournament games. And it could air a "Selection Show" when the NCAA Tournament pairings were announced. Viewers noticed that there were fewer

Aussie Rules football games and more NBA games, including some in the playoffs.

And then came the great jujitsu move.

As ESPN built its audience, Werner came to think of the network as somewhat akin to a men's magazine. It would generate some of its revenue with advertising dollars. But it would also make revenue, ideally as much as half, through the equivalent of subscriptions. ESPN had paid the cable systems a "carriage fee" for the right to be included among their array of offerings. How else, after all, was it going to get on the air?

Now that was about to change. When consumers were subscribing to cable expressly *because* they wanted ESPN, didn't the network have the leverage? And if so, shouldn't the cable providers be paying the network and not vice versa? And if ESPN was operating at a loss and facing this existential threat, couldn't that doom the entire industry?

In an audacious move, ESPN attempted a complete reversal of the business model. In 1983, it began seeking to charge its affiliates a modest fee of a few cents per subscriber per month. ESPN was in roughly 25 million homes at the time. At 60 cents per home (five cents times 12 months) times 25 million homes, that would bring in $15 million in annual revenue. Presto — one line in the budget would wipe out the operating loss for the year.

Reflexively, the cable system resisted. *You pay us; now you're asking us to pay you?* They pointed to contracts, most of them years from expiring, under which ESPN had agreed to pay the distributors.

ESPN had a response. *If we don't get some value, we might go out of business, which means you might go out of business. Or we will make it, which means we'll have even more power. So we can renegotiate now and we'll lock this in at a modest price. Or we can let the contract play out and when it comes time to renegotiate, we will not be as generous.*

Most affiliates grudgingly recognized the economic reality and paid up, reaching the conclusion that ESPN had a loyal audience that would complain — or, worse, drop their cable subscriptions entirely — if they didn't have access to *SportsCenter* or NASCAR or the NFL Draft. *Other networks have viewers; we have fans.*

By the summer of 1984, ESPN resembled a player on the trading block, subject as it was to daily rumors. Ted Turner — who already owned the lone *profitable* cable network in America at the time, WTBS in Atlanta — had requested financial information on ESPN in preparation for making a bid. This inspired fear in Bristol. If he purchased the network, Turner surely would either fold it into his eponymous Turner Broadcasting System in Atlanta or kill the network entirely and keep the technology.

Turner even invited Roger Werner and ESPN's CEO, Bill Grimes, to discuss ESPN, in the hope that they would align themselves with his bid. Werner recalls that Turner was alternately "threatening and cajoling, throwing every goddamn thing at the wall that he could think of to try to get us to share proprietary information." They wanted no part of Turner or of being part of his media portfolio. But they would still laugh years later recalling how bizarrely Turner had acted and how wildly optimistic his projections for the network were.

Unknown, though, to the concerned ESPN rank-and-file: Years before, ABC had provided ESPN with various programming in exchange for the right to buy up to 49 percent of the company. In January of 1984, ABC had quietly exercised this option and bought 15 percent of ESPN for $25 million. More important, it would turn out, the deal came with a clause that ABC held a right of first refusal to buy more of ESPN if Getty wanted to exit the cable business.

After determining that the contract still applied after the sale to Texaco, ABC sprang to action. On April 30 the network paid Texaco $202 million to acquire the 85 percent of ESPN it did not already own. It paid an additional $14 million for the satellite broadcasting facilities.

Bob Ley was working an overnight *SportsCenter* show at the time and had gone to bed shortly before sunrise. At nine in the morning, his phone rang. It was Elaine Truskoski, the secretary for the newsroom. Groggily, he picked up the line.

"We're going to live!" she gushed. "We're going to survive!"

Roused from his sleep, Ley had no idea what this meant.

"We've been sold to ABC!" she said. "We're going to be okay!"

In Atlanta, Turner was livid. He released a statement claiming that he had been excluded from making a bid. "The sale of ESPN was completed without the solicitation of bids from any parties other than ABC."

Emboldened, both by new ownership and by data that suggested that cable subscribers *really* wanted ESPN, executives resumed the strategy of charging affiliates a subscriber fee. And while this didn't even merit a footnote in the trade press, it would prove to be a critical maneuver that gave rise to tens of billions of dollars in revenue.

In the summer of 1984, ESPN announced that the rate card fee would be raised to 19 cents per subscriber per month. And by now there were 35 million cable homes in the United States. Even if few cable distributors paid that, and the average price was "only" 10 cents a month, some back-of-the-envelope calculations: at this rate, ESPN would make $40 million in subscriber fees alone. By the summer of 1984, ESPN's cumulative losses were roughly $80 million. In other words, one rate hike would single-handedly wipe out half of its losses.

Not only that; it was self-perpetuating, a virtuous cycle. More revenue meant that ESPN could spend more on rights fees, buying more appealing sports properties. And more appealing properties meant that more viewers—er, fans—would watch. If ESPN had leverage over the cable companies when they televised America's Cup sailing races and Davis Cup tennis matches and thoroughbred horseracing . . . well, imagine the leverage they would wield when they televised NBA playoff games and college football bowl games.

Then, in October of 1984, ESPN received still another squirt of jet fuel when Congress passed—and a president wedded to deregulation signed — the Cable Communications Policy Act. Introduced by Senator Barry Goldwater, the legislation provided for full deregulation of fees. In other words, cable operators were free to charge whatever they wanted for their basic cable packages. Which meant that networks on those packages (like ESPN) were now free to charge whatever *they* wanted in subscriber fees, escalating, seemingly, in perpetuity.

By 1985, ESPN — this upstart network, begun on a lark, that five years earlier had lacked a business plan — was turning a profit. That same year, sure enough, Tom Murphy and Capital Cities acquired ABC for $3.5 billion and, with it, ESPN. By 1987, ESPN signed a breakthrough contract with the NFL to air games on Sunday nights. The number of Americans with cable grew year after year. And ESPN's subscriber fees grew in lockstep, passing $1 per home per month, then $5. With its dual revenue streams — "the secret sauce," as it became known at HQ — ESPN bypassed and surpassed networks like HBO that didn't have commercials.

In 1984, Roger Werner thought he was being optimistic when he forecast subscriber fees growing to become comparable to the network's advertising revenues. By 2012, when ESPN was getting roughly $7 a month per household — or more than $8 billion a year — from subscription fees, they constituted roughly 75 percent of the network's revenue. By 2012, ESPN was worth in excess of $40 billion — at the time, roughly the value of every team in the NBA *combined*. When *Forbes* called ESPN "the world's most valuable media company," there wasn't much disagreement. By then, CBS, NBC, and Fox (which had once abandoned cable) all had their own cable sports networks. As did each sports league, as well as tennis, golf, and auto racing. And even most major college conferences. And while Ted Turner may have missed out on the chance to buy ESPN, his eponymous networks, Turner Network Television (TNT) and Turner Broadcasting System (TBS), would become largely driven by sports programming as well.

ESPN would come to build a global workforce of more than 8,000 employees. Part of this growth meant paying to retain talent. Berman may have started at $16,500 in 1979, but after several overtures from other networks, he would eventually earn more than $5 million a year. "They underpaid me for the first half of my career," he says, "and over-paid me for the second."

And Bodenheimer, who had started in the mailroom and spent the early eighties selling ESPN to cable providers in the heartland? He would become the network's long-serving president. Bob Ley, who started in 1979? For four decades, he would still be a face of the network, a stalwart journalist and figure of credibility. The network that had begun by airing softball and Aussie Rules football and kickboxing would come to air *Monday Night Football,* NBA and MLB playoff games, the college football National Championship, and Wimbledon.

Like a big game, the ascent of ESPN was marked by key plays and critical moments. Between the purchase by ABC and the full embrace of the subscriber fee, the summer of 1984 marked what Werner calls "a pivotal, pivotal time." As the cliché-prone sportscaster might put it, ESPN had broken through the line and was in the open field.

18

THE BRAWL TO END IT ALL

As absurdist story lines go, this one was right out of a pro wrestling writers' room.

In the early 1980s, a struggling female pop singer and a veteran athlete meet by happenstance on a flight headed to New York from Puerto Rico. She's in her early twenties, a singer chasing stardom. He's in his early fifties, and looking for a final act. She is five-three, swallowed up by her first-class seat, and speaks in a cartoonishly squeaky voice that recalls Betty Boop in the Queensiest of Queens accents. Her style of dress might be described as thrift-shop chic. She wears her heavily teased hair and eyelashes in assorted colors of the rainbow.

He verges on obese. On this day, he is without his signature accessory — rubber bands dangling from a biblically long beard and safety pin piercing his cheek — but still cuts a striking figure with his chaotic ringlets of hair, his unbuttoned Hawaiian shirt. He speaks in a New York accent as well — his a thick baritone.

Neither recognizes the other. But as they talk, they realize they like each other, that their commonalities outstrip their differences. They are both extroverts — the kind of people who talk to their seatmates on flights. They are both from the New York area. Both are in show business. Both are working in industries buffeted by change. Together they will help form an unlikely alliance, enter new arenas, and help each other's careers. In the process, their pairing — an unlikely tag team — will play an outsized role in building one of the most valuable franchises in sports.

She is Cyndi Lauper, a singer in search of a big break. Growing up, she paid a price for her weirdness, her otherness. "People used to throw rocks at me for my clothes," she told *Rolling Stone* journalist Kurt Loder, in what Loder described as "her appealing Queens-side wheeze."

He is Lou Albano, a galoot born in Rome, once a football star at the University of Tennessee before he was kicked out of school for bad behavior and cheating on a final exam. He then joined the Army, but aggravated a football injury and was honorably discharged. Back in New York, he tried to become a boxer, leaning on a cousin in the promotion business, Lou Duva, to help get him fights. When that didn't work, Albano transitioned to professional wrestling.

In the fifties and sixties, "Leaping Lou" was a ponderous wrestler — a "stiff," in the vernacular — who didn't always execute his moves with technical expertise. He did, however, master the performative part of the job. He looked the part and dressed the part and acted the part. He also relished playing a heel, a wrestling villain. Partnered with Tony Altomare, Albano was half of "the Sicilians," a tag team so convincing in their hijinks that, as they toured the Midwest, they elicited actual threats from organized crime in Chicago.

The Sicilians appeared on *The Jackie Gleason Show* and wrestled for various promotions. When they broke up, Albano transitioned into becoming a manager. "Captain Lou" Albano — a reference to his time in the Army, and, in the tradition of pro wrestling, exaggerating his rank — played his pulpy role masterfully, stomping around the ring as his hairy chest and assorted gold chains protruded from his unbuttoned silk shirts.

But by the early eighties, pro wrestling was an industry in transition.

For decades, the sport had existed in the United States under a patchwork "territory system," whereby different regions of the country had their own promotions. One might liken this to college sports conferences, but without the NCAA to unify all of them.

Boundaries were inexact, but each promotion had its own roster of stars. Like wrestlers ricocheting off the turnbuckle, the Spandex-clad band would bounce from one testosterone-soaked arena to another. Each promotion would make its own television deals — usually with local stations — at strange hours. Hulk Hogan worked primarily for the American Wrestling Association (AWA) in Minnesota. Ric Flair (d/b/a Nature Boy) wrestled mostly for the National Wrestling Alliance. André the Giant, a seven-foot-four, 500-pound French leviathan, toiled mostly in the World Wide Wrestling Federation (WWWF).

The WWWF was the main promotion for the Northeast. The head of the organization, Vincent J. McMahon, was not a ruthless businessman. He was known to share gate receipts with his wrestlers. He openly told the media that wrestling was fake. Though unhappy about it, he allowed one of his up-and-coming "babyfaces," Hulk Hogan, to film a cameo as Thunderlips in *Rocky III*.

But in 1982, Vincent McMahon sold his business to his ambitious, hard-charging son, Vincent Kennedy McMahon, known to all as Vince Jr. or Vinnie. Vinnie's vision and his disposition were nothing like his father's. Then in his late thirties, Vinnie had ambitions that went beyond the Northeast. He put forth an acquisition strategy. The new federation would, in effect, roll up all the balkanized territories and create one streamlined pro wrestling organization. He shortened the name of the promotion to World Wrestling Federation, the WWF, making his ambitions clear. (If the new acronym had the potential to cause confusion with the World Wildlife Federation, which had trademarked WWF in 1961, so be it.*)

---

* After a series of settlements and legal battles over the acronym, the World Wildlife Fund prevailed over the World Wrestling Federation. In 2002, the conservation group

McMahon's empire-building acquisition strategy was centered around the same principle that David Stern was using concurrently to expand the power of the NBA: television. Specifically, cable television. One TV deal would knit it all together. Why restrict your product to a region when the technology existed to expose it to an entire country —and beyond?

"In the old days there were wrestling fiefdoms all over the country, each with its little lord in charge," McMahon would later explain to *Sports Illustrated*. "If I hadn't bought out my dad, there would still be 30 of them, fragmented and struggling."

McMahon began to negotiate putting the WWF on nationwide cable. Suddenly viewers throughout the country were able to watch McMahon's product. And the top wrestlers, predictably, followed. Why would an up-and-comer like Hulk Hogan, for instance, limit himself to the Midwest when he could decamp to the WWF and find national exposure on television? "TV is the most important part of our profession," said Big John Studd, who stood six-ten, weighed 364 pounds, and starred in the eighties for the WWF. "It's actually more important than what we do in the ring."

For a sport predicated on violence, with so many stories on themes of revenge, the men in power were remarkably passive. Promoters disparaged McMahon behind his back. They hated McMahon for violating a code. For weaponizing television. For disrupting their business.

According to McMahon, on multiple occasions, the little lords warned that he'd "end up in the bottom of river" if he kept up his turf war. But apart from idle threats, he faced remarkably little resistance.

With typical pro wrestling bravado, when McMahon heard that other promoters had gathered at the Hilton Chicago O'Hare hotel to discuss how to thwart his ambitions, he laughed. "The first meeting they had, all they could agree on was that they hate me and that they're going to

---

kept the initials; Vince McMahon rebranded his organization as the WWE, World Wrestling Entertainment.

do everything possible to put us out of business," McMahon said. "The second meeting, they couldn't even agree on ordering lunch."

McMahon had already taken over the Sunday morning time slot on the USA Network. For more than a decade, a Saturday night slot on Ted Turner's SuperStation WTBS was devoted to *World Championship Wrestling,* featuring the cast of Georgia Championship Wrestling. McMahon approached Turner with an offer to buy the Saturday night slot. Perhaps still chastened by his unsuccessful bid to buy ESPN weeks earlier, Turner was in no mood to negotiate. He rejected McMahon. Undeterred, McMahon had another plan: he would buy the Georgia Championship Wrestling promotion, which owned the time slot. McMahon found enough willing sellers, and soon the WWF had a controlling stake in the Georgia promotion.

July 14, 1984, marked what would be known as Black Saturday, another McMahon victory, at least in the short term. At 6:05 p.m. that night, wrestling fans tuning in to TBS realized that Georgia Championship Wrestling had been taken over by the WWF. The loyalists hated it. They hated that McMahon had made an end run around Ted Turner and gotten his promotion on cable. They hated the WWF style of wrestling, as well as the cartoonish characters. They hated McMahon and his preening.

Callers flooded the TBS switchboards to complain. The ratings of *World Championship Wrestling* began to tank. Turner, to his credit, began to investigate how he could expand into wrestling and put up some competition. Eventually, McMahon would end up selling the slot. But at the time, Black Saturday was still a sign of Vince McMahon's ambitions. And like wrestlers in compromised positions, the competition appeared helpless to escape and survive the WWF stranglehold.

If professional wrestling was being buffeted by change and shifts in media, so was pop music. The industry had been in a slump in the early 1980s. It was starting to emerge from the chill, thanks in part to a new television network in the expanding cable universe.

Music Television, soon shorthanded MTV, was predicated on a new art form: the music video. As the "veejay" Mark Goodman explained it when the network first went live, "This is it, the world's first 24-hour stereo video music channel. . . . Behold! A new concept is born, the best of TV combined with the best of radio!"

For decades, pop stars and mainstream bands had been recording songs, arraying them on an album, and then releasing them one by one, hoping they would find favor on the radio. The video delivered another sensory experience that could enhance the listening. "Think of it as the movie of your song," one MTV executive explained during a seminar for a music label. Scientists described it, more high-mindedly, as "synesthesia," a process whereby sensory impressions are carried over from one sense to another. The Associated Press was both less scientific and less charitable. The video was a capitulation to "peachfuzzy viewers, notorious for their bite-size attention spans."

The artists (and their labels) would have to foot the bill to produce the videos. They would then deliver the video to MTV. The network's roster of veejays — including Loder, the *Rolling Stone* writer — would air these videos, interspersed with commercials. The artist would receive no revenue. But what they received in exchange for donating these song-movies had value: marketing and promotion. At the beginning and end of the video, graphics listed the name of the song, the artist, the album, and the label, a free bit of advertising that, ideally, would motivate the viewer to buy the single or, better yet, the album.

MTV officially launched on August 1, 1981, rolling out a video by the Buggles, a British new wave band, for their single "Video Killed the Radio Star." It was a clever meta joke; but it was also a bit of prescience. Why listen to the radio when you could *see* the artist perform the song you were hearing?

Soon the video became as essential to an artist's success as radio play. Artists who took advantage of this new platform could break through — and sell millions of albums — based as much on the visual impact as the merits of the music itself. As in professional wrestling, the visual performance and the image of it all — the wardrobe, the appearance, and the ability to "sell the move" — became as essential as underlying talent.

Not all artists embraced this new medium. For some, this video craze was an annoyance, a new job responsibility that went beyond the scope of their employment. Some simply provided live concert footage and called it a video. Though this, too, could be effective: when, in the summer of 1984, Bruce Springsteen cast a young actress named Courteney Cox as a fan who would come onto the stage during the video for "Dancing in the Dark," it helped turn the song into a smash hit.

Other artists were thrilled for the new opportunity to express their creativity. Often at great expense, artists would experiment with concept and hire Hollywood directors. (Even "Dancing in the Dark" was directed by Brian De Palma.) From Duran Duran to Madonna to Michael Jackson, the most successful acts of the era, not coincidentally, put out the most inspired videos.

By the summer of 1983, Lauper's career had gained traction. She had broken with her band, Blue Angel, and, after a dispute with the band's manager, had been forced to file for bankruptcy. As a solo artist, she had a new manager, David Wolff, who became her boyfriend. Having been in a band himself, Wolff knew music, and he helped Lauper land a deal with Portrait Records, a sister label to Epic.

Lauper was 30 and, with Wolff's guidance, treated this as both her big break and perhaps her last chance at stardom. For her album — titled, appropriately, *She's So Unusual* — she hired the estimable photographer Annie Liebovitz to shoot the cover image. Lauper and Wolff devoted great care to the video for the album's first single, "Girls Just Want to Have Fun," a winsome, upbeat, doo-woppish tune with a feminist message. Lauper and Wolff storyboarded the video. Lauper would star as a carefree young woman living at home, whose parents couldn't abide her lack of serious purpose. Lauper's mother, Catrine, would portray herself. But with the Laupers divorced, who would play her father?

Wolff had an inspired idea. A fan of professional wrestling, Wolff figured the video could use a cartoonishly over-the-top figure. One wrestler in particular came to mind. "There's this guy, Lou Albano —"

Lauper nearly did a spit take.

"I know Captain Lou!" she squealed, recalling the nice man she'd sat alongside on the flight from Puerto Rico. "We swapped numbers when we were on a plane together."

Albano, too, had fond recollections of that flight from Puerto Rico. He was happy to appear in the video. But there was a hitch. "You need to ask permission from my boss, Vince McMahon."

Unlike his father, McMahon *wanted* his wrestlers branching out into pop culture. If wrestling was going to grow beyond smoky ballrooms and off-hours TV and its blue-collar fan base, it would need to move from the margins to the mainstream. And there was no faster way to do that than to get on television. "You got him," McMahon responded.

While labels and musicians and artists themselves were beginning to invest in videos, "Girls Just Want to Have Fun" was a bare-bones production, made for less than $35,000. (Michael Jackson's "Thriller" video was made around the same time for $800,000.) Lauper and her team wrangled friends to waive their fees and called in favors. Wolff appears in the video. So does Lauper's brother, Butch. Lauper's attorney, Elliot Hoffman, did a turn as well, as a dancing lawyer. Hoffman had another client, Lorne Michaels, then nearly a decade into his run overseeing *Saturday Night Live*. Michaels generously agreed to provide state-of-the-art digital editing equipment at no charge. The video was filmed on the Lower East Side, and most of the interiors were shot in Lauper's bedroom.

Scene-stealing Albano, dressed in a white undershirt, his elaborate curls bouncing, scolds Lauper for her insolence. She accepts his criticism at first.

My father yells, "What you gonna do with your life?"
Oh Daddy dear, you know you're still number one

But she then rotates and—*foreshadowing!*—with the skill of a professional wrestler, manipulates his wrist and pins him against the wall. He surrenders and retreats, a defeated man.

"Girls Just Want to Have Fun" was released in the fall of 1983. It received little fanfare. Frank DiLeo, head of promotion for Epic Records—trivia: he later played Tuddy Cicero in the Martin Scorsese film *Goodfellas*—summoned Wolff to his office. "I hate to tell you this," DiLeo said, "but 'Girls Just Want to Have Fun' is a stiff. We're closing this single down and we're going to release the next single."

"Hang in there!" Wolff protested. "Don't bail on it yet!"

"Fine," said DiLeo. "I'll give you and Cyndi two more weeks to figure out how to turn this around."

Two weeks later, Wolff was back at Epic and saw a woman in the promotions department running up the hall. "We're on KIIS-FM!" she shrieked. "We're on KIIS-FM!"

Epic had placed the single in the rotation of KIIS-FM, Los Angeles's biggest Top 40 station. And, like that, the song and Lauper's career took on escape velocity. Two weeks later, every pop station in the country was playing "Girls Just Want to Have Fun." In the spring of 1984, it reached No. 2 on the charts—topped only by Van Halen's "Jump." And the video may have been an even bigger hit, playing on heavy rotation throughout 1984. Lauper won the MTV Best Female Video award for 1984.

As Lauper's career blossomed, so did her friendship with Albano. They would speak on the phone and meet socially in Manhattan. Lauper and Wolff would drive to the suburbs and spend the day with Lou and his wife, Geraldine. Lauper would describe him as a favorite uncle.

Recognizing opportunity, Wolff wanted to keep the cross-promotion going. He set up a meeting and drove to WWF headquarters in Stamford, Connecticut—ironically, Wolff's hometown—to strategize with McMahon.

McMahon, happy for any and all crossover promotion, listened intently. Accounts of what follow vary, but we'll stick with Wolff's. He recalls pitching McMahon on a "Rock 'n' Wrestling" strategy, an extensive blueprint for marrying the spandex-clad wrestlers with spandex-clad rock stars, for twinning the WWF with pop music. And Lauper, of course, would figure prominently. When she went on Johnny Carson's *Tonight Show*, for instance, she would mention pro wrestling. "I love it," said McMahon.

Then Wolff went to Les Garland, who oversaw programming at MTV.* Wolff's big idea: the WWF would put on an event at Madison Square Garden in the summer of 1984. And MTV would broadcast the event live — the first time wrestling had ever been broadcast live on nationwide cable television.

Wolff was asking the network to interrupt its rotation of videos and air a professional wrestling event? Live? It was bizarre. It was off-brand. It was also a broadcast scheduled for a Monday night in the dead of summer, a few days before the start of the 1984 Olympics. MTV had little to lose.

Garland said, "I love it."

Hype and promotion are essential components of pro wrestling, as they are of pop music. Wolff, Vince McMahon, and MTV already had a name for their summer wrestling event: The Brawl to End It All.

They even had a basic plotline that pivoted on feminism — "women's lib," Lauper insisted on calling it. Reinforcing the fact that, under Vince McMahon, professional wrestling was going to become something entirely different and more inclusive, the headline match would pit two women against each other. Lauper would play the manager of a young and progressive female wrestler, while Lou Albano would play a misogynist who managed the opponent. This wasn't just a battle for wrestling supremacy; it would be a battle over ideology.

---

* A longtime DJ, Garland has a lengthy list of other claims to fame, including serving as the radio voice in the Starship single "We Built This City."

Now all they had to do was sell it.

In May of 1984, Wolff and Lauper left a vacation on Martha's Vineyard and drove in a rainstorm to Pennsylvania, eight or so hours away. The show *All-Star Wrestling* filmed at the Allentown Agricultural Hall, taping three or four episodes at once.

One of the most popular segments was titled "Piper's Pit," hosted by "Rowdy" Roddy Piper, the bombastic kilt-clad wrestler, one of the most gifted "heels" ever. (Though Canadian, for the purposes of character, he passed himself off as Scottish.) "Piper's Pit" was designed to feature interview segments between wrestlers, managers, and other WWF figures. But inevitably, this devolved into trash talk and brawls.

When the cameras started rolling, Piper did his part. He introduced Lauper, noting that she had "flown seven thousand miles to come here and see us." Lauper explained that she had been in Europe, England, and London. She then corrected herself. "London. England. Same thing." Piper then introduced Lauper's manager, "Lou Albano, who brought you from nothing."

Lauper cut him off. "I love Lou, but Lou's not my manager!"

With that, Albano walked onto the set, wearing an unbuttoned leather vest and earrings dangling from both lobes. "Cyndi, tell these people how I found you in Queens and made you a superstar," he said. Referencing Lauper's hit singles, Albano continued, "Tell them how I wrote the words for 'Time After Time' and 'Girls Just Want to Have Fun.'"

"He's only kidding," Lauper said as the audience began booing.

Albano was not subtle in escalating the fight, ad-libbing, "Tell them women belong in the kitchen and pregnant, Cyndi. That no woman has ever accomplished anything without a man behind her. . . . How all women are nothing, Cyndi. . . . They're slime!"

After a few more exchanges, in one of which Albano used the word "broad," Lauper mock-angrily flipped over the table, grabbed her handbag, and conked Albano on the head. Lauper played her role to perfection. Almost. Clad in ridiculous attire and over the top in her delivery, she fit perfectly into the wrestling tableau. But she had forgotten to remove a bottle of perfume from her bag. When she struck Albano with the bag, it left a welt. Unfamiliar with the thermodynamics of professional wrestling, the entertainment media saw only the clip and didn't realize the context. In particular, the television show *Entertainment Tonight* assumed that the feud was real.

The premise was ridiculous, even by wrestling standards. But it fed the hype machine before the big show. This was Vince McMahon's vision unfolding in real time. That the taping occurred the same weekend as the death of his father — who likely would have despised precisely this kind of cross-pollination of wrestling and pop culture — seemed somehow fitting.

As the crowd filed into Madison Square Garden on Monday, July 23, 1984, for the Brawl to End It All, there was a palpable sense of uncertainty. It was only nine days after Black Saturday, when McMahon and the WWF took over the wrestling cable spot on WTBS. Wrestling fans weren't sure what awaited and how closely this glamorized, mainstream, made-for-live-TV event would align with pro wrestling as they had known it. The mainstream music fans, meanwhile, didn't always know that pro wrestling was scripted theater.

The Brawl to End It All offered 10 matches chock-full of the brightest stars in the WWF's roster. The headliner, though — which would be the only match airing on the main MTV broadcast — featured two women, who operated far from the mainstream.

Mary Lillian Ellison (aka the Fabulous Moolah), a battle-ax from South Carolina, had been a champion since the 1950s and was a favorite of Vince McMahon Sr. Recognizing that Vince Jr. was about to monopolize pro wrestling, she had recently sold her championship rights to the WWF. In exchange for a payout, she joined the WWF, aware that they could script her out of her belt at any moment. For the Brawl to End It All, Moolah would enter as the champion, and she would be managed by Albano. Her challenger was far younger and more obscure, Wendi Richter, from Dallas, managed by Lauper.

Gene Okerlund was a bald-pated Minneapolis TV and radio executive, who occasionally served as a ring announcer for local pro wrestling events. Soon he came to like wrestling more than office work. He rose in the ranks of the American Wrestling Association and joined McMahon's WWF as its interviewer and television commentator. Okerlund was nicknamed "Mean Gene" by a Minnesota wrestler, Jesse Ventura, who fifteen years later would become the state's governor. Working the Brawl to End It All — partnered with 400-pound sidekick Gorilla Monsoon — marked a career apotheosis for Okerlund, just as it did for the wrestlers. Meanwhile, Dave Wolff — conflicts of interests be damned — worked the television broadcast as well.

The night began as a conventional wrestling card. On the fifth match, the WWF introduced its rising star, Hulk Hogan, who had left Minnesota for the national stage. Still best known to the mainstream for his *Rocky III* cameo, Hogan emerged to the strains of "Eye of the Tiger," not the song that would become his anthem, "Real American."

He wore red, white, and blue, not his trademark red and yellow. Though he was only 30 years old, his hairline was already in a state of retreat. Curiously, as the ring announcer intoned, "Weighing three hundred and two pounds," graphics listed him at 235.

Discerning fans may also have noticed that the wrestlers were nervous. They knew that this was a new audience and, potentially, a significant cultural moment.

Discerning fans also noticed something else. The wrestlers were playing for the television cameras. Television had long been an essential part of wrestling. But for the low-budget broadcasts under the promotion system, a few static cameras were planted in the rafters, shooting down at the ring. In some cases, there was a remote camera ringside, but it often panned the crowd or was trained on the announcers. Wrestlers barely thought about the cameras. And why should they have? Weeks later, a broadcast — often edited to conceal any screwups — would air on some regional network.

Now the setup was completely different. MTV brought an array of cameras to the broadcast. It reinforced the point that the prime audience was no longer the fans in the stands — in this case 15,000 or so, not even a sellout. It was the millions at home. So it was that, time and again, wrestlers like Hogan would be doing their bit wearing a mask of earnestness. Then, clearly realizing the camera was fixed on them, they switched their expression to exaggerate pain and give a villainous wink. Video, you might say, killed the wrestling star.

The main event was pro wrestling at its most over the top. Captain Lou emerged, saliva spraying, selling the match as only he could. "This woman can never be defeated! Often imitated, never duplicated. . . . This woman has had the belt for — what is it? — 12 years!"

Moolah, who had turned 61 years old the day before, gently corrected him. "Twenty-seven years."

Richter then emerged, to predictable walkout music: "Girls Just Want to Have Fun." She was trailed by Lauper, wearing sunglasses and dressed, as ever, outrageously. Richter's face was caked with inexpertly applied makeup. (She claimed after the match that Lauper has been teaching her how to dress fashionably and wear cosmetics.) As Richter was being introduced, Captain Lou paced around the ring, ranting and heckling fans, calling one, memorably, "a prefabricated dog biscuit."

The match itself was not a technical masterpiece. Moolah got the action started, executing an arm drag that Richter strenuously sold to the crowd. Moolah choked Wendi directly in front of Lauper. Wendi writhed free somehow, headbutted Moolah, and applied a half nelson. The crowd urged Lauper to take a few shots at the hated champion. Lauper smiled but declined. But moments later she got another opportunity, and this time couldn't resist, wrapping her hands in a towel and unloading.

Then it was Moolah's turn. Somehow she managed to apply a full nelson to Richter, all the while pulling her hair. Captain Lou then climbed onto the ring apron. Moolah, though, had mounted Wendi and appeared to have pinned her opponent. The crowd grew noticeably quiet as Moolah pranced around the ring with Albano, both of them with their arms elevated. *Wait, what? All this hype and the villainous Moolah wins?*

But hold on! The referee grabbed the mic for the official decision and . . . determined that Wendi had managed to get her shoulder off the mat. And then he quickly declared Wendi the champion. Pandemonium ensued.

Moolah kicked the referee to the ground. Albano taunted the crowd, which began giving the middle finger, which forced the folks in the MTV production truck to switch quickly to a different camera angle. "Total chaos!" yelled Mean Gene Okerlund. "Total chaos!"

Even given the low standards of professional wrestling, this was a patently ridiculous sequence. And if the overarching goal of the night was to demystify professional wrestling for a new audience, why not end the match with Wendi beating Moolah, or pinning her more conventionally and winning decisively?

But it was also undeniably entertaining. And undeniably successful. The wrestlers knew instinctively that this had been a winning performance and that the new crowd was, as McMahon would later put it, "eating up what we're serving." The anecdotal evidence was soon supported by the data. MTV scored a phenomenal 9.0 rating, making it *the* most watched program in the history of the network.

After the show, Lauper and Wolff repaired to the apartment they were sharing in Lower Manhattan. Still wired and unable to sleep, Wolff arranged a conference call with Albano and Roddy Piper. "We did it!" Wolff screamed. And they spent the next hour replaying the night and sharing their excitement.

Predictably, the Brawl to End It All did nothing of the sort. It only fueled interest in professional wrestling and the WWF and convinced McMahon that he was onto something, courting crossover audiences. Suddenly wrestling was no longer the province of the benighted, long on tattoos and low on teeth. As *Sports Illustrated* framed it: "Knuckle draggers who traditionally made up wrestling crowds have been booted out of the bleachers and replaced by Wharton graduates."

The ratings success of the Brawl to End It All caught the eye of more networks. Within months, four of the country's top 10 cable shows were devoted to professional wrestling, two of them produced by McMahon himself. McMahon had effectively choked off the competition. He had gained scale by taking his product mainstream. And he was on his way to becoming a billionaire.

The other big winner was Hulk Hogan. He was on his way to becoming pro wrestling's leading light and began negotiating a cartoon series on CBS, titled, appropriately, *Hulk Hogan's Rock 'n' Wrestling.* (It paled in comparison with Hogan's signature cartoon series, but Albano came to be well-known to a new generation as the voice of Mario in *The Super Mario Bros. Super Show!*) There could be no better example of the WWF's crossover strategy. "Rock and wrestling is not a dream," Hogan said. "It's the way we live."

Seven months later, the WWF was back in Madison Square Garden for another Rock 'n' Wrestling card that would air on MTV. This one was titled the War to Settle the Score, and it drew a sellout crowd of 22,000. Again, there was a vague feminist theme, as Gloria Steinem and Geraldine Ferraro both were recruited to tape promos.

Lauper again played a prominent role, managing two wrestlers this time. Bob Costas called the action for the main event, which featured Hulk Hogan against Rowdy Roddy Piper. With Lauper in his corner, Hogan defeated Piper by disqualification. In the obligatory brawl afterwards, Lauper was kicked in the head by Piper. Backstage, a motley crew that included Mr. T., Hogan, and Piper continued their act in a room under the Garden. While Gene Okerlund attempted to broker peace, Andy Warhol walked into the frame. Warhol, the eccentric pop artist and a closet pro wrestling fan, had been in attendance. Okerlund grabbed him for an impromptu interview.

A year earlier, Warhol would have required a lengthy introduction to the wrestling fan base. Now he was just another celebrity in the stands.

"Your impressions of the Rock 'n' Wrestling connection?" asked Mean Gene.

"It's the most exciting thing I've ever seen in my whole life," Warhol said flatly.

Not everyone was as fond of Rock 'n' Wrestling. To the pro wrestling tribalists, this was viewed as the ultimate commercial sellout. The *Los Angeles Times* ran an article headlined "Wrestling Has Gone Hollywood and It's Ruining the Sport."

But that was a minority view. Professional wrestling was now squarely in the mainstream. It was regular cable television fare. McMahon had, as planned, effectively clotheslined the competition and established a monopoly for the WWF. In 2019, the weekly show *WWE Smackdown* aired on the Fox network on a Friday night—media galaxies removed from regional cable outlets—and drew nearly four million prime-time viewers.

So much of it owed to a strange female pop star, her ambitious manager, and a quirky show in the summer of 1984.

Emboldened by this success, a few weeks later, in 1985, McMahon went bigger still, returning to Madison Square Garden yet again, for still another supershow. This one wouldn't air on MTV, but on closed-circuit television.

In keeping with McMahon's philosophy, mainstream stars figured prominently. Muhammad Ali was a referee. Billy Martin, then the New York Yankees' manager, was a ring announcer. Liberace, naturally, was the timekeeper.

Of course, the two unlikely mascots of this era were there, too. Captain Lou Albano managed the tag team, the U.S. Express. Lauper again managed Wendi Richter, who, in a rematch, defeated Leilani Kai to win the WWF Women's Championship. (Richter was paid $5,000, while comparable male wrestlers allegedly made up to $100,000. She protested and was essentially drummed out of the WWF.*)

In the main event, Hulk Hogan and Mr. T. defeated Paul Orndorff and Roddy Piper. More than a million fans paid to watch the broadcast, making it, at the time, one of the largest pay-per-view buys in history, setting it on track to become the biggest annual franchise in sports after the Super Bowl.

WrestleMania, they would call it.

* Let the record reflect: she would not speak for this book project unless she was paid a fee.

19

THE SUMMER OF THE MAC

On January 22, 1984, at the end of the third-quarter break of Super Bowl XVIII, the game telecast was interrupted by a bit of entertainment far more arresting than the football itself. It was, notionally, a very long TV commercial. But it played out as a futuristic sci-fi movie in miniature.

The first scene was set in a dark gray, austere matrix of tubes. Inside the tubes, a Big Brother–type leader pontificates on a video screen. Faceless, soulless subjects march into a hall and watch the leader — entranced. Except for one strikingly athletic woman.

Having broken free of the ritual, she outruns storm troopers in pursuit and throws a hammer at the leader's image on the screen, causing an explosion. Drone-like figures stand with mouths agape, blown back by the impact, as a voiceover intones, "On January 24, Apple Computer will introduce Macintosh. And you'll see why 1984 won't be like *1984.*"

Decades later, of course, the release of even the smallest Apple product gives rise to an unofficial national holiday. Tribalists camp out overnight at signature stores, waiting for new releases. But in 1984, Apple was a minor player in the tech sector. It would have been a stretch to call the company a rival of IBM, when Big Blue was generating 50 times Apple's sales revenues. Apple's young and ambitious CEO and co-founder, Steve Jobs, was tasked with the rollout of the company's new computer. The Macintosh was seen as a last gasp for Apple to avoid acquisition. And Jobs bet big. He hired Ridley Scott, fresh off of *Blade Runner*, as director; he devoted a generous budget of $750,000 to the commercial; and he commissioned 90 seconds of airtime during the Super Bowl. (Days before the game, at the behest of Apple's horrified board of directors, the spot was whittled to 60 seconds.)

The commercial was, in a word, genius. At a time when America was still trying to form an opinion about technology, the ad positioned the personal computer as an unmistakable force of good, an instrument of enlightenment and liberation.

Technology, as a term, came shrouded in vagueness in 1984. It was often used in conjunction with space exploration and futuristic robotics, a domain for engineers and scientists but hardly a driving force in everyday life. According to the National Center for Education Statistics, the four most popular areas of concentration for students graduating in 1984 were liberal arts, business, education, and natural science/medicine.

Electrical engineering/computer science — bundled as one category — was fifth but growing, luring students with the promise of future employment. "It is a chance to spend your life working with devices smarter than you are and, yet, have control over them," said Paul M. Kalaghan, dean of the College of Computer Science at Northeastern University, in 1984.

In addition to helping to demystify technology — and solidify the phenomenon of the Super Bowl commercial as a cultural event — this spot, which would never run again, transformed Apple. Other brands were fascist; Apple was democratic. PCs might be cold, harsh, *products;* the Macintosh was a household good, an "information appliance," Jobs, the original disruptor, later called it. (Not for nothing, the first Mac was based on the design of the Cuisinart food processor.) The reigning incumbent, IBM, was the oppressive regime; Apple was the people's party, making a populist and accessible product.

Macs weren't cheap, originally priced at around $2,500—roughly $6,000 in 2020 dollars—more than the median American household earned in a *month*. But, demystified, the Macintosh sold briskly throughout the year. With a block of June-July-August free time, Americans familiarized themselves with what was less a machine than a functional, friendly toy. The Mac smiled at you when you turned it on. It was accompanied by a quaint appendage whose very name—"mouse"—suggested cuteness. Americans spent that summer learning how to draw on a machine, how to publish from a desktop, how a personal computer could truly be personal.

The year 1984 did not, of course, cement Apple's dominance. Within a year, Jobs would fall out of favor with the board and would be looking for new employment. IBM and then Microsoft would consign Apple to underdog status for many more years. But that year, Apple came into vogue, and that summer Americans played with their well-designed appliance and realized that a high-tech future doesn't have to be dystopian at all.

In the summer of 1984, Jobs predicted that Apple could one day be a $10 billion company. In the summer of 2020, it was valued at $2.0 trillion. And, yes, that previous sentence was typed out on a Mac, some 35 summers after the product made its debut.

Even after accounting for the popularity of the cute and cube-like Macs, the vast majority of Americans still did not own a personal computer in 1984. Writing was something done by hand or on a typewriter. So-called word processing called to mind medieval punishment. Driving directions were obtained via paper maps. Inasmuch as people searched for information, they did so by consulting an encyclopedia.

And Americans certainly didn't get their news from computers. In the summer of 1984, newspaper circulation hit a historic high. Combined readership for various U.S. dailies hovered around 63.3 million — and many cities published both morning and afternoon papers. Though no one knew it at the time, this was the portrait of an industry peaking.

Advertisers, as they always do, followed eyeballs. On July 18, 1984, *Sports Illustrated* published its Olympic preview edition, the thickest issue in the brand's history. It was fat as a phone book, pregnant with advertisements interspersed among 23 feature stories, most of which had entailed international travel by the journalists and photographers. The final article in the issue — the long and lyrical piece known as "the bonus" — by the great Gary Smith, profiled the Chinese high jumper Zhu Jianhua. It ended on page 533.

Yet the 1984 Summer Olympics offered a glimpse into the future of media and communications — and the decline of print. When competitors and coaches checked into the Olympic Village at UCLA, they were handed assorted "swag bags." (The one provided to all U.S. athletes by Levi Strauss contained *54* different articles of free attire.) The competitors were also given a password to an Electronic Messaging System (EMS) connecting more than 50,000 members of the "Olympic Family," from the athletes themselves to media members to volunteers. Records would reveal that most people given these passwords never actually activated them, thereby missing their first email experience.

Before the Los Angeles Games, technology was a scarce commodity at the Olympics. At Montreal in 1976 — the most recent Summer Games held in North America — the distances of discus throws had been determined with tape measures. Boxing scores were tabulated by hand. An army of messengers hand-delivered memos and sheets of information from venue to venue.

Organizers in L.A. were determined to prove that the intersection between technology and sports was, at least potentially, a busy one. Some of this was by necessity. With 23 separate sites spread across 4,000 square miles, information couldn't be transported via messenger.

But this pivot to technology was also philosophical. A few hours south of Silicon Valley, Peter Ueberroth and his team were intent on showing off American innovation and the practical application thereof. More than once, Jim Murray, vice president of technology for the L.A. Olympic Organizing Committee,* proudly announced, "We wanted to do some things that have never been done before." The organizers estimated that the committee spent $50 million on technology.

Even before the Games started, it was hard not to notice the wires and cables and gadgets unfurled at the venues. As a press release breathlessly put it, "Personal computers help tabulate results quickly; electronic timers clock swimming and track races . . . Mass spectrometers and gas chromatographs test athletes for banned substances and drugs; state-of-the-art pagers remind competitors of team meetings and event starting times; and sophisticated radio communications equipment carried by security personnel aid efforts to protect Olympic athletes."

Sponsors helped defray the costs and set up the infrastructure. IBM provided monitors at the boxing venue. Motorola distributed pagers. Maybe most significantly, AT&T set up the Electronic Messaging System. The networks entailed 1,700 terminals and 7,000 paging devices connected by 300 miles of light-guided cables. Without picking up a phone, those on the network could instantly message one another. "The Olympics EMS will be one of the largest area communications networks developed," said Jack Scanlon, Western Electric's vice president for processor and software systems.

"The scale of the system is Olympian in itself," Bob Ford, a spokesman for AT&T Bell Laboratories, added. "Most of these people, especially the foreign athletes, have never even seen a computer before."

Mark Houska, then a USC student on summer break, was a volunteer for the basketball events held at the Forum, where there were a half dozen terminals near the media seating. He recalls them going unused. "You were going to leave your work area to check in at a computer ter-

* Not, as he often had to explain that summer, the *L.A. Times*'s beloved sports columnist of the same name.

minal during the day? So you could get messages from someone you already worked with? It was a foreign process."

One of the television production assistants working for ABC Sports, Jay Bilas, an L.A. native, had finished his sophomore season at Duke. Given his interest in media — and given that he was the starting forward on his school's basketball team — he was a natural for the position. Bilas was not, however, tech savvy. During the training session for "electronic messaging," Bilas casually shared his password with mischievous colleagues. Later that day, female production assistants were surprised to receive strikingly personal messages from "Jay Bilas."*

When they weren't hacking one another's accounts, the production assistants gradually took to this instant electronic communication. They realized that they could send each other short messages, arrange meetup times, and gossip, without worrying about remembering phone numbers or getting busy signals.

The few Olympic volunteers and media members who took the time to use these accounts realized another benefit. As the Games were unfolding, it was fun to send messages back and forth, firing off staccato bursts of observations, issuing predictions, making offhand remarks, and cracking snarky jokes. In retrospect, they were using email to have a second-screen experience.

The heading was jarring enough. But then came the content of the letters, sent in early July of 1984 to various Olympic organizing committees for countries in Asia and Africa.

> African Monkeys!
>
> A grand reception awaits you in Los Angeles!
>
> We are preparing for the Olympic games by shooting at black moving targets.

---

* So it is that Jay Bilas might rightfully claim to be among the first people ever catfished.

> In Los Angeles our own Olympics flames are ready to incinerate you.
>
> The highest award for a true American patriot would be the lynching of an African monkey.
>
> Blacks, Welcome to the Olympic games in Los Angeles!
>
> We'll give you a reception you'll never forget!
>
> We shall put an end to this. The blacks and yellows will not be permitted to defile America's stadiums. We shall not permit the apes to be present either. If your cubs dare to come to the Summer Olympics in America, they will be shot or hanged.

The letters were signed simply: "Ku-Klux-Klan."

The threatening, anonymous missives triggered panic among the recipients, but also among members of the Los Angeles Olympic Organizing Committee.

If the organizers were prepared for the Soviets not to show up, they were not prepared for the Soviets to meddle and interfere. The foreshadowing and parallels to today are so obvious they scarcely merit mention. But KKK letters posed a new wrinkle.

As word began to spread about this batch of vile, racist hate mail, Ueberroth raised the issue of the letters at multiple staff meetings. Anita DeFrantz, a bronze-medal rower at the 1976 Games in Montreal—and vocal critic of the 1980 boycott—served as a vice president of the LAOOC. Her official job mostly entailed planning and organizing the Olympic villages, especially the main one, on the campus of USC. But, as with most employees under Ueberroth in the critical, frantic weeks before the Games, her duties were vast and her hours of sleep were few.

She assumed she had been chosen for this role, at least in part, because she was African American. But she got to work, calling sports ministers from African nations. She told them, "The Games will be secure. Your athletes will be safe." She then made a self-deprecating joke: "One of the only things the U.S. government does for sport is to protect the events."

As much concern as these repugnant letters prompted, they also prompted suspicion. Targeting Olympic athletes from other countries hardly seemed consistent with the aims of the Ku Klux Klan, which, since its founding immediately after the Civil War, had a domestic agenda. The letters were sent to the specific addresses of organizing committee members, implying a high level of sophistication. They were postmarked from suburban Washington, D.C., not exactly a known hotbed for virulent racist groups.

There were also physical characteristics that put their authenticity in doubt. The letterhead did not match that of the KKK. The letters appeared to have been produced on a rare typewriter used by businesses. The grammar and phrasing and erratic use of exclamation points suggested that the writer spoke a foreign language. Maybe most perplexingly, in the letters the name "Ku-Klux-Klan" was, unaccountably, hyphenated. As word of the letters seeped out, the KKK denied involvement.

If the letters were inconsistent with the M.O. and goals of the KKK, they *were* thoroughly consistent with the M.O. and goals of the Soviets. In the months after the announced boycott, the Soviets had explained their nonparticipation in Los Angeles not on political grounds but safety ones. One dispatch from the Soviet "news" outlet TASS, justifying the boycott, declared, "There is an epidemic of thefts in Los Angeles, where Olympic ideals have been subordinated to business, where an atmosphere of violence reigns supreme, where bandits shoot at Olympic buses and one feels as if in prison."

TASS eagerly reported on the letters. But instead of reporting, accurately, that the notes had been signed "Ku-Klux-Klan" — noting the strange and off-brand hyphens — the TASS reports attributed the letters to "the Invisible Empire, the Knights of the Ku Klux Klan."

Sourcing these mysterious letters was the ideal project for the Active Measures Working Group, an interagency group under the State Department that had been set up during the Reagan administration to counteract Soviet propaganda. An FBI source embedded in the KGB confirmed the origin and even confirmed that he had helped prepare the racist leaflets. The grammatical mistakes were not the handiwork of an uneducated Klansman but of someone whose first language was Russian. The letters' Maryland and Virginia postmarks were traced to two of the few counties where Soviet nationals were permitted to live (see the FX network spy thriller series *The Americans*) and were likely mailed by Soviet embassy personnel.

Fearful that revealing the details of the investigation would "compromise the informant and lead to his death," the Active Measures Working Group came up with ways to expose the hoax without exposing the source. Without sharing specifics, the FBI and the State Department permitted LAOOC employees to state unequivocally to the recipients that the letters were fake.

The KKK hate mail did not have the desired effect. Only two of the 44 African nations boycotted outright: Ethiopia and Angola, both of which had ties to the Soviet Union and declined to send athletes to Los Angeles in a show of solidarity, not because of fears of racial attacks.

The "letters scare," as Ueberroth called it, was not mentioned at all during ABC's coverage of the opening ceremonies. But U.S. attorney general William French Smith spoke at a conference of the American Bar Association on the subject of the Communist "threat to the international rule of law." In the course of his speech, he mentioned "openly racist and disgusting" letters that had been mailed to the national Olympic committees.

He added that the letters "were not produced or sent by the Ku Klux Klan. They were instead manufactured and mailed by another organization devoted to terror: the KGB. . . . Although I cannot detail all of what we know about these documents for fear of helping the authors to refine their efforts, a thorough analysis — including linguistic and forensic techniques — reveals that they are classic examples of a Soviet forgery or disinformation operation."

TASS dismissed the accusation as "delirious myths." And this strange event was lost to the folds of history. The Soviets had clearly attempted to hack a sacred institution and destabilize America. They had failed abjectly. Lesson learned. Surely they would never again try to hack an American institution . . .

20

LET THE GAMES BEGIN

Peter Ueberroth approached the 1984 Summer Games much like an athlete would. He and his team had been preparing for years, knew their strengths and vulnerabilities, and had established a clear path to success. He evinced a sense of guarded confidence.

Then came the Soviet boycott, and Ueberroth had to switch tactics, playing more defense and less offense. First he set his sights on stanching the flow of boycotting countries. Just as he couldn't lean on taxpayer dollars to fund these Games, he wasn't going to get much diplomatic help from the government. So Ueberroth and his team of envoys flew all over the globe meeting with world leaders and sports officials. He ensured the safety of the athletes and vowed that the L.A. Games would not be politicized. And he did so with considerable success.

In Cuba, Fidel Castro explained that he couldn't defy the Soviet boycott. But he agreed not to pressure other Latin American countries to stay home. Ueberroth prevailed on Yugoslavia and Romania to send their athletes. Maybe most important, he and his minions helped encourage China to send its first full athletic delegation to a Summer Olympics.*

In the summer of 1984, the narrative was simple: the Soviets boycotted the Olympics as a retaliatory punch. "The Soviet withdrawal from the Los Angeles Olympics is nothing more than paying America back in kind for its boycott of the 1980 Games in Moscow," a *New York Times* masthead editorial put it. "It has also proved that if the modern Games are to continue, their form and location needs to be thoroughly rethought."

But documents, later declassified, would suggest something quite different. The Soviet Union had devoted billions of rubles to sports excellence. Defeating the Americans at the Games they were hosting — a few minutes from Hollywood, no less — would be the ultimate narrative, the ultimate expression of supremacy.

So why stay away? A confluence of events. For one, leader Yuri Andropov, who had supported Olympic participation, was replaced by hard-liner Konstanin Chernenko in February of 1984. Beyond that, the Soviets were concerned about terrorism and the possibility of defection. A fringe group in Southern California, the Ban the Soviets Coalition, announced plans to set up safe houses for defectors and line the freeways with billboards aimed at Soviet athletes, encouraging them to seek asylum. The Soviet media latched on to this "threat." The *Literary Gazette*, the Kremlin weekly house organ, wrote that if the Soviets sent Olympic delegations, athletes "will be seized and whisked away to clandestine hideouts. And there, all conceivable methods will be used to extort from them betrayal of their motherland. They will be wrapped in the Stars and Stripes — all in the light of the Olympic flame."

The Kremlin claimed other dangers as well, citing everything from the possibility of earthquakes to another flare-up of the Watts riots to the Manson murders. When it was reported that the LAOOC was hiring

* China sent a small delegation to Helsinki in 1952, a token gesture of participation.

gang members to scrub graffiti around Los Angeles, the Soviets stressed not the beautification effort but the affiliation with gangs.

When Ueberroth wasn't trying to persuade other countries to attend his party, he was busy convincing ABC that, even without the Soviets, its $225 million bid for the television rights was money well spent. The day the Soviet boycott was announced, ABC's stock plunged as investors acted on fears that the Olympics would be a ratings bust. Ueberroth put forth a theory that the boycott would result in *more* American medals, which would goose ratings. ABC was covered. Shrewdly, the network had negotiated rebates from the LAOOC if a "substantial" number of countries boycotted and ratings fell below estimates. But concerns lingered.

Ueberroth also had to appease the Olympic sponsors, reassuring them that the boycott would not hurt their investments. And none more so than McDonald's. Earlier in 1984, the Wendy's hamburger chain had scored big with its wildly successful "Where's the Beef?" marketing campaign. McDonald's saw the 1984 Olympics as an opportunity to claw back some market share.

In the run-up to Los Angeles, McDonald's offered a promotional game. Customers were given a scratch-off card revealing a sport. If the United States won a gold medal in the sport listed on the game card, the bearer was entitled to a free Big Mac. A silver medal in the indicated sport was good for a regular-size French fries. A bronze entitled you to a regular soft drink. "Now you can compete in the Olympics, too! If the U.S. wins, you win!" gushed the television commercials that aired nonstop throughout the summer.

One problem: the marketers did not account for an Eastern Bloc boycott. With the absence of all those East German track stars and Russian weightlifters and Cuban boxers, the United States was likely to win that many more medals.

Meanwhile, the torch relay continued westward, ginning up much interest, and more goodwill. Americans would line two-lane roads, applauding and giving a thumbs-up as the torch passed. As 3,636 torch-bearers spent 82 days taking the torch on a zigzagging 9,300-mile tour —for what could have been 2,500 miles on the interstate—one in four Americans looked on. (Someone cleverly determined that the relay was witnessed by more people "than any live event in history.") The progress report gave nightly newscasts an easy, feel-good feature. Local newspapers devoted untold column inches to the relay. *Time* magazine gushed: "The flame came fluttering out of the darkness, into an early morning light. Americans in bathrobes would sometimes stand by the sides of two-lane roads . . . For Americans, the moment was powerfully emblematic."

Given the location, it was fitting that the Los Angeles Games were inaugurated by an opening ceremony orchestrated by a Hollywood producer. David Wolper, whose credits included *Roots* and *Willie Wonka and the Chocolate Factory,* staged a show inside the L.A. Coliseum that was somehow, at once, understated and over the top.

The nods to America were sometimes subtle and sometimes not —Gershwin music, rock-and-roll, an ersatz NASA astronaut descending into the stadium via jetpack—but the overarching theme was one of unity, not American superiority. White doves, Beethoven's "Ode to Joy," balloons in neutral colors. The most affecting moment may have come when planes scrawled Olympic rings in the crystalline blue California sky.

The great climax came when Gina Hemphill, Jesse Owens's granddaughter, who had run the torch through the streets of New York, burst through the crowd carrying the kindled Olympic flame. She handed it to Rafer Johnson to light the cauldron—the same cauldron that Los Angeles had used when it hosted the 1932 Olympics.

Johnson was an ideal choice. He was an extraordinary athlete (decathlon gold medalist in 1960) and humanitarian (the head of the California Special Olympics) and even a significant historical figure (the man who ripped the gun away from Sirhan Sirhan after he shot Robert Kennedy).* Johnson, then 48, was suffering from a bad case of shin splints the week of the ceremony and had slipped in practice. Ueberroth made the unusual decision to have a relief climber ready to go up the stairs in case Johnson was unable to ascend them. Bruce Jenner wasn't needed. But he was waiting just in case.

Johnson lit the main flame, igniting five interlocked rings as an orchestra played "The Olympian," a piece composed and conducted by Philip Glass. The Chinese shooter Xu Haifeng won the first event staged, the 50-meter pistol competition. It may as well have been both a literal and metaphorical starting gun. The 23rd Summer Olympics were off, and each day brought a slate of achievements.

For decades, Pauley Pavilion had been most closely associated with giant men, most notably the UCLA basketball teams that won 10 national titles in 12 seasons under coach John Wooden. But on August 3, 1984, Pauley belonged to a four-foot-eight-inch waif with size 3 feet, a 16-year-old who, as the *Los Angeles Times*'s peerless columnist Richard Hoffer put it, "restored *pixie* to our vocabulary."

Mary Lou Retton of Fairmont, West Virginia, something other than a gymnastics hotbed, was so transfixed by gymnastics as she watched Nadia Comaneci of Romania in the 1976 Olympics that she would sleep in a leotard. Within a few years she was being coached by Bela Karolyi, the austere Romanian who had trained Comaneci. Here Retton was, eight years later, herself in the Olympics, with a chance at gold, pitted against Comaneci's heir apparent. Trailing Romania's Ecaterina Szabo by five one-hundredths of a point in the women's all-around, Retton headed to Karolyi. "You need a 10," he told her flatly. She nodded, took a breath, and executed a vault.

Already smiling before she landed flawlessly, Retton became the first American woman gymnast ever to win the all-around gold. She also be-

---

* The former NFL player Rosey Grier, as well as writers Pete Hamill and George Plimpton, also helped disarm the assassin.

In the summer of 1984, Michael Jordan soared above the competition. Bob Knight, his coach on the Summer Olympic team, declared, "I think he's the best athlete I've ever seen play basketball."
Heinz Kluetmeier / Sports Illustrated

After limbering up, Michael Jordan would inevitably dazzle on the court.
Manny Millan / Sports Illustrated

Bob Knight, at the peak of his powers, coached the 1984 men's basketball team to an undefeated record against teams of NBA stars, and then to an Olympic gold. At the Los Angeles Games, the team's average margin of victory was 32 points. Peter Read Miller / Sports Illustrated

The rivalry between Larry Bird and Magic Johnson grew ever more textured as they met in the NBA Finals for the first time. The series spanned seven games — to the delight of the NBA — with the Celtics prevailing. Richard Mackson / Sports Illustrated

When the Celtics' Kevin McHale clotheslined the Lakers' Kurt Rambis, it sparked a brawl, marked a pivot point in the 1984 NBA Finals . . . and only intensified the Celtics-Lakers rivalry.
Peter Read Miller / Sports Illustrated

In the summer of 1984, Donald Trump went from a New York real estate magnate to a full-blown American celebrity, not least because he became the bombastic, self-promoting owner of a pro football team, the USFL's New Jersey Generals.
Lane Stewart / Sports Illustrated

Above: Though Wayne Gretzky had already been anointed the Great One, it wasn't until 1984 that he won his first Stanley Cup. Neil Leifer / Sports Illustrated

Below: Amid an MVP season, Ryne Sandberg brought joy to Wrigleyville, suggesting that maybe, just maybe, the perennially misbegotten Chicago Cubs might not be cursed after all. Walter Iooss Jr. / Sports Illustrated

A lefty in every sense of the word, Martina Navratilova nearly went undefeated in 1984, turning in one of the great tennis seasons of all time, along with . . .
Walter Iooss Jr. / Sports Illustrated

. . . fellow lefty John McEnroe, who won both Wimbledon and the U.S. Open and came within a few games of winning his only French Open — all the while keeping his famously volcanic temper in check.
Walter Iooss Jr. / Sports Illustrated

Above: In the summer of 1984, in his first months on the job, David Stern began redefining the role of the modern sports commissioner. Meanwhile, in the span of weeks, Ted Turner, the Atlanta media magnate, had opportunities to purchase both the WWE and ESPN.
George Tiedemann / Sports Illustrated

Below: After a terrorist attack at the 1972 Games in Munich, heroic cost overruns at the 1976 Games in Montreal, and the U.S.-led boycott of the 1980 Games in Moscow, the Olympic movement was in peril before 1984. The 1984 Summer Games in Los Angeles changed that.
Rich Clarkson / Sports Illustrated

One of the darlings of the 1984 Olympics stood four feet nine inches and weighed less than 100 pounds. Mary Lou Retton won Olympic gold in the all-around gymnastics competition, still another shining moment that negated the Soviet boycott.
Jerry Cooke / Sports Illustrated

After his leadership role in the blazingly successful (and profitable) 1984 Olympics, Peter Ueberroth went on to become both the sixth commissioner of Major League Baseball and *Time*'s Man of the Year. Jerry Cooke / Sports Illustrated

A sweet, modestly budgeted movie about martial arts in the valley, starring Ralph Macchio, waxed the competition at the box office and became an archetype for the underdog sports movie.
Erick W. Rasco / Sports Illustrated

Michael Jordan started the summer unsure whether he wanted to leave college. He ended it with an Olympic gold medal, the third pick in the NBA Draft, a new home in star-hungry Chicago, and a signature Nike basketball shoe.
Manny Milan / Sports Illustrated

came, instantly, one of the figures most closely associated with the Los Angeles Olympics.

This was in keeping with a theme that rang throughout the Games. In many respects, this was the Women's Olympics, an event that would represent a hinge point for women's sports.

In the mid-eighties, the sports public — fans, media, sponsors — still had an uneasy relationship with women's sports. Title IX, then 12 years old, was supposed to have created equal opportunity for women, but for college administrators and athletic directors it was a piece of federal legislation that went largely ignored. The column inches and broadcast windows devoted to women's sports were vanishingly small. At the 1984 Games, only 23.1 percent of the participating athletes were female. Which, still, set a new high for the Olympics.*

How could it be that for every female Olympic athlete there were three males? Fewer events, for one. Until 1960, women's Olympic track races were never longer than 200 meters, with one notable exception. Women competed at 800 meters at the 1928 Olympics in Amsterdam. Several of those runners collapsed from exhaustion. For decades, the IOC — overwhelmingly male, it scarcely needs mentioning — declined to expand competitive opportunities for women in sports or events that were seen as (their word) un-feminine. By 1980, the longest women's race was still only 1,500 meters.

But in Los Angeles, after a groundswell of protest from groups asserting that XX chromosomes did not preclude long-distance running, the International Association of Athletics Federations (IAAF), track's international governing body, added both a 3,000-meter run and a marathon for women. Both came wrapped in controversy.

Maybe the most anticipated event of the Games, the 3,000 meters pitted U.S. star Mary Decker against a young South African runner, Zola Budd. Decker had been named *Sports Illustrated*'s Sportswoman of the Year in 1983, when she won two thrilling races, the 1,500 and the 3,000

---

* By the 2016 Olympics, in Rio, a full 45 percent of the competing athletes were women.

at the World Championships in Helsinki. South Africa had been excluded from the Olympics because of its apartheid policies, but thanks to a hastily delivered passport, Budd was able to run for Great Britain.

This was billed as one of the Games' great showdowns. But five minutes into the race, Budd, unforgettably, clipped the leg of her rival, sending Decker to the infield of the track in a fit of pain and a fit of rage. Thanks to the power of television, Decker's expression — a cocktail of anguish, anger, and agony — became perhaps *the* enduring image of the Games.

Like that, Decker's Olympic ambitions had been squelched. Budd never won one, either. Though she had the lead in the L.A. race, after Decker's fall she relinquished it, as if weighted from the guilt of exterminating the medal hopes of the American golden girl. She finished seventh. Budd was eventually exonerated — if she had tripped Decker, it was inadvertent — but she was never again the same runner.*

The marathon debuted at the first modern Games in 1896. But the *women's* marathon debuted in L.A. Joan Benoit, of Maine, won the race with a time of 2:24:52, faster than 13 of the 20 *men's* Olympic champions — and proof of women's ability to run far longer than 800 meters. She rightly said, "Once I passed through that tunnel [of the L.A. Coliseum, site of the final leg], I knew things would never be the same."

Meanwhile, when Nawal El Moutawakel of Morocco won the 400-meter hurdles, she became the first female gold-medal winner from a Muslim country. (She also became the first Olympic champion from Morocco, male or female.) Jackie Joyner, a converted UCLA basketball player, announced herself in the heptathlon. By the time the women's basketball team had won gold and their coach, Pat Summitt, had been hoisted in the air, many speculated that Cheryl Miller, the team's Jheri-curled star, was the most dominant player — female or male — on the planet.

Women also provided some of the more memorable and poignant

---

* Budd did win the world cross-country title twice.

human-interest stories, an Olympic staple. Right after the gold-medal ceremony, Pam McGee, a six-three forward on the basketball team, headed into the stands. There she found another six-three player who bore a striking resemblance. Paula and Pam, identical twins, had played together — and alongside Cheryl Miller — at USC. Paula was among the last players cut from the team. Pam handed her medal to her sister, her way of saying their bonds were stronger than ever.*

Joan Benoit was right. Things *would* never be the same. The percentage of female athletes would rise in each Olympics thereafter and is currently crowding 50 percent. Never mind a women's Olympic marathon — eventually there would be women's wrestling and boxing and rugby and curling. Just as critically, the L.A. Olympics offered proof that sports fans — and, no less crucially, networks and sponsors — could, and would, warm to women in competition.

In other events . . .

- Carl Lewis won four gold medals in track and field, equaling Jesse Owens's record from the 1936 Games in Berlin. At age 23 and in the blazing prime of his career, Lewis won the 100 meters, the 200 meters, the 4 x 100 relay, and the long jump, establishing himself as one of the great titans of the sport.

  Lewis's ambitions went beyond athletics. He craved not just admiration but adoration. Before the Olympics, Lewis was paid by Nike but turned down a significant deal with Coke — these being the days of pseudo-amateurism in track and field — because he reckoned he could attract more commercial interest after the Olympics. As his manager, Joe Douglas, explained, Lewis wanted to be "as big as Michael Jackson."

  Lewis didn't want to be the biggest star in track and field; he wanted to be bigger *than* track and field. After winning each of his

* A few years later, in January 1988, Pam would give birth to a son, JaVale, who would take her surname and grow up to become a cultish NBA fan favorite.

first three gold medals in L.A., Lewis did not appear for press conferences. Instead he tape-recorded answers to anodyne questions posed by Douglas. Maybe because of his imperious personality, Lewis never fully capitalized on his Olympic feats. And neither did track and field.

- An Olympic alternate, Mike Tyson had come achingly close to making the team and now had to mask his disappointment as best he could and prepare for the remote possibility that he could be summoned to compete. He maintained his fitness level, sparred with team members, and envisioned himself winning a gold medal. But there were plenty of other reminders that he was not actually on the team and that his time in Los Angeles would most likely be spent cheerleading — a reality that other members were happy to stress.

  After meeting at the Colorado Springs training center, the boxing team flew to L.A. At the airport, a well-meaning woman offered best wishes to Tyson: "Good luck with your fight!" Tyrell Biggs, the team's superheavyweight, overheard and chuckled merrily. "You mean on this *flight,* not his *fight,*" Biggs said. "He's not fighting at the Olympics!"

  With Tyson looking on in conflicted frustration — the fate of the alternate — the U.S. boxing team won 11 medals, nine of them gold. (Ironically, one of the few Americans *not* to win gold would go on to become the most decorated professional; Evander Holyfield, then a light heavyweight, took bronze on account of a controversial disqualification.) Biggs, who teased Tyson about not making the team, would take gold in the superheavyweight division. As would Tyson's vanquisher, Henry Tillman, in the heavyweight division.*

---

* Tyson would later find motivation in the disappointment of the Olympics and the personal slights. In 1987, his pro career already in full blossom, he faced Biggs, who not only had teased him but had once failed to show up for their scheduled sparring sessions. Tyson turned Biggs's face into tartare, winning by knockout in the seventh

And that wouldn't be Tillman's only success at the Games. Inadvertently, he delivered one of the more memorable lines of the Olympics. An L.A. native, he was asked where he lived in relation to boxing's host venue, the L.A. Sports Arena. "Three and a half to four miles, depending on the traffic," he responded. Tillman also watched Gina Hemphill carry the torch for the opening ceremonies. He got her number, they met, they fell in love, and they married three years later. By which point Hemphill was working as a producer for an up-and-coming television talk show host, Oprah Winfrey.

- China's first full Olympic delegation yielded 32 medals, including 15 golds. While sports had already been used as a crowbar to pry open diplomatic relations with China, the success at the 1984 Games did something else: changed China's self-perception.

For centuries in China, there had been a sense of physical inferiority and an unfamiliarity with — if not an outright skepticism toward — team sports. Susan Brownell, once a nationally ranked U.S. heptathlete, spent time in Beijing in the 1980s undertaking research for a dissertation on the anthropology of Chinese sport. She quickly noted that Chinese athletes were often convinced that they were physically inferior to other races, that Caucasians were significantly superior to them and Blacks dramatically so. This served, she told *Sports Illustrated*, "as the basis for self-fulfilling defeatism."

Inasmuch as Chinese athletes were successful, they had excelled in "technique sports," such as shooting, archery, and table tennis. Chen Weiqiang, the featherweight weightlifting champion, not only won gold, but then held aloft the hand of the bronze medalist, who happened to be from Taiwan. Li Ning won three golds in gymnastics at the L.A. Games. He would have won the all-around title,

---

round. After the weigh-in, Tyson told his handlers, "If I don't kill him, it don't count." Tyson didn't *kill* Biggs that night. But not for lack of trying.

too, but for a careless mistake on the parallel bars, when he bent his knee on an elementary move, a stutz to a handstand.

China's success in Los Angeles also activated a desire to host its own Olympics, where it could reveal its might to the world. "The lid," *Sports Illustrated* wrote, "has been torn off the cheerless world Mao made. Life is full of change, full of wonder, full of promise."*

Li Ning also used the 1984 Olympics to launch himself. After his gymnastics career, he founded what would become China's largest sportswear company and one of the largest in the world. At its height in 2007, Li Ning Company Limited boasted 4,300 retail stores across the globe, a new commercial model for a blossoming economy. It was only fitting that he lit the torch during the opening ceremonies of the 2008 Games.

- Before 1984, the Olympic soccer competition was open only to amateurs. This had the consequence of ensuring that the World Cup would remain the sport's quadrennial tournament, open, as it was, to all players. It also meant that the Olympic format gave advantage to players and teams behind the Iron Curtain, where the entire concept of professionalism in sports scarcely existed.

For the 1984 Games, though, the Fédération Internationale de Football Association (FIFA), the sport's governing body, allowed professionals to compete, provided they had no prior World Cup experience. Given that Carl Lewis — the great star of the Games — had been flagrantly taking money from meet promoters and sponsors, this slight nod to professionalism seemed a small concession.

The tournament was a terrific success. France defeated Brazil, 2–0, in a spellbinding gold-medal game that played out before 101,799 spectators at the Rose Bowl, then the largest American

* China launched a bid to host the Olympics in 2000 but lost out, narrowly, to Sydney. The Games returned to their ancestral homeland, Athens, in 2004. But Beijing submitted a successful bid to host in 2008.

crowd to watch a soccer game. Among those in attendance were dozens of IOC officials, who, apart from a gripping game, saw the potential for marketing dollars that could come from a loosening of the amateurism rules.

The door ajar, within eight years the best professional players in the NBA — the Dream Team, which included Michael Jordan, Larry Bird, and Magic Johnson — were the stars of the Barcelona Olympics. Two years after that, the United States, having demonstrated an ability to support international soccer, hosted the 1994 World Cup. The final was played in the Rose Bowl. As was the decisive game of the historic 1999 Women's World Cup.

- And then there was Michael Jordan. At the L.A. Games, he was not yet a pro. But he was also no longer a college kid playing against Clemson and Duke. Performing on a global stage, Jordan, for the first time, offered the world a whiff of his coming superiority.

Even with his restricted minutes, in game after game Jordan was, quite obviously, the best player on the court. He could score from any coordinate on the floor. He could defend the other team's best player. He could dribble and rebound and deliver the perfect pass when double-teamed.

And he could levitate — he seemed able to resist the laws of physics, gravity, and geometry. Leon Wood, a sharp-shooting guard from Cal State Fullerton, was a teammate of Jordan's and another awed onlooker: "I've talked with other athletes who have been watching our games here. A lot of them are saying Michael is the best athlete they've seen here, in any sport, from any country. I tell them they ain't seen nothing yet."*

Jordan's personality also took flight. He may have distinguished

---

* After a 274-game NBA career, Wood became an NBA referee, making him the only person to both foul Jordan and call a foul on Jordan. While playing for Philadelphia, Wood was also a road trip roommate of Charles Barkley's.

himself from his teammates with his play, but he did not distance himself from his teammates socially. Quite the opposite. While there was no formal captaincy, Jordan became the leader. He spoke openly, with confidence and often on behalf of the entire team. But this was an exercise in soft power. In private, Jordan led with a smile. Everyone got a nickname. Everyone got a pat on the back.

Jordan also took on the role of unofficial spokesman, happy to make glorifying statements on behalf of the entire team. As the U.S. team breezed through game after game, Jordan said flatly, "It would take an all-world, all-star team to beat us. . . . We've been winning by big scores, but we're still motivated." And: "Put this team in the NBA right now," he said, "and we'd be .500, I think."

During an off day, George Raveling brokered a meeting between Jordan and Sonny Vaccaro, of Nike. Rudy Washington, a longtime Vaccaro acolyte, picked Jordan up at the team hotel. They met at Tony Roma's, a rib joint in Santa Monica not far from the team hotel.

Vaccaro was at his companionable best, explaining that Nike was already revolutionizing basketball and that Jordan would be best served by this cool company that was "running circles around the other guys" when it came to marketing and promotion. Intentionally, Vaccaro didn't even deign to mention the competitors by name.

Later that afternoon, Raveling asked Jordan what he thought of Nike and his pal Sonny. "I told you," Jordan said, "I'm an Adidas guy."

But he said it with a smile, implying that Nike had made an impression.

Meanwhile, a few days later and a few miles away, Jordan's footwear situation was discussed more formally. A group of Nike executives attended the Olympics, mostly to watch Nike's vast stable of stars, including Carl

Lewis, compete in track and field. But the name Michael Jordan had a way of worming its way into every conversation.

Before the closing ceremonies of the Olympics, David Falk, Jordan's agent, headed to the tony Viceroy L'Ermitage Hotel, in Beverly Hills, to meet with Nike. Falk was keenly aware that Jordan's stock was in ascent, and he had been doing his due diligence. He believed that Adidas would be reconsidering its offer to Jordan of $100,000 per season. And there were other suitors.

Spot-Bilt, an offshoot of Saucony, was looking to make a big play and even hired a popular and reputable former athlete, O. J. Simpson, to work as a frontman to help recruit clients. To Simpson's credit, he was an early Jordan apostle. A vice president of sales and promotions for Spot-Bilt, Simpson watched Jordan throughout the summer of 1984 and declared to colleagues, "This kid at North Carolina, he's the next me. We should go for him."

Falk understood his unique leverage. Basketball was a sport on the upswing. If the NBA had once been dismissed by marketers as "too Black," that odious view was splintering. And now here was this wholesome client from a middle-class family in North Carolina whose default expression was a smile and whose deep, rolling voice exuded warmth and likability. He was heading to Chicago, an attractive, if untapped, market. And it was becoming clear that Michael Jordan was, potentially, a transformative player. Distinguishing yourself as the best player on the floor in college was one thing. Doing that against NBA stars on a barnstorming tour and then again in international competition was something else entirely.

Already in agreement that if Jordan came to Nike, his arrangement would be like no other, Falk and Nike's Rob Strasser talked about the architecture of an Air Jordan deal. The terms, assuming Jordan agreed, would be for five years. Nike offered $250,000 per year and a cut of the revenues. Seeking more up front, Falk countered with $500,000 a year and a smaller cut of revenues.

Nike wanted some protection and came up with a clause whereby it could cancel the contract after the third year if Jordan didn't make an All-Star team, win Rookie of the Year, and average 20 points a game, or if certain sales thresholds weren't met. On the other hand, if Jordan achieved none of the basketball goals, but the shoes brought in more than $4 million, the last two years would still be paid.

Falk and Strasser shook hands. They were on their way to a deal that would single-handedly change Nike *and* change sports marketing. They, of course, had no way of knowing that within a year, Jordan would already be an All-Star and Air Jordan would be nearing $100 million in sales.

Now Nike just needed to convince Jordan.

Meanwhile, Jordan continued to dominate games. And he continued to display a similarly deft touch when dealing with Knight. Before the gold-medal game, Knight asked Willie Davis to address the team. A former Green Bay Packers star who had turned corporate titan — and a director of the 1984 L.A. Olympic Committee — Davis had a simple message: "You're too young to appreciate it now, but this game will define you for the rest of your lives. Embrace the pressure." Jordan looked on, nodding in agreement.

Knight had prepared a similar spirited pep talk, reinforcing that this would be the most important game of his players' young lives. They would not only be representing the country, but avenging the injustice visited upon past U.S. basketball teams. They were playing against history and playing for history.

Knight walked into his office to find a note written on yellow paper affixed to his chair. The missive read "Coach — don't worry. We've put up with too much shit to lose now." It was signed "The Team," but Knight and his assistants recognized Jordan's handwriting. When it came time to address the team, Knight said simply, "Let's go out and win."

Which they did. The gold-medal contest against Spain was less a game than a showcase.

At halftime, Knight sidled over to Jordan's locker for one last bit of repartee.

"Mike, when the hell are you going to set a screen?" Knight barked in mock anger. "All you're doing is rebounding, passing and scoring. Dammit, screen somebody out here."

By this point, Jordan could hold his own. As Knight tells the story, Jordan turned, looked up, and smiled. "Coach, didn't I just read last week, you said I may be the quickest basketball player you've ever been around?"

"What the hell has that got to do with you screening?" Knight snapped.

"Coach," said Jordan, "I think I set 'em quicker than you can see 'em."

The final score of 96–65 somehow managed to *overstate* the level of competitiveness. The U.S. team didn't bother to call a single timeout the entire game. The Americans' defense was so formidable that Spanish players twice retreated off the court and attempted shots from behind the backboard.

Like accolades from giddy reviewers filing out of a Hollywood screening, the raves about Jordan were endless. Asked to name America's best player, Spanish coach Antonio Diaz-Miguel smiled. "Michael Jordan. Ees not a difficult question." The coach continued with an analogy that Nike was seizing on as well. Jordan, he said, "can be in the air like an airplane. When he is in the air, I don't know how he remains there. Everyone else is going down."

George Raveling, the assistant coach who'd grown close to Jordan, gushed, "In two or three years there's going to be a major controversy in the NBA. It will concern how Michael Jordan was allowed to be drafted only third instead of first or second. . . . I don't think the pros realize how good he is. They're in for a surprise. It's like a kid waking up on Christmas morning and expecting to get a bicycle and finding out it's a 10-speed."

The 1984 Summer Games could scarcely have been scripted better. They played out amid perfect weather, free of smog, ideal conditions for virtually every outdoor event. None of the doomsday predictions came to pass. There were no terrorist attacks, no mass shootings, no financial scandals, no political uprisings, no riots, no earthquakes. So many Angelenos had fearfully left town that the freeways might never have been *less* congested.

Thanks in part to an army of 35,000 civic-minded volunteers, the Games were remarkably well coordinated and organized. Television ratings started strong and only improved. Even the McDonald's giveaway promotion ultimately worked out. Midway through the Games, there were reports that at some of McDonald's 6,600 American locations, franchises were running out of hamburger buns, trying as they were to accommodate all the scratch-off game winners. "With all the gold medals that the U.S. is winning, we're swamped," a company spokesman told the *Los Angeles Times*.

The prizes on the cards were valid throughout the fall. Stories abounded of families collecting the winning cards and redeeming them for weeks, heading to McDonald's and eating for free. While McDonald's would not reveal the exact losses occasioned by the promotion, executives later conceded that the game had cost twice what the company originally anticipated.*

Yet maybe McDonald's didn't lose after all. The most costly promotion was also the most successful. At the next Summer Olympics, in 1988, the company again featured the scratch-off game, with the same rules and prizes.

The Games weren't *flawless*. A rehearsal for the opening ceremonies featured a bald eagle, inauspiciously named Bomber, recruited from the Patuxent Wildlife Research Center, in Maryland. Bomber had been trained to fly over the spectators and land on the Olympic rings. Like an athlete who had neglected his training, the bird arrived overweight

---

* Years later, the 1984 scratch-off game was still being mocked on *The Simpsons*. ("Not to worry, [Krusty]. We rigged the cards. They're all in events Communists never lose." Krusty [*reading newswire*]: "Soviet boycott. U.S. unopposed in most events. How does this affect our giveaway?")

and out of shape. Before the ceremony, Bomber died of what was called "vascular collapse."

Early in the Games, fire alarms were triggered at the athletes' village in Santa Barbara, where most of the rowers and canoeists were staying. The cause? A group of South Korean athletes were cooking a snake on a hibachi grill. July 29, the first day of competition, featured the women's cycling road race in Mission Viejo. Officials there soon realized there were not enough press phones available at the venue, preventing journalists from filing their stories. U.S. cyclist Connie Carpenter-Phinney beat countrywoman Rebecca Twigg to the line by less than a bike tire to win the two-hour, 11-minute event. The venue press chief hastily arranged for reporters to make calls from private homes near the race site.

The following day, a reception was held to celebrate the 70th birthday of past IOC president Lord Killanin. Midway through the meal, Killanin began choking on a piece of food, and an LAPD officer stepped in to save the day by administering the Heimlich maneuver.

Other miscues didn't come to light until later. On August 11, ABC was supposed to air the final track and field events, including Carl Lewis's last race. Moments before, race chaos arose behind the scenes. ABC was running behind schedule. And Al Michaels's broadcast partner, Wilma Rudolph, was nowhere to be seen. When it was determined that Rudolph's handler had given her the wrong call time, ABC producers frantically ordered their other track and field commentator to scramble to the broadcast booth and join Michaels.

So it was that O. J. Simpson saved the day, calling a relay race for which he'd done no prep work.

But ABC still hadn't synced up its coverage to the race. A producer yelled in Michaels's ear to start.

Michaels was confused. "Start what?"

"Start talking! We'll tape the race."

Tape the race? *This is nuts,* Michaels thought to himself. *Carl Lewis is going for a record four gold medals and we're not showing this live?*

Michaels and O. J. Simpson offered a brief setup. They called the

400-meter relay race. Lewis and the Americans literally ran away with the relay — as ABC broadcast preliminaries from platform diving. Almost 15 minutes after it had ended, the race aired on ABC. None of the millions of viewers knew they were watching a tape delay of a race that had already been run. And ABC didn't feel the need to disclose this. Two days later, word leaked out and ABC grudgingly apologized — auguring a day when tape delay would not pass muster with sports viewers.

Far more serious: while the details didn't seep out until months later, the L.A. Games were also, ominously, the site of a blood-doping scandal.

With school out for summer, the dorms on UCLA's campus served as one of the athletes' villages for the Games, the lodging facilities for most of the 7,000-plus Olympians. This was a great convenience. For sports like gymnastics, held at UCLA's Pauley Pavilion, athletes sometimes left their quarters, avoided the transport buses, and simply walked to their events.

The cycling events, though, were held at the velodrome in Carson, 20 miles south of the UCLA campus. The U.S. men's cycling team athletes accepted their rooms in the village, but then messed up their beds and scattered some dirty clothes so the rooms would appear occupied. They then headed to the Ramada Inn a mile from the velodrome, where they would stay during the days of competition.

To traffic in considerable understatement, this was the lesser stealth operation involving American cyclists and the Ramada Inn. For it was there, in that featureless motel, that the team dedicated one room at the end of a hall to administer blood transfusions to riders as the athletes lay supine on a double bed. Dr. Herman Falsetti, a professor of cardiology at the University of Iowa, found a vein and transferred fresh blood into the riders' arms. Then they would race.

Heading into the L.A. Games, the United States had not won an Olympic cycling medal since 1912. A new coach was determined to end this dry spell. Edward Borysewicz — known to all as Eddie B. — had been an assistant coach on Poland's 1976 Olympic cycling team. After defecting to the West, he became the U.S. national team coach, applying training and methods and philosophies he'd learned in Eastern European academies and training centers.

Eddie B. spoke virtually no English, and in order to communicate with his riders he often needed to seek out translators, including the children of Polish immigrants. But this also had the effect of adding to his mystique. He had a different perspective and an outsider's mentality. Eddie B. made sure the team had the most cutting-edge Raleigh bicycles, and personally put helium in the riders' tires. He hired the pioneer of aerodynamic cycling, Steve Hed, to design the team's wheels. "We're not going to fall behind the Russians and East Germans anymore," Eddie B. declared.

And before the 1984 Games, Eddie B. allegedly encouraged the American cyclists to seek a competitive advantage through blood transfusions. In advance of competition, they would have one or two pints of their blood — or the blood of a relative with the same type — withdrawn and placed in cold storage. In the intervening time, the athlete's body would replace its own withdrawn blood. Days before the race, the frozen blood would be thawed and reinjected into the athletes.

The operation was risky, this being when the term "AIDS epidemic" was just starting to enter the lexicon. But the underlying theory was quite simple. The "donated" blood would boost the athletes' red blood cell count, which would get more oxygen to tiring muscles, which would increase endurance, which would increase performance. And while it was, by most measures, deeply unethical and deeply unsafe, it was not, astonishingly, expressly *prohibited*.

Blood doping had been a clandestine practice for years in international sports, rumored to have been used systematically among Eastern Bloc athletes in the 1970s. In the months before the Games, the cycling team's technical director, Ed Burke, presented the suggestion to the U.S. Olympic Committee, seeking its blessing. The USOC punted, neither condoning blood boosting in sports nor condemning it. And the International Olympic Committee had never seen fit to outlaw the practice. (Besides, the testing at the time, mostly done via urine, all but ensured that no blood-boosting athletes would fail an anti-doping control.) The IOC's doping policy specifically prohibited "any physiological substance taken in abnormal quantity or taken by an abnormal route of entry into the body, with the sole intention of increasing in an artificial and unfair manner performance in competition."

Anabolic steroids, amphetamines, and other stimulants would fall squarely under this. But blood doping? Using a loose interpretation, one could argue that accepting a transfusion of blood before competition would fall into this category. But since blood doping didn't involve a "drug" or "substance," under a strict interpretation, the practice didn't technically run afoul of the rules.

Emboldened by these loopholes — and the low probability of getting caught — Eddie B., Burke, and the other rogue operators pressed on. While riders were not forced to take part in blood doping, the team coaches and administrators knew they wouldn't have to do much persuading.

A win-at-all-costs mentality had long been embedded in innumerable elite athletes. Though there were, astonishingly, zero athletes caught doping at the 1980 Games in Moscow, within a decade they were ridiculed as "the Chemists' Games" after it was revealed how many athletes were doping. A member of the IOC Medical Commission, Manfred Donike, privately ran additional tests with a new technique for identifying abnormal levels of testosterone by measuring its ratio to epitestosterone in urine. Twenty percent of the specimens he tested, including those from 16 gold medalists in Moscow, would have resulted in disciplinary proceedings had the tests been official.

Before the 1984 Olympics, researchers presented athletes with a hypothetical: *There's a pill that would guarantee you winning an Olympic medal, but it will reduce your life by 10 years. Would you take it?* Incredibly, 87 percent said they would.

They were then asked: *There's a pill that will guarantee you an Olympic gold medal, but it will lead to a 50-50 chance you'll be dead in 10 years. Would you take it?* This time, 93 percent answered yes. This research —

shorthanded the Goldman Dilemma, after the researcher, Bob Goldman—would be forever cited in support of anti-doping testing.

A month before the Olympics, U.S. rider Danny Van Haute experimented with blood doping prior to the Trials in Colorado Springs. A solid rider but hardly a star, Van Haute suddenly burned up the track, winning the points race and turning in some of the best times of his life.

Van Haute decided not to blood-dope during the Olympics. But teammates had taken note of his dramatically improved performance. At least eight members of Team USA took part in the scheme. Some of them were able to recycle their own blood. Others who waited—and missed the window for a safe self-transfusion before the start of the Games—relied on the transfused blood of a sibling or other family member.

In the case of at least one U.S. rider, the result was disastrous. After receiving a transfusion from his brother, Mark Whitehead, a top U.S. medal hope, came down with a 103-degree fever that lasted for 50 hours before it broke, by which point he had lost 10 pounds. He managed to race but failed to qualify for the finals.

But, overall, the team succeeded, not only winning its first Olympic cycling medal in 72 years but taking a total of nine, including four golds. Some of this surely owed to the absence of the Soviet Bloc competition. Some of it surely owed to the sheer talent of some American cyclists. But some of it also surely owed to the blood doping. At least four medals were won by riders who had taken part in the practice.

By the end of the year, a whistleblower had come forward: Thomas Dickson, a team doctor who had initially declined to be part of the scheme. The United States Cycling Federation president, Rob Lee, resigned over the Olympic transfusions. After an investigation, the IOC announced that it would not discipline the American cyclists, much less strip them of their medals. They had, after all, technically broken no rules. The USOC and the USCF also declined to punish the cyclists, though both Eddie B. and Ed Burke were suspended for 30 days for what were called "serious errors in judgment."

At the next annual meeting of the IOC, executives announced that, though a test for detection was still unavailable, the transfusion or re-infusion of blood or red blood cells was banned. Soon the committee added to the list of banned drugs a list of banned *procedures*.

Significantly, the IOC recognized that the appetite to gain an advantage was so severe that rules would have to go further in closing loopholes. The IOC showed that it was willing to ban practices even if detection or reliable tests were yet to exist. "Ban first, test later" represented a departure in strategy, as well as a realization and an acceptance that performance enhancement was only going to become more widespread.

Blood doping would, of course, become as much a part of professional cycling as flat tires and lactic acid buildup. Three decades later, Lance Armstrong would, disgracefully, concede that much of his success owed to cheating. The United States Anti-Doping Agency (USADA) called Armstrong the ringleader of "the most sophisticated, professionalized and successful doping program that sport has ever seen." It was not hard to trace the lineage.

John Gleaves, a professor at Cal State Fullerton and an anti-doping expert, put it this way in a paper he published in *The International Journal of the History of Sport:* "The use of blood transfusions by certain members of the 1984 U.S. cycling team significantly altered the IOC's attitudes and policies toward doping. . . . One of the legacies of the 1984 Olympic Games is its role in shaping a fundamental and lasting change to how the IOC and later the World Anti-Doping Agency (WADA) approached and understood the issue of doping."

Overall, though, the L.A. Olympics made for one of the most wondrous sports spectacles in history, a thundering success by any measure. The Games featured almost 7,000 athletes from 140 countries and awarded 688 total medals in 221 events. The United States was the runaway winner and unquestionably the biggest beneficiary of the Communist boycott. At the 1976 Montreal Games, American athletes had won 94 medals, 34 of them gold. In 1984, with so many rivals absent, Americans won 174 medals, 83 of them gold. Yet there was little sense that the competition had been diluted. The gold medalists had competed better than anyone else in the competition, and fans seized on this, not on the absentees.

For all the new stars minted, none shone brighter than a 46-year-old man who wore loafers and a suit, ate entire meals while walking, and survived on astonishingly little sleep. Before the Games had ended, the legend of Peter Ueberroth was already being recounted. With little budget and lots of challenges, and with military precision, Los Angeles had staged an Olympics that would become the new standard-bearer. Beyond that, the alloy of sports and commerce and television would become a new blueprint. If the Olympics had suddenly been transformed from pure amateurism to a commercial enterprise, few seemed to mind.

Ticket sales came in at 5,797,823, a new record and nearly double the 3.2 million sold for the Montreal Games just eight years earlier. The television ratings were astronomically high. More than 180 million Americans watched, making the 1984 Summer Olympics the most viewed event in television history. Ninety percent of all U.S. households had tuned in to the Games at some point. (The "boycott rebate" ABC had once mentioned had become a laughable concept.) The sponsors that had committed roughly $150 million were thrilled with the association. Los Angeles was plump with civic pride and, by extension, the United States swelled with national pride.

During the closing ceremonies, Ueberroth was saluted with a standing ovation from the crowd of 93,000 at the L.A. Coliseum. When the final balance sheets were prepared, the Los Angeles Olympics showed a *profit* of more than $250 million. Ueberroth was awarded a richly deserved $475,000 bonus. He gave the money to charity.

After L.A., it suddenly became desirable to host an Olympics, and bidders began lining up for future Games. Ueberroth and his team had managed to reawaken the entire Olympic movement. When observers would later claim that Ueberroth had "saved" the very concept of the Olympics, they were not guilty of exaggeration.

The 1984 Olympics ended on August 12. Within weeks, Ueberroth reported to his new job as commissioner of Major League Baseball. For his efforts, he was named *Time*'s Man of the Year for 1984. While he had granted *Time* an interview and posed for a photo, he didn't quite grasp the concept. He found out about the honor by walking by the magazine section of a Circle K convenience store. He bought seven copies.

And what of that profit? Much of it was reinvested in sports programs and facilities in Los Angeles, through the LA84 Foundation. Over the years, one of the projects funded a series of after-school football teams in Compton. With his father serving a life sentence for a murder conviction, Caylin Moore availed himself of the program. He ended up going to Texas Christian University on a football scholarship and then becoming a Rhodes Scholar. Nearby, a youth basketball program was also subsidized by the LA84 funds. One of the players taking advantage of this program: a hard-nosed and stubborn guard named Russell Westbrook.

Also in Compton, LA84 supported a program called National Junior Tennis and Learning, operated by the SoCal Tennis Association and designed to introduce the sport to kids from low-income neighborhoods. At NJTL events in Compton, volunteers watched, awestruck, as a pair of sisters in the program already showed more than a passing familiarity with tennis.

It turned out that when they were younger, their father used to wheel a shopping cart filled with tennis balls onto the Compton courts and put the girls through a series of drills. In the retelling, they would sometimes have to cut sessions short when gunfire between rival gangs broke out.

But day after day, the sisters would return and practice on the courts. And they would often take part in the NJTL programs funded by the surplus from the 1984 Olympics. And one day, those sisters, Venus and Serena Williams, would—among many other achievements—win Olympic gold medals themselves.

21

SUPER SATURDAY

You can blame Martina Navratilova. She made such fast work of Chris Evert Lloyd in the 1983 U.S. Open women's final, winning 6–1, 6–3, that CBS was forced to fill its broadcast window with replays and second-rate programming. And now, in 1984, CBS was not going to risk another Saturday afternoon of television dreck. Not on this valuable weekend after Labor Day. Not with the next day's NFL game broadcast to promote.

So executives seized on a new idea for the network's tennis coverage. Instead of playing both the men's semifinal matches on a Friday, the tournament — taking its orders from the television gods paying all that money for coverage — would sandwich the women's final in between the two men's semifinals and create one generously stuffed Saturday session. If a match, even two, were stinkers, there would still be plenty to fill the broadcast window.

In theory, anyway, it sounded good. And optimism was unbridled when play kicked off on Saturday, September 8, 1984. With summer finally bleeding into fall and cloudless skies overhead, fans settled in.

The session started at 11:00 a.m. with a bonus warm-up act of a match from the Men's Legends division, between two former Wimbledon champions: Australia's John Newcombe and Stan Smith, an American who had lent his name and likeness to an Adidas shoe. The minimalist footwear had sold surprisingly well, perhaps especially so when you consider Smith's unassuming personality. Smith's own son, Ramsey, had recently informed his father of a coincidence: "Dad, you share your name with a guy whose name is on a shoe!"

Because the match between Newcombe and Smith went longer than expected, it was nearly 1:00 p.m. when Ivan Lendl and Pat Cash, a 19-year-old Aussie, came on-court for the first semifinal. Lendl, emboldened by his defeat of John McEnroe at the French Open in June, was the clear favorite. But he and Cash split the first two sets, and the New York fans grew restless, to say nothing of the two players in the women's locker room, next on the bill.

Chris Evert and Martina Navratilova, the women's finalists, sat a few feet from each other. By this point, Navratilova had beaten Evert 12 straight times and hadn't lost a match to *anyone* since January. Still, they had grown closer, not more distant, on account of the rivalry. This would mark their 61st match, and their head-to-head record was, remarkably, tied, 30-30. Navratilova was only half-kidding when she suggested that they never play again, so that neither could claim superiority over the other.

How did these combatants while away the time in the locker room before squaring off in one of the weightiest matches of their careers? They shared a bagel.

A few weeks earlier, Cash had played disastrously in the Los Angeles Olympics. Tennis was an exhibition sport, and Cash admitted that he had lost on purpose — tanked, in the tennis locution — so he could stick around, use his free tickets for other events, and meet girls. But on this afternoon he was sensational, attacking the net and executing crisp volleys. Lendl, though, had a response for every question and prevailed in a dramatic insta-classic, 3–6, 6–3, 6–4, 6–7, 7–6.

It was after 4:00 p.m. when Evert and Navratilova finally took to the court. If they were both annoyed from having to wait around for their match — a major final — until the men were done, it did not show in their play. In possibly the most compelling of their dozens of matches, Evert won the first set, 6–4. That in itself was a breakthrough, and the crowd roared its approval. Evert executed a fist pump, a wildly self-aggrandizing gesture by her standards.

While the crowd was, perhaps, simply supporting an underdog, Navratilova interpreted it differently. Here was another reminder that she was "other," that she would never be totally accepted. Later, she would recall the match as "one of the hardest things I've ever been through, all those people wanting me to lose."

She funneled this hurt into her play. Dictating rallies with her power and athleticism — overcoming the fans who, sensing her displeasure, began cheering her errors — she won the second set, 6–4. In the third set, Evert's play suggested, *This time you're really going to have to beat me.* Navratilova obliged and won, 4–6, 6–4, 6–4. For Evert, a day soaked in hope ended bitterly. "It's just not enough to play a good match against her anymore," she sighed. For Navratilova, the day marked her *sixth*-straight major singles title. And still, it felt somehow incomplete.

After an abbreviated trophy presentation ceremony, it was 7:28 p.m. when John McEnroe and Jimmy Connors took the court. "Ridiculous," McEnroe muttered about the start time as he walked on. If the McEnroe-Connors rivalry did not conjure the warmth of the Evert-Navratilova rivalry, it often caused both men to summon their best tennis.

Which they did this night.

Though Connors was more than six years older than McEnroe and had turned 32 just a few days earlier, he looked just as fresh as his opponent for the first three hours. McEnroe won point after point with his sidewinding lefty serving and artistry at the net. But Connors, too, won point after point with his defense and backhand, a flat two-hander that sent passing shots whistling by McEnroe.

Finally, after they had split the first four sets, it was Connors who blinked. Early in the fifth, his level dropped and McEnroe pounced. It was 11:14 p.m. when McEnroe hit his last sharply angled lefty serve to put away Connors, 6–4, 4–6, 7–5, 4–6, 6–3. By then, every match on the Saturday docket had gone to a decisive set and fans had been treated — some might say subjected — to more than 12 hours of tennis encompassing 16 sets, 165 games, and 979 points. CBS was like the farmer who prayed for rain and then got a flood.

The following day, McEnroe, showing fine powers of recovery, beat Lendl in the final, pushing his match record on the year to 66-2, almost as absurdly good as Navratilova's 61-1. But the talk still centered on what was instantly christened Super Saturday. CBS even announced, triumphantly, that it was the longest continuous coverage of a sporting event in American television history.

But it would end up being something much more: the high-water mark for tennis in the United States. The tennis boom that started in the late seventies had reached its height on Super Saturday.

Though only 25 years old, McEnroe would never win another major singles title. (He would also never again face Connors in a big match.) Soon enough, his genius would revert to the tortured variety, and other players would surpass him. Navratilova, too, would lose in December's Australian Open, forestalling a Grand Slam of all four majors in a calendar year, tennis's holy grail. And she would even lose to Evert the next time they played.

Super Saturday marked one of the last official days of summer. Symbolically, it was for an entire sport as well.

22

MIKE AND NIKE

When Michael Jordan returned home to North Carolina, friends and family assumed that he would be exhausted from the Olympics and the increasing demands on his time that came from his swelling profile. He smiled and disabused them of that idea. "I wish [the NBA] opened tomorrow," he said sunnily. "That's how excited I am."

Jordan was less excited, though, about getting dressed up and sitting in conference rooms taking boring meetings. Donald Dell, the head of ProServ and, notionally, Jordan's agent, was hashing out his client's playing contract with the Bulls, Jordan's leverage having increased after his Olympic showing. "I wouldn't say we've got the Bulls over a barrel," Dell told the *Chicago Tribune.* "[But] they certainly know Michael is a dynamic young man who turns people on. He's never going to be a head case or get involved in drugs."

David Falk paid a visit from Washington, D.C., to discuss Jordan's marketing plan. He was growing close to James and Deloris Jordan. Unlike so many parents Falk encountered, who thought their kid was a unicorn, the Jordans "pushed Michael to improve at everything he did."

Falk's spirits were further lifted when he popped by the UNC campus. Though Jordan had spent the entire summer playing basketball, he went to Woollen Gym to play pickup with a group of former UNC players already in the NBA, among them James Worthy, Walter Davis, and Dudley Bradley. Falk watched slack-jawed as Jordan looked to be playing an entirely different sport. He recalls thinking, "He made these guys look like a high school team. And these were established NBA players — the same guys he'd be going up against soon."

By this point Falk was beyond eager for his client to sign with Nike. It was, as he saw it, the perfect match of a creative, entrepreneurial, ascending company and a creative, up-and-coming athlete. Besides, Falk had already named the damn shoe. When Falk broached the subject, Jordan cut him off. "Just get it done with Adidas," he told him.

Jordan's parents had explained to him that there was more to being a professional basketball player than putting a ball in a hoop. "Take care of your business," James Jordan told his son with a laugh. "And be happy you have business to take care of." Specifically, Jordan Sr. told his son that he needed to attend meetings about what product would his adorn his feet. The next of these "shoe meetings" was at Nike, and Michael would be attending, whether he wanted to or not. So it was that the day after Labor Day, Jordan accompanied his parents and Falk on a cross-country flight to Portland.

To say that Nike unfurled the red carpet for the Jordans would be selling short their hospitality effort. When the family arrived, a limousine was waiting and Sonny Vaccaro got out and held the door open for Deloris Jordan. There were fancy meals at the downtown Portland restaurant Broadway Revue and a golf outing at the posh Oswego Lake Country Club.

The Jordans arrived to the pitch meeting at Nike's campus, in Beaverton, held at the "Murray Two" building. (Soon Nike would begin naming buildings after the top athletes it shod, Jordan included.) They were greeted by a printed banner: THE NIKE FAMILY WELCOMES THE JORDAN FAMILY.

The Jordans sat with Falk. The Nike contingent included Rob Strasser, Sonny Vaccaro, and Peter Moore, the star Nike designer. But Phil Knight, Nike's eccentric CEO, told colleagues he "would pop in later."

The meeting started inauspiciously. Howard White, the lone African American Nike executive, arrived late. The Nike team had created a highlight video of Jordan's various dunks and anti-gravitational moves, scored to the 1984 pop song "Jump," by the Pointer Sisters. When an executive popped the cassette into the video player, the machine jammed. Awkwardly, the Jordans waited.

The video finally played, ending with Moore's wings logo and the tagline "Air Jordan, Basketball by Nike."

Rightly proud of his handiwork, Moore smiled, as did everyone else in the room. Except one 21-year-old. While the design was in keeping with the color scheme of the Chicago Bulls, Jordan was a tough critic. "Devil's colors," he muttered, adding that he wished the prototype of the shoes could be tinted in Carolina blue.

Late in the meeting, Phil Knight walked in. There was uncertainty whether it was a good thing that the CEO of the company had arrived, or a bad thing that he'd walked in late, clearly having prioritized something else.

Strasser, the companionable, rotund marketing man, took it upon himself to break the ice.

"We know you like cars," he said to Jordan.

Jordan nodded, expressionless.

"Well," Strasser said, dramatically reaching into his pocket, "I thought you might like this."

Other Nike executives, not least Knight, weren't sure where this was going. It was not beyond Strasser to reach into his pocket and hand Jordan — whom the company hadn't even signed — keys to a new car.

As suspense mounted, Strasser pulled out two plastic toy cars and said words to the effect of *Sign with us and you'll have plenty of money to buy the real thing.* Everyone laughed. Except for Jordan.

The meeting was mostly about Jordan becoming his own brand, having, yes, a signature shoe, and also having an image all his own. But it also came with the potential for vast wealth. Falk made clear that Jordan wanted more money from Nike up front, even if it meant less in back-end earnings. Still, if the Air Jordan shoe took off, the royalties alone could pay Jordan more than his NBA contract.

The other key to the meeting: Nike asked for Jordan's input and opinion, making it clear that this was a partnership and that Air Jordan would truly be *his* signature line. No one, of course, knew it then, but the meeting marked one of the hinge-point moments in the history of sports business, never mind in Nike's corporate history.

Falk wasn't sure how to read his client. He knew that Jordan was less than thrilled about having been dragged across the country, a few weeks after the Olympics and a few weeks before his first NBA training camp. He didn't smile once during the meeting. Then again, Falk also knew that — a legacy of all those late-night poker games at UNC, perhaps — Jordan was masterful at negotiating and revealing nothing with his expression. Falk would call it "Michael's business face."

When the meeting broke up, Falk asked Jordan what he thought of the presentation.

Finally the young man smiled. "I don't want to see anyone else."

As a courtesy, Falk reached out to his contact at Adidas and explained what Nike had offered, aware that Adidas would not be able to match the offer. As another courtesy, Falk and James Jordan took one last meeting at Converse in Massachusetts.

It was as though they had gone from watching color TV to black-and-white. Converse whipped through a dutiful presentation. They showed images of all the other stars they represented. Nike was determined to make Jordan a stand-alone star and give him a signature shoe line. At Converse, clearly he would be just another car in the garage. James Jordan couldn't restrain himself. "Don't you have *any* new, creative ideas?"

By the first week in September, Michael Jordan had signed with Nike, and Air Jordan had gone into production.

23

WAIT TILL NEXT YEAR

As the summer rounded third base, the Chicago Cubs, remarkably, were still in first place, their flag highest, for a change, among those Wrigley Field pennants. Inside the ballpark, site of so much gallows humor and fatalism, was an unlikely theater of optimism. Would this — *could* this? — finally be the year the Cubs overcame their history and exorcised the Curse of the Billy Goat?

Overcoming a slumplet in September, Chicago would win the National League East by six and a half games, holding off the Mets and their star rookie pitcher, Dwight Gooden. The Cubs would finish the regular season with a record of 96-65. Ryne Sandberg would bat .314, win another Gold Glove, and be named the National League's Most Valuable Player.

After his trade from Cleveland to Chicago, big Rick Sutcliffe would go 16-1 and win the National League Cy Young Award. For good measure, he and Tommy Lasorda, his former manager, reconciled. "Every time Sutcliffe's name is mentioned, somebody asks me about what happened,"

Lasorda fumed to reporters that season. "That's history. Why don't you ask me about the Lindbergh baby?"

In the summer of 1984, the Cubs were a sensation in Chicago, but also beyond. For years, the Tribune Company had owned Chicago's WGN, a local television station that grew to become a "superstation" available to cable subscribers throughout the United States, and ranked among the most popular outlets in the country outside of the three broadcast networks.

WGN had carried Cubs and White Sox games since the late 1940s. But when Tribune bought the Cubs in 1981, it took advantage of the synergy and began broadcasting more and more Cubs games. Following the 1981 season, the network hired Harry Caray, who had been working as a broadcaster for the White Sox, making him the voice (and face) of the Cubs.

Caray was equally unintelligible and endearing, slurring his way through the latter innings and shredding what would later become political correctness. It wasn't uncommon for him to invite an attractive woman to sit on his lap in the booth. Or to enthuse, "They're dancing in the streets of San Juan!" when a Latin player, regardless of their country of origin, hit a home run. But Caray became a national celebrity. Fans would surround the Cubs' bus in Pittsburgh or San Diego and Caray would draw more interest than many of the players.

Another consequence: the superstation created an entire generation of Cubs fans who lived nowhere near Illinois. On most days, WGN was one of only two networks in the country broadcasting live baseball. (The Atlanta Braves on Ted Turner's TBS was the other.) So the Cubs became a sort of national team. WGN was how Sandy Sandberg, marooned in eastern Washington State, managed to watch his son Ryne play every day. It was how Eddie Vedder got his Cubs fill on the West Coast. And how young Theo Epstein watched in the Boston suburbs.

The Cubs' presence on the Superstation also minted a young audience, on account of the day games. Countless American kids — myself among them — would return from school and reflexively turn on the TV.

Apart from cartoons, the other television option was afternoon baseball. If you could endure a horrible jingle ("Kids in Chicago, having a good time. / They're all watching Channel 9!"), Harry Caray and the Cubs were the de facto babysitters until parents returned from work.

Cubs fans tended to come in three varieties. There were the Chicagoland natives, whose families passed their fandom — and longtime suffering — down through generations. There were the national fans, who grew up watching the Cubs on WGN and were converted. And then there were those who had no particular affinity for the Cubs or even perhaps for baseball, but attended a game at Wrigley and got seduced.

Tom Ricketts — who came up with this classification model — put himself squarely in the third category. Ricketts grew up a baseball fan in Nebraska, collecting baseball cards and reading box scores in the morning newspaper. He was a fan of the Kansas City Royals, mostly because the team's minor league affiliate played in Omaha.

In 1984, though, Ricketts fell in love. He was 18 years old and had been accepted to the University of Chicago. Instead of whiling away the summer in Nebraska, he figured he'd move up to the city and live with his older brother Pete, a rising junior at U of C.

The Ricketts boys came from means. In the 1970s, their father, Joseph Ricketts, founded First Omaha Securities, among the country's largest discount brokerage firms. But, hell-bent on making sure that his kids established themselves independently, Joseph Ricketts set a policy: none of his four children could join his company — it would later change its name to TD Ameritrade — until they turned 30.

So it was that Tom and Pete spent the summer of 1984 living a life that belied the family wealth. They shared a hovel of an apartment above Sports Corner, a low-rent sports bar perfumed with stale beer and body odor. The redeeming feature: the apartment was on the corner of Addison and Sheffield, across the street from Wrigley Field.

That summer, young Tom Ricketts spent incalculable hours at Wrigley. Living on a budget, he sat in the sun-splattered, beer-splattered bleacher seats. And loved it. The ballpark blended major league games with the intimacy of the minor league experience he knew from Omaha. The ivy latticing the outfield walls. The old-timey organ. The absence of lights and presence of bonhomie . . . It all fed something in him.

It was a magical summer for Ricketts. As the team seemed to improve with each passing month, his affinity spread to the players themselves. "You have this team that no one expected to be that good and it kept winning," Ricketts recalls. "You had compelling young players, you had great veterans. All these likable personalities. You had the best pitcher [Sutcliffe] and the best hitter [Sandberg]. It all had this special charm."

When he wasn't at the ballpark, Ricketts worked at the Chicago Board of Options Exchange. Offhandedly, he wondered whether some of the numbers and probabilities that the pit traders used might have an application in baseball. *Could you use data to measure a player's performance or make in-game decisions?* By the end of the summer, Ricketts had been baptized. He was a Cubs fan. That summer, he says, marked "an inflection point."

During his undergraduate summers, as he eyed attending business school, he would continue to work at the Chicago Board of Options. And he would continue to attend games in the Wrigley bleachers. (It was there that he met the woman who would become his wife.) He would also continue to wonder how the Cubs could use data to take advantage of inefficiencies and give themselves the best possible chance of finally winning the damn World Series.

When the 1984 National League playoffs commenced—the team's first postseason appearance in 39 years—the Cubs faced the winner of the National League West, the San Diego Padres. Before Game 1, the Cubs summoned "Mr. Cub," Ernie Banks, to throw out the first pitch, announcing that Banks had "waited his entire major league career for this moment." Banks took the mound, theatrically bowing to everyone in the ballpark. At age 53, he threw a trick underhanded pitch, the perfect representation of the Cubs' insouciance.

In the actual game, the Cubs played perhaps the best nine innings of their entire season. Sutcliffe pitched masterfully and hit a home run. Which was not a unique feat that day. With the wind blowing out at 20 miles an hour, the Cubs hit five home runs and won 13–0. They won again the following day, scoring in the first inning and never trailing. They were now a game away from the World Series; but the celebration was muted. Both teams headed to O'Hare airport for a cross-country flight, as Game 3 would be played in San Diego the very next day.

The Cubs took an early lead, but the Padres responded, shelling the Cubs' fantastically mustachioed pitcher, Dennis Eckersley. In Game 4, both teams held and then relinquished leads. In the bottom of the ninth inning, with the score tied 5–5, the Padres' young hitter Tony Gwynn reached first base. Steve Garvey came to the plate against Lee Smith, the Cubs' reliever and the best closer in baseball that season. Smith left his second pitch out over the plate and Garvey took a massive swing, sending the ball beyond the reach of the Cubs' leaping right fielder.

For the Cubs and their fans, it was still another reminder that the franchise had done something to truly piss off the Baseball Fates. For Garvey—a man of athleticism, striking good looks, and then-unimpeachable character—it was the latest in a life of successes. "I think our future senator picked up a few votes tonight," quipped Padres teammate Champ Summers.

A few minutes before Game 5, Ryne Sandberg headed to the team's Gatorade canister for a quick drink. Sandberg was the epitome of surehanded. He had committed only six errors that season and would win his second of *nine* straight Gold Gloves, on his way to retiring with one of the highest fielding percentages in major league history. But on this afternoon, he clumsily knocked over the cooler, soaking Leon Durham's first baseman's glove in the process.

Sandberg would recall that Durham tried everything to dry off the leather glove, first dabbing it with dugout towels and then seeking a hair dryer from the clubhouse. The mitt was still sticky when the game began. So much so that he asked the Cubs' third-base coach/yoda, Don Zimmer, if he thought he should still use the glove.

A hard-bitten baseball lifer, Zimmer shrugged, "It might bring you good luck."

The Cubs struck first in Game 5 when Durham hit a home run in the first inning, giving Sutcliffe a cushion. San Diego chipped away at the lead, but Chicago was still ahead 3–2 in the seventh inning, nine outs from the World Series. And then it came, a singularly Cubsian conclusion.

In the seventh inning, San Diego's Tim Flannery hit a ground ball to the right side of the infield. Durham positioned himself perfectly for what was likely a double play. He bent his knees and dropped his hands for the kind of ground ball he would field as routinely and uneventfully as he might tie his shoes or deposit a letter in the mailbox. This was Durham, a player who — in the kind of irony that only the Cubs could deliver — had made *Bill Buckner,* of all people, expendable as a first baseman.

The ball hugged the field and squirted through Durham's legs and into the outfield. Perhaps this was the curse of Durham's Gatorade-soaked glove. Owing entirely to the four runs they scored in the seventh inning, the Padres won, 6–3. Having taken the last three games from the Cubs, they headed to the World Series, where they would lose to the Detroit Tigers.

For the Cubs, baseball's lovable losers, here was another chapter in their compendium of heartbreak. Maybe this was the Baseball Fates offering some foreshadowing for Buckner. Or just the Cubs Curse, the encapsulation of the remark from Jack Brickhouse, the Cubs' longtime announcer before Caray, that "everyone's entitled to a bad century."

In Chicago, young Tom Ricketts was among the disconsolate. How, he wondered aloud, could a summer of baseball that contained so much sweetness have ended with such bitterness? But, befitting a student at the University of Chicago, he was entirely too rational to attribute the Cubs' disappointment to a curse. His new favorite team didn't win that season, but they showed that, one day, they could. Maybe they just needed the right management and ownership.

24

BE LIKE MIKE

One might have thought that when the team's top draft pick — fresh off winning an Olympic medal, and recent recipient of a signature shoe deal — arrived in Chicago, the Bulls would have arranged an airport pickup. But in the last week of September 1984, as summer faded from view, Michael Jordan was the last passenger to get off his flight to Chicago. And while he assumed the Bulls would be sending someone to meet him at the gate, no greeter was forthcoming.

Jordan had started walking absently around O'Hare when he was spotted. A few weeks earlier, George Koehler had left his job at a swanky Chicago hotel and opened a new company, Prestige Limousine. There was one limo in the fleet, and Koehler, 29, was the driver. He, too, had been stood up at O'Hare that day, waiting for a fare that never showed up. He was about to go home when he recognized a large man looking as though he needed a ride. *Was this the Bulls' rookie? And what's his name again?*

"Hey," Koehler said, impulsively. "You're Larry Jordan."

Michael Jordan turned and smiled, thinking it was a clever joke. Jordan's older brother Larry was his basketball idol. Michael Jordan, the story goes, chose uniform number 23 because Larry had worn number 45 and Michael aspired to be half the player his brother was. (Presumably, number 22½ was unavailable.) Larry, though, stopped growing at five-eight.

"Wait," Jordan asked Koehler, "how do you know my brother?"

Koehler sheepishly admitted that he had misspoken and didn't know Jordan had siblings, much less one named Larry. But when Jordan added that he needed a taxi to get to the North Shore hotel the Bulls were using for training camp, Koehler offered to drive him there.

"How's twenty-five dollars sound?"

"Deal."

Though Jordan was in the back and Koehler in the front, the two men chatted easily. Koehler managed to conceal that he wasn't entirely sure where he was going. Jordan hadn't spent much time in Chicago — or riding in limos, for that matter — and, he, too, tried to conceal his apprehension. When they finally arrived at the intended destination, Jordan handed over $50. *Keep the change.*

Koehler thanked Jordan, handed him a business card, and added, "If you need to know of any places to live, restaurants to eat at, you want to go out for a beer . . . you've got a friend in Chicago."

Two weeks later, Koehler's phone rang.

"Georgie, my boy!"

"Who's this?"

"It's MJ."

"I don't know any MJ."

"Yes, you do."

"I'm not going to argue. I don't know who this is."

"Dumbass, it's Michael Jordan."

MJ had a request. Could Koehler pick up Deloris and James Jordan the following day? Koehler could. And for the rest of Michael Jordan's time in Chicago, Koehler served as the driver, assistant, and friend of the greatest basketball player there ever was.

• • •

Though situated just a few miles away on Chicago's North Side, the Angel Guardian Gym was everything that Wrigley Field was not. Indoor. Dank. Cheerless. Alcohol-free. The recreation space of a longtime orphanage, the gym doubled as the site of the Chicago Bulls' practice facility. It was chosen by the team mostly because it was equidistant from downtown and the northern suburbs, where most of the Bulls players and coaches lived.

As the Bulls gathered at Angel Guardian during the 1984 off-season for summer drills and then, officially, for training camp, optimism was in short supply. Coming off a dreadful 27-55 season, the Bulls reigned as one of the worst teams in the NBA.

The Horri-Bulls or Laugha-Bulls or Abomina-Bulls, as they were openly mocked in the Chicago media, averaged around 6,300 fans a game — barely one-third the capacity of their arena — making them 21st out of 23 teams in the NBA in attendance. Their home court, Chicago Stadium, was a charm-deprived concrete barn built in the late 1920s. It was an open secret that members of the Bulls' ownership group were looking to sell; but prospective buyers balked at the $10 million valuation.*

From the Bulls' coaches to the ticket manager to the public relations staff, there was an unmistakable current of job insecurity. Compounding matters, one of the team's best players, David Greenwood — the second pick in the 1979 NBA Draft, after Magic Johnson — was locked in a bitter contract dispute with Bulls management and threatening not to play.

But, as an immutable sports rule, all training camps must open with *some* sense of promise and potential. In the case of the Bulls arriving at Angel Guardian in 1984, the buoyancy came from the team's top draft pick. During the NBA off-season, while other players were luxuriating

* In 1985, with Michael Jordan on the roster, Jerry Reinsdorf led a group that bought 56.8 percent of the team for $9.2 million, effectively valuing the Bulls at $16 million. In 2020, *Forbes* put the Bulls' valuation at $3.2 billion.

poolside, Michael Jordan had won an Olympic gold medal. Word was spreading through the NBA grapevine that Jordan was going to get his own *personalized* basketball shoe, part of a groundbreaking, if vague, deal with Nike that might pay him more than even the $550,000 in base salary he would get from the Bulls.

About that playing salary . . . As it had turned out, both Jordan's soaring play at the Olympics and the grounded state of the Bulls had helped Jordan in his contract negotiation. His deal, finally signed in mid-September, called for him to make roughly $6 million over five years, including a $1 million signing bonus. In retrospect, it was not an especially generous deal, but it did make Jordan the highest-paid player in Bulls history. (It famously contained a clause permitting him to play pickup games in the off-season; it also contained incentives if the Bulls hit certain attendance thresholds.)

If Bulls players and employees expected the team's rookie to swagger into his first day of work, a new star illuminated in neon, they were pleasantly surprised when it wasn't the case at all. A smile welded to his face, unable to conceal his giddiness about being in the NBA, Jordan took the initiative in introducing himself to everyone and projecting his easy confidence without crossing the median into overconfidence.

He also managed the balancing act that entailed projecting hope without casting himself as the savior. "I've seen a winning attitude here in camp, and all I can do is be a part of it, not the reason for it," he said during his first week on the job. "If we play hard and prove we can win, our fans will get behind us, the same way everyone in Chicago is now pulling for the Cubs."

The Bulls did their part to tamp down expectations. The team's head coach, Kevin Loughery, a former NBA player from Brooklyn, talked of bringing in Jordan as a reserve. He also spoke flatly of trying to "cover up" Jordan's "problems with one-on-one defense" by emphasizing offense. Loughery let it be known that Jordan would likely be coming off the bench, a bit of psychological warfare deployed both to motivate Jordan and to assure the veterans that the rookie would have to earn his place.

Then training camp officially opened.

Wearing red Nike Air Ship shoes — his stand-ins until the Air Jordan model rolled off the assembly line — Jordan ran faster, jumped higher, and hung in the air longer than anyone else. He also shot more accurately, made savvier decisions, and defended better.

Loughery and his assistant Fred Carter had been NBA teammates in the 1960s and '70s. Between them, they had guarded the best backcourt players of their era: Elgin Baylor, Pete Maravich, John Havlicek, Dave Bing. Yet they were reduced to giggles as they stood against the walls of the gym watching Jordan. Recalls Carter, "We thought we had seen a lot. Well, Michael was doing things we had never seen before."

"Can you believe how good he is?" Carter muttered to Loughery.

"Nope," Loughery said flatly, looking straight ahead.

Another Bulls employee approached Loughery that first week, looking downcast.

"Um, we seem to have a problem, Coach."

"What's that?" Loughery asked, bracing himself for news of a player's knee injury or drunk driving arrest.

"Well," the employee said, smiling and motioning to Jordan, "there's a young kangaroo loose in the gym."

Soon this kangaroo was moved to the starting lineup. When the first team scrimmaged against the second unit, Jordan was at his most ruthlessly effective. Loughery and the other coaches began calling phantom fouls and violations on Jordan. Mostly it was just to keep the game competitive. But it was also to test Jordan and prepare him for the occasional injustices of NBA officiating. Jordan smiled and, running downcourt, detoured to the sidelines to smack Carter on the butt. "Cheat all you want," he said. "It's not gonna work. And they're not gonna win."

After an early practice, Quintin Dailey, Chicago's veteran — and sometimes troubled — shooting guard, challenged Jordan to a game of one-on-one. It was classic alpha male stuff, the proud incumbent trying to *not-so-fast* the ambitious rookie. Jordan didn't just beat Dailey. He broke him. So much so that by the end of the game, Dailey was flashing a look of resignation. "I'm good," Dailey conceded to Carter. "But I'm not good the way *he's* good."

Early in the training camp, Loughery asked his assistants to take some notes and jot down their impressions of the players, especially the new ones. Taking the measure of Jordan, Carter wrote words to the effect of *Warm and engaging. He knows there is something within him, but does he know how good he can be? There's no arrogance. There's nothing not pleasurable about him.*

The media shared in this assessment. As word of Jordan's prowess spread through the basketball cosmos, NBA writers from all over the country angled for interviews. Tim Hallam, the Bulls' young head of PR, would hand Jordan a stack of "While you were out" pink memo sheets, detailing the various requests and including the reporters' phone numbers. *USA Today. New York Post. Dallas Morning News.* Jordan would scowl and smirk and give Hallam some grief. ("You're paying me extra for this, right?") Then he would take the stack, head to an office, and begin dialing, charming the writers on the other end of the line.

On October 15—a month to the day from the signed contract date—Jordan played an exhibition game against the New York Knicks in Glens Falls, New York. Wearing his red-and-black Nike Air Ship shoes, Jordan caught the disapproving eye of NBA shoe police, who had two concerns. The shoe was not predominantly white, and it violated the "uniformity of uniform" rule demanding that "a player must wear shoes that not only matched their uniforms, but matched the shoes worn by their teammates."

The Bulls played the Knicks again three days later at Madison Square Garden. Word came down that Jordan couldn't wear the shoes. Falk, the agent, called Rob Strasser, deeply concerned. Did this mean the entire Air Jordan concept needed to be rethought? When Falk told Strasser about the potential for a $10,000 fine for each game Jordan wore the offending Nike shoes, he heard gleeful cackling on the other end of the line.

"Great!" Rob Strasser yelled.

"Great?" asked Falk.

"Write a check for $82,000," said Strasser, whose math skills weren't the equal of his marketing skills. (A $10,000-per-game fine over an 82-game NBA season would come to $820,000.) "It'll be the cheapest marketing campaign ever!"

The controversy would be sorted out by adding a band of white. Though, as Strasser predicted, this bit of controversy was marketing gold. When the Air Jordan was released weeks later, it was accompanied by a television commercial beginning with a faux-ominous voice intoning, "On October 15, Nike created a revolutionary new basketball shoe. On October 18, the NBA threw them out of the game. Fortunately, the NBA can't keep you from wearing them."

By then, the Bulls had won their first six preseason games and Michael Jordan was already achieving cruising altitude.

"You know," Loughery said to Carter. "Honest to goodness, I really do think he can fly."

"We're going to look back at this as a good summer," Carter replied. "A *very* good summer."

Conclusion

In the spring of 2019, David Stern sat across a desk from me. Since leaving the NBA commissionership five years earlier, he'd kept an office off Columbus Circle, in Midtown Manhattan. Stern had started his own sports-themed investment fund, titled, appropriately, Micro-management Ventures. And while the mustache was long gone and his sport coat was perfectly tailored to fit him this time, his energy level was comparable to what it had been in 1984 when he first assumed the job of overseeing a floundering pro basketball league.

Stern being Stern, he was eager to learn more about this book — and ended up being a main source. And, Stern being Stern, he immediately asked me to defend its premise. But then, marveling at how much sports had changed over the past 35 years, he said, "It *is* pretty amazing how many of the organizing principles were established that summer of 1984."

When we spoke that particular morning, the 2019 NBA Draft was coming up and, 35 years after Stern announced Akeem Olajuwon as the first pick, 8 of the 60 players selected would come from Africa — joining more than 100 NBA players born outside of the United States. The NBA Playoffs, broadcast the world over, were winnowing to a final that would pit a team from Canada (run by a British-born Kenyan-Nigerian) against a team from the tech hub of the Bay Area recently valued at $5 billion. NBA league-wide revenues that season hovered around $9 billion, a mere 76-fold increase from the $118 million the league made when Stern became commissioner.

As Stern had predicted, television, specifically *cable* television, had transformed sports. More than $3 billion of the NBA's revenue came from various TV deals. And this was dwarfed by the NFL's TV package. Individual NFL *games* sold for hundreds of millions of dollars — more than any Hollywood blockbuster. The legacy of the summer of 1984 Supreme Court decision in the *NCAA v. Board of Regents* case, college sports became billion-dollar television properties as well.

In the secure hands of Disney after its sale in the summer of 1984, ESPN had become the most profitable media company in history, elevated by its "secret sauce" — capitalizing not just on selling commercial time but on charging a monthly subscriber fee, which had risen from a dime or so in the summer of 1984 to roughly $7.50 in 2019.

Also buoyed by television rights — and its fantastically successful WrestleMania franchise, incubated in the summer of 1984 — the WWE was a publicly traded company, and Vince McMahon was a billionaire. Still looking to cause disruptions in his mid-seventies, McMahon was busy preparing to (re)launch a football league to challenge the NFL. "I wouldn't put it past him," Stern said, smiling.

Stern was less charitable talking about the former owner of the New York/New Jersey Generals of the USFL. Relying on the same media savvy and cavalier relationship with the truth that he had first betrayed during his national emergence in the summer of 1984, Donald Trump had, improbably, been elected president of the United States. Stern seemed to take particular umbrage at Trump's disdain for the growing cohort of athletes who channeled their "inner Navratilova" and used their platforms to become activists and speak about matters beyond sports.

As Stern realized in the summer of 1984, as Magic Johnson and the Lakers played Larry Bird and the Celtics, rivalries are spindles on which sports are wound. And whether it was an NBA team or the New England Patriots during Bob Kraft's ownerships, sports also thrive in the presence of dynasties. And just as Stern presciently foresaw sports being run as businesses and not as hobbies, owners used data-driven analytics to make decisions, ranging from the price of tickets to the wisdom of signing a particular free agent. One such franchise: the Chicago Cubs. Tom Ricketts — who had been seduced by the Cubs as a kid sitting in the right-field bleachers during that magical summer of 1984 — would lead a bid to buy the team for $900 million in 2009. Seven years later, the Cubs would exorcise one of the great sports curses and win the World Series for the first time since 1908.

And then there was Michael Jordan. If Wayne Gretzky winning his first Stanley Cup and Magic-Bird playing a captivating seven-game NBA Finals defined the importance — and value — of the superstar athlete, Jordan redefined it. He was the ideal star for the era. He was howlingly talented, but also blazingly intense and committed to the craft of basketball. He was cool and subversive, but sufficiently mainstream to endorse Chevrolet and mustard. And besides, he smiled too damn much to cut the figure of a rebel.

Like all towering figures in their field, Jordan would transform basketball, showing — if not demanding — that top players could excel on offense *and* defense. They could dunk but also shoot. Jordan would completely transform the moribund Chicago Bulls — winning three titles, retiring, unretiring, and winning three more, he would awaken the NBA.

But beyond basketball, Jordan redefined the model of the superstar athlete. Telegenic at a time when sports became relentlessly visual, Jordan would become sport's truly global superstar. His playing salary would mirror the growth of sports. The rookie contract David Falk and Donald Dell negotiated paid $550,000; in his final season in Chicago, Jordan was paid north of $33 million.

And his basketball income was dwarfed by his off-court income. The signature shoe that Peter Moore at Nike had designed in the summer of 1984 grew to become the appropriately named Jordan Brand. In 2019 — with Jordan in his mid-fifties and more than 20 years removed from his Bulls heyday — his signature brand turned in a $1 billion *quarter* in revenue. By then Jordan was also majority owner of the Charlotte Hornets. (When, in the summer of 1984, James Jordan encouraged his son to leave North Carolina and turn pro, in part because the kid could start building his own portfolio, he didn't know how right he'd turn out to be.)

As Stern reminisced, all that history reappeared. Like so many other subjects I spoke to for this book, Stern smiled as he recollected. The past kept crashing into the present. The summer of 1984 was in that sweet spot: recent enough that he could recall names and figures and events that would take on great meaning; sufficiently far removed that he could speak candidly with the perspective of 35 years. He wondered aloud, "Hey, wait, wasn't that around the time the Mac came out?" (It was.) "And I think that was the summer Boris Stankovic [the Serbian head of various international basketball organizations] talked about broadcasting more games in Europe and letting pros play in the Olympics, which led to the Dream Team."

Stern, tragically, passed away a few months later, in early 2020. He was, rightly, recalled as the most capable, powerful, and effective commissioner in the history of American sports. He was also the most visionary. In our last conversation, we talked about how many of the trends he glimpsed in the summer of 1984 — his first few months on the job — did indeed come around the corner. In other cases, these seismic events were unforeseen. "Did I know on draft night that Michael Jordan would be this transforming player? No, I did not."

More than once, Stern would pause his thoughts to speak, almost evangelically, about the power of basketball, specifically, and sports in general. Of *course* sports would become such appealing content for television. "Nothing is guaranteed," Stern said, "and anything is possible." Sports are unscripted, unchoreographed, and play out in real time.

What this also means: the plot points—the great pivotal moments that echo for decades—can unfold at any time. It just so happens that many were bunched together in one magical summer.

Acknowledgments

Scott Price — longtime colleague, friend, and as fine a writer as you will find — once offered me a sage bit of advice: "If you have a book idea in your head and it would crush you to realize someone else had written it, that's a good sign you need to start writing."

I had long thought there was a book to be written about the summer of 1984. The more time I'd spent in sports, the more it'd become clear that this 90-day interval was the moment we went from black-and-white to Technicolor — with Dolby sound. Break down sports the way NFL coaches screen film and you would single out the summer of 1984 as the pivotal moment, the equivalent of the game-changing play.

Stars like Jordan and Barkley and Bird and Magic and Gretzky and Hulk Hogan and McEnroe and Navratilova and Sandberg . . . the peripheral players, the seminal moments, the events that scarcely drew mention at the time but would loom large for decades . . . a Supreme Court decision and the rise of cable TV and ESPN and the marriage of sports and commerce . . . the chance encounters . . . the bits of foreshadowing . . . the many moments that would echo in the future and in this present. Put it all together and, if nothing else, it would sure be a hell of a lot of fun to write.

In 2018, I shared this idea with Susan Canavan at Houghton Mifflin Harcourt, the editorial equivalent of a player's coach. By week's end, we were signing a contract.

And, damn, this was a book to write.

Authoring a nonfiction book is such a strange and contradictory exercise, at once deeply solitary and deeply collaborative, crucially dependent as it is on the kindness, time, recollections, and expertise of others. Like any other author, I consulted dozens of books; banked scores of interviews; and read hundreds of accounts.

I am intensely biased, but one source stood out. I joined *Sports Illustrated* in (gulp) 1996 as a summer intern, seeking an exile from big-firm law practice. This was the tail end of the golden age of magazines, a time when reporters went anywhere to chase a story and expense accounts were exercises in creative writing.

In the last quarter century, the changes at *Sports Illustrated* are too numerous — and sometimes too painful — to recount. But through it all, this has been unswerving: a commitment to journalism; a commitment to writing; a fundamental decency.

Sports Illustrated was — and is — more than a collection of first-rate journalists. It comes with its own built-in value system, a pride of ownership and sense of community. That was reinforced as I read so much of the magazine's coverage of events and figures from 1984. But that's also made manifestly obvious in reading my colleagues today, in various platforms, in pixels as well as on paper. Being part of this institution, this family, is one of the great joys of my life.

At the risk of sounding like a clumsy Oscar winner, I am reluctant to go down this road, lest I forget someone. But so many people come in for so much gratitude here. Thanks to:

Susan Canavan, for getting the concept immediately. It's a pity she couldn't see it through, but her tag-team partner for this book, Rakia

Clark, came off the top rope, and it was a pleasure to work with her and with Will Palmer, the Michael Jordan of copy editing. Speaking of . . .

David Shoemaker, Dave Wolff, Jimmy Traina, and Justin Barrasso: all were kind enough to help a WWE novice — and here we mix sports metaphors — get up to speed.

Brian Cazeneuve and his peerless grasp of all things Olympics.

Alex Prewitt, a rising star in the field, wrote an excellent piece for *Sports Illustrated* on *The Karate Kid*, and he graciously crane-kicked his notes over to me.

Bob Hammel, my mentor when I was a teenager in southern Indiana, a shining exemplar that sports journalists could (a) make an honest living and (b) be mensches. Decades later, he was no less generous in helping with this project.

Al Michaels and Bob Costas were generous with their time, remembrances, and insight, as were Bob Ley, Jay Bilas, Chris Berman, and Charley Steiner.

David Stern passed away before the final draft of this book was completed. But his generosity of time, candor, and (grudging) recollection were deeply important — and deeply appreciated.

Draggan Mihailovich, whose sorcery as a television producer is matched by his informed passion for UNC basketball.

For decades, *Sports Illustrated* and its writers were profoundly lucky to have access to the editing chops of Rich O'Brien. As was I for this project.

Malka Wickramatilake, Cristina Gallotto, and Jeff Spielberger were wonderful as eagle-eyed readers and fact-checkers.

Chris Stone and Steve Cannella and the *SI* front office for their encouragement and collegiality. Bill Owens and the *60 Minutes* front office, for theirs.

In no order but alphabetical: Seth Abraham, Teddy Atlas, Jeff Austin, Tracy Austin, Larry Bird, George Bodenheimer, Fred Carter, Andy Coats, the late and peerless Frank Deford, Anita DeFrantz, Donald Dell,

Phil de Picciotto, Joel Drucker, Richard Evans, Chris Evert, David Falk, Mike Farber, Lee Fentress, Mike Fraysse, Tim Hallam, Frank Hawkins, Mark Heisler, Keith Hernandez, Hank Hersch, Mark Houska, Stacey James, Robert Mark Kamen, Joe Kleine, Michael Lewis, Ralph Macchio, Jack McCallum, John McEnroe, Patrick McEnroe, Brian McIntyre, Gabe Miller, Dave Nagle, Martina Navratilova, David Newman, Gabe Oppenheim, Jeff Pearlman, George Raveling, Scott Reames, Tom Ricketts, Ted Robinson, Tom Ross, Brad Ruskin, Ross Schneiderman, Pam Shriver, Stan Smith, Ken Solomon, Mike Tollin, Mike Tyson, Sonny Vaccaro, Herschel Walker, Randy Walker, Roger Werner, Matt Williams, Alex Wolff.

Finally: to Ben, Allegra, and Ellie. I am profoundly fortunate to be on your team.

Notes

Introduction

page

6 *"the chucklingest president in history"*: Lincoln Mitchell, "Which Republican Candidate Is Most Like Ronald Reagan?" *New York Observer,* August 27, 2015.

7 *It was suggested that Clara Peller*: Benjamen Walker, "1984 (the Year Not the Book) Expanded Version," *Benjamen Walker's Theory of Everything,* Soundcloud, 2014, https://soundcloud.com/bwalker/1984-the-year-not-the-book.

Steve Rushin: Steve Rushin, *Knights in White Castle: A Memoir* (New York: Little, Brown, 2019).

1. Be Like Mike

14 *Barkley's physique:* Curry Kirkpatrick, "They're Second to None," *Sports Illustrated,* February 21, 1983.

15 *Mark Halsel:* Malcolm Moran, "Players: A Powerhouse on the Court," *New York Times,* April 24, 1984.

16 *Bob Knight deadpanned:* David Halberstam, *Playing for Keeps: Michael Jordan and the World He Made* (New York: Three Rivers Press, 2000), p. 797.

17 *"Where did you get your granddaddy's shoes?"*: Sam Smith, *The Jordan Rules* (New York: Pocket Books, 1993).

19 *"They said they was gettin' the best 72"*: Curry Kirkpatrick, "It Was Trial by Fire," *Sports Illustrated,* April 30, 1984.

21 *"It was almost eerie"*: Curry Kirkpatrick, "They're Second to None," *Sports Illustrated,* February 21, 1983.

2. The Great One

24 *"as normally proportioned as the newspaperboy"*: E. M. Swift, "Greatness Confirmed: Four of the Best Players in NHL History Assess the Supremacy of Wayne Gretzky," *Sports Illustrated,* December 27, 1982.

"hearing Mozart play a piano at five": Mike Pesca, *Upon Further Review: The Greatest What-Ifs in Sports History* (New York: Twelve, 2018).

27 *In 1982, he was named:* E. M. Swift, "The Best and Getting Better," *Sports Illustrated,* October 12, 1981.

28 *"After they won, they were too beat up"*: "Gretzky Recalls Great Rivalry," New York Islanders website, NHL.com, March 8, 2009.

3. Are the Games Dead?

38 *"What is a velodrome?"*: Gregory L. Williams, *The Campus Series: California State University, Dominguez Hills* (Charleston, SC: Arcadia, 2010).

4. Johnny Mac and Martina

42 *"I have transcended another level"*: Curry Kirkpatrick, "Worthy of Really High Fives," *Sports Illustrated,* June 18, 1984.

45 *Navratilova's "tumultuous year"*: Skip Bayless, "Millionairess in Search of Happiness," *Daytona Beach Morning Journal,* August 1, 1981.

5. The Trump Card

50 *The accompanying article:* Graydon Carter, "Donald Trump Gets What He Wants," *GQ,* May 1, 1984.

51 *"Donald J. Trump is the man of the hour"*: William E. Geist, "The Expanding Empire of Donald Trump," *New York Times,* April 8, 1984.

52 *"a miracle man"*: Robert H. Boyle, "The USFL's Trump Card: Builder Donald Trump, Owner of the New Jersey Generals, Has Bid Big Bucks to Make His League a Winner," *Sports Illustrated,* February 13, 1984.

53 *his "truthful hyperbole"*: Jia Tolentino, *Trick Mirror: Reflections on Self-Delusion* (New York: Random House, 2019).

56 *"A few guys had a few beers"*: *30 for 30,* season 1, episode 3, "Small Potatoes: Who Killed the USFL?," directed by Mike Tollin, ESPN, aired October 20, 2009.

58 *"Steinbrenner is Burt Reynolds"*: Mike Lupica, "Trump Making Steinbrenner Run Scared in NY," *New York Daily News,* May 4, 1984.

62 *"take Donald Jr. and his classmates"*: Tim Rohan, "Donald Trump and the USFL: A 'Beautiful' Circus," *Sports Illustrated,* July 12, 2016.

63 *Philadelphia Stars beat the Arizona Wranglers:* Ralph Wiley, "They're Loaded with Trump Cards: The New Jersey Generals Now Have More than Herschel

Walker, As They Proved in a Win Against Birmingham," *Sports Illustrated,* March 5, 1984.

64 *A Canadian industrialist:* Jeff Pearlman, "The Day Donald Trump's Narcissism Killed the USFL," *The Guardian,* September 11, 2018.

66 *A quarter century after:* Dylan Howard, "Never-Before-Seen Medical Records Reveal How Pepsi Fire Started Michael Jackson on the Road to Addiction," *Radar Online,* October 21, 2013.

6. Larry Versus Magic

73 *"If you were Raquel Welch":* Bruce Newman, "Together at Center Stage," *Sports Illustrated,* June 4, 1984.

As he later told fellow Hoosier: Royce Young, "Video: Larry Bird and Magic Johnson on Letterman," CBS Sports, April 12, 2012.

75 *"spinning in slow motion":* Anthony Cotton, "Green and White and Red All Over," *Sports Illustrated,* June 25, 1984.

76 *At the hospitality room at the Marriott:* Ian Thomsen, "Memories of Los Angeles Lakers–Boston Celtics Rivalry Come to Mind as 2017 Finals Near," NBA.com, June 1, 2017.

80 *"White boy, I'll kick your ass":* Dave Feschuk, "Celtics-Lakers Doc Highlights NBA's Uncivil War," *The Star,* June 10, 2017.

82 *"nobody will remember the score":* Bob Ryan, "In Sweltering Boston Garden, Larry Bird Was On Fire," *Boston Globe,* June 8, 2012.

"je ne sais quoi": George Vecsey, "One Bad Game for Lakers," *New York Times,* June 10, 1984.

87 *"something very special was happening here":* E. M. Swift, "From Corned Beef to Caviar," *Sports Illustrated,* June 3, 1991.

7. Heir Jordan

91 *"it's more fun to be noticed":* Roland Lazenby, *Michael Jordan: The Life* (New York: Back Bay, 2015), p. 214.

95 *James Jordan, Michael's father:* Lazenby, *Michael Jordan: The Life,* p. 217.

8. There's a Draft in Here

97 *the Felt Forum:* Filip Bondy, *Tip-Off: How the 1984 NBA Draft Changed Basketball Forever* (Philadelphia: Da Capo Press, 2008).

98 *Another devastating blow:* Chris Cobbs, "Widespread Cocaine Use by Players Alarms NBA," *Los Angeles Times,* August 20, 1980.

Steve Mills, who had played basketball: E. M. Swift, "From Corned Beef to Caviar," *Sports Illustrated,* June 3, 1991.

99 *"relentless pursuit of perfection":* Chris Ballard, "Pressing Forward: David Stern Is Not Looking Back," *Sports Illustrated,* October 24, 2018.

101 *"stature of an ant":* Swift, "From Corned Beef to Caviar."

104 *a "Slumlord Billionaire":* Dave Zirin, "Donald Sterling: Slumlord Billionaire," *The Nation,* April 26, 2014.

107 *his friend Stu Inman:* Bill Simmons, "Let's Go to Tape," ESPN, July 22, 2002.

110 *One agent who did not pay Barkley:* Sam Galanis, "Charles Barkley on Ex-Agent Lance Luchnick: 'I'd Blow His Damn Brains Out,'" NESN, August 28, 2015.

111 *"I signed with a scumbag":* Jake O'Donnell, "The Story Behind Barkley's Sour Relationship with His Ex-Agent," *SportsGrid,* August 28, 2019.

"I didn't leave school to make $75,000": Charles Barkley on *The Late Show with Stephen Colbert,* March 10, 2020.

9. Joy in Wrigleyville

115 *"The fun, the game, the sunshine":* Peter Golenbock, *Wrigleyville: A Magical History Tour of the Chicago Cubs* (New York: St. Martin's Griffin, 1996).

13. Swooshing In to Woo Jordan

157 *Strasser had always grasped:* David Wolman, "This Man Reinvented Nike, Seduced Adidas, and Helped Make PDX the Sports Gear Capital of the World," *Portland Monthly,* June 13, 2016.

159 *what this new rollout should be called:* David Falk, *The Bald Truth* (New York: Gallery Books, 2010), p. 174.

14. Down Goes Tyson

163 *"I probably wouldn't be alive today":* "Mike Tyson vs. Henry Milligan 1984-06-09 (Amateur)," video, 6:08, uploaded by 0gc00l, July 25, 2012, https://www.youtube.com/watch?v=FD8E2bC5TnA.

Tyson faced Henry Tillman: Tim Reiterman and Mitchell Landsberg, "An Olympics Boxer's Long, Hard Fall," *Los Angeles Times,* January 26, 2000.

166 *"Come at me":* Pat Putnam, "Their Fists Did All the Talking," *Sports Illustrated,* July 16, 1984.

15. The Dream Team

174 *he and Jordan began play-wrestling:* Jack McCallum, *Dream Team: How Michael, Magic, Larry, Charles, and the Greatest Team of All Time Conquered the World and Changed the Game of Basketball Forever* (New York: Ballantine, 2013).

175 *"I'm going to hug every mean person":* Scott Howard-Cooper, "For Tisdale, Playing for Bobby Was Knightmare" *Oklahoman,* April 23, 1991.

16. The Victory Tour

181 Thriller *had sold more copies:* Michael Goldberg and Christopher Connelly, "Michael Jackson: Trouble in Paradise?," *Rolling Stone,* March 15, 1984.

182 *"I think he's creepy":* J. Randy Taraborrelli, *Michael Jackson: The Magic, the Madness, the Whole Story, 1958–2009* (New York: Grand Central, 2010).

183 *the Jacksons would invest the money:* J. Randy Taraborrelli, *Michael Jackson: The Magic and the Madness* (New York: Birch Lane Press, 1991).

193 *"Was I scared?":* Peter King, "Kraftwork," *Sports Illustrated,* February 6, 2012.

17. The All-Sports, All-the-Time Network

197 *ESPN story in short strokes:* James Miller and Tom Shales, *Those Guys Have All the Fun: Inside the World of ESPN* (New York: Little, Brown, 2011).

198 *the transfer of "electronic mail":* Joann S. Lublin, "Dogfight in Space: Competition Heats Up in Domestic Satellites as Technology Gains," *Wall Street Journal,* September 8, 1978.

199 *"until the world ends":* Dylan Byers, "CNN When the World Ends," *Politico,* January 5, 2015.

$34,167 a month: Jim Shea, "Father-and-Son Dream Team," *Hartford Courant,* September 26, 1993.

200 *As for the matter of financing:* James Andrew Miller and Tom Shales, *Those Guys Have All the Fun: Inside the World of ESPN* (New York: Little, Brown, 2011).

204 *networks had effectively given up on cable:* "Double Play: ABC Buys ESPN Cable Service," *Time,* May 14, 1984.

206 *averaged a 2.4 rating:* Larry Stuart, "ESPN Still Afloat in Uncharted Water," *Los Angeles Times,* May 6, 1992.

207 *In an audacious move:* Dave Nagle, "1984 in Review," ESPN, January 2, 1985.

18. The Brawl to End It All

213 *Partnered with Tony Altomare:* David Shoemaker, *The Squared Circle: Life, Death, and Professional Wrestling* (New York: Avery, 2013).

214 *allowed one of his up-and-coming "babyfaces":* Mike Mooneyham and Shaun Assael, *Sex, Lies, and Headlocks: The Real Story of Vince McMahon and World Wrestling Entertainment* (New York: Broadway Books, 2002).

McMahon sold his business: Mooneyham and Assael, *Sex, Lies, and Headlocks.*

215 *Big John Studd:* Bruce Newman, "Who's Kidding Whom?," *Sports Illustrated,* April 29, 1985.

216 *known as Black Saturday:* Mooneyham and Assael, *Sex, Lies, and Headlocks.*

217 *"peachfuzzy viewers, notorious for":* Steve Rushin, *Knights in White Castle: A Memoir* (New York: Little, Brown, 2019).

227 *"Knuckle draggers who":* Bruce Newman, "Who's Kidding Whom?," *Sports Illustrated,* April 29, 1985.

19. The Summer of the Mac

231 *said Paul M. Kalaghan:* Gene I. Maeroff, "College Students Flock to Computer Science," *New York Times,* January 14, 1985.

233 *around 63.3 million:* Dennis F. Herrick, *Media Management in the Age of Gi-*

ants: Business Dynamics of Journalism (Albuquerque: University of New Mexico Press, 2012).

Advertisers, as they always do: "The Great Leap Upward," *Sports Illustrated,* July 18, 1984.

234 *"We wanted to do some things":* Frank Thorsberg, "Business Today: What Happens to High-Tech Olympics Hardware Now That the Show Is Over?" United Press International, August 13, 1984.

"The Olympics EMS": B. Feiner, "EMS at the 1984 Olympics," *Emergency Medical Services* 13, no. 2 (March-April 1984).

237 *Active Measures Working Group:* Fletcher Schoen and Christopher J. Lamb, "Deception, Disinformation, and Strategic Communications: How One Interagency Group Made a Major Difference," *Strategic Perspectives* 11 (June 2012).

238 *William French Smith spoke:* "Smith Says Soviet Forged Threats," *New York Times,* August 7, 1984.

239 *TASS dismissed the accusations:* "Tass Mocks Smith Charge," *New York Times,* August 9, 1984.

20. Let the Games Begin

241 *"The Soviet withdrawal":* "Moscow Settles a Score," *New York Times,* May 9, 1984.

The Literary Gazette: Brianna Nofil, "The California Activists Who Scared the Soviets Away from the 1984 Olympics," History.com, February 21, 2018.

243 Time *magazine gushed:* "Peter Ueberroth: The Achievement Was Olympian," *Time,* January 7, 1985.

244 *"restored* pixie *to our vocabulary":* "Retton Vaults Past Szabo to Win Gold Medal," *Los Angeles Times,* August 4, 1984.

247 *"as big as Michael Jackson":* Jim Lassiter, "Lewis a Thriller, But Bigger than Jackson?" *Oklahoman,* June 23, 1984.

249 *Chinese athletes were often convinced:* Frank Deford, "An Old Dragon Limbers Up," *Sports Illustrated,* August 15, 1988.

250 *"the cheerless world Mao made":* "The Image Has Altered," *Sports Illustrated,* August 15, 1988.

252 *"all-star team to beat us":* David Halberstam, *Playing for Keeps: Michael Jordan and the World He Made* (New York: Three Rivers Press, 2000).

253 *Spot-Bilt, an offshoot:* Darren Rovell, "How Nike Landed Michael Jordan," ESPN, February 15, 2013.

254 *"Coach — don't worry":* Bob Knight with Bob Hammel, *Knight: My Story* (New York: Thomas Dunne, 2002).

255 *"Ees not a difficult question":* Alexander Wolff, "In the Driver's Seat," *Sports Illustrated,* December 10, 1984.

256 *running out of hamburger buns:* David Wharton, "Remember When McDonald's Lost Big at 1984 Los Angeles Olympics?" *Morning Call,* June 16, 2017.

261 *At least eight members:* Robert Sullivan, "Triumphs Tainted with Blood," *Sports Illustrated,* January 21, 1985.

21. Super Saturday

266 *meet girls:* Curry Kirkpatrick, "They Did Their Things," *Sports Illustrated,* September 17, 1984, https://vault.si.com/vault/1984/09/17/they-did-their-things.

23. Wait Till Next Year

274 *"ask me about the Lindbergh baby?"*: John Garrity, "The Trade That Made the Cubs," *Sports Illustrated,* September 3, 1984.

Bibliography

"1984 Olympics to Rely on Private Enterprise." *New York Times,* December 6, 1981.

Ajemian, Robert. "Master of the Games: Peter Ueberroth." *Time,* January 7, 1985.

Badenhausen, Kurt. "Why ESPN Is Worth $40 Billion as the World's Most Valuable Media Property." *Forbes,* November 9, 2012.

Ballard, Chris, "Pressing Forward: David Stern Is Not Looking Back." *Sports Illustrated,* October 24, 2018.

Barbash, Fred. "U.S. Ties 'Klan' Olympic Hate Mail to KGB." *Washington Post,* August 7, 1984.

Barnard, Bill. "Bird Named MVP; Magic a Distant 3rd." *Los Angeles Times,* June 26, 1984.

Bayless, Skip. "Millionairess in Search of Happiness." *Daytona Beach Morning Journal,* August 1, 1981.

Bird, Larry, and Earvin (Magic) Johnson, with Jackie MacMullan. *When the Game Was Ours.* New York: Houghton Mifflin Harcourt, 2009.

Blockus, Gary. "Blood in Their Veins, Medals in Their Closet: The Success of the U.S. Cycling Team at the 1984 Olympics Was Tarnished by Reports That Athletes May Have Enhanced Their Performances by Blood Doping." *Morning Call,* June 2, 1996.

Bodenheimer, George, and Donald T. Phillips. *Every Town Is a Sports Town: Business Leadership at ESPN, from the Mailroom to the Boardroom.* New York: Grand Central, 2015.

Bondy, Filip. *Tip-Off: How the 1984 NBA Draft Changed Basketball Forever.* Philadelphia: Da Capo Press, 2008.

Bonk, Thomas. "Angry Riley Says Celtics Creating 'an Ugly Situation.'" *Los Angeles Times,* June 8, 1984.
———. "Celtics Steal One from Lakers, 124–121." *Los Angeles Times,* June 1, 1984.
———. "Lakers Explode and Roll Past Celtics, 137–104." *Los Angeles Times,* June 4, 1984.
———. "Lakers' Fast Break Leaves the Celtics Broken Down." *Los Angeles Times,* June 4, 1984.
———. "Lakers' Sprinters Could Sweep, but Boston Plans on a Marathon." *Los Angeles Times,* May 31, 1984.
———. "Lakers Wilt in the Heat of the Night." *Los Angeles Times,* June 9, 1984.
———. "Sinking Lakers Are Rescued by the Sky Hook: Ailing Abdul-Jabbar Gives Pep Talk, Big Performance to Beat Celtics, 119–108." *Los Angeles Times,* June 11, 1984.
Boyle, Robert H. "The USFL's Trump Card: Builder Donald Trump, Owner of the New Jersey Generals, Has Bid Big Bucks to Make His League a Winner." *Sports Illustrated,* February 13, 1984.
Burke, Monte. "Robert Kraft Has Used Business Sense and a Fan's Blind Faith to Turn the Once-Laughable New England Patriots into One of the Richest Franchises in Sports." *Forbes,* September 19, 2005.
———. "Unlikely Dynasty." *Forbes,* September 19, 2005.
Byers, Dylan. "CNN When the World Ends." *Politico,* January 5, 2015.
Callahan, Tom, Lee Griggs, and Joseph Kane. "One Last U.S. Victory Lap." *Time,* August 27, 1984.
Carter, Graydon. "Donald Trump Gets What He Wants." *GQ,* May 1, 1984.
Champlin, Charles. "Morita's Long Road to Miyagi." *New York Times,* June 22, 1986.
Cobbs, Chris. "Widespread Cocaine Use by Players Alarms NBA." *Los Angeles Times,* August 20, 1980.
Cohen, Rich. *The Chicago Cubs: Story of a Curse.* New York: Farrar, Straus and Giroux, 2017.
Conconi, Chuck. "Time's Man of the Year." *Washington Post,* December 31, 1984.
Cotton, Anthony. "Green and White and Red All Over." *Sports Illustrated,* June 25, 1984.
Cummings, Darron. "U.S. Open's First 'Super Saturday' Still Resonates." *USA Today,* September 11, 1984.
Deford, Frank. "An Old Dragon Limbers Up." *Sports Illustrated,* August 15, 1988.
———. "Talk About Strokes of Genius." *Sports Illustrated,* July 16, 1984.
———. "You'll Get a Kick Out of 'Karate Kid.'" *Sports Illustrated,* July 9, 1984.
"Double Play: ABC Buys ESPN Cable Service." *Time,* May 14, 1984.
Ebert, Roger. "The Karate Kid" review. RogerEbert.com, 1984.
Eskenazi, Gerald. "U.S.F.L. Set for Fall Play in '86." *New York Times,* August 21, 1984.
Falk, David. *The Bald Truth.* New York: Gallery Books, 2010.
Feiner, B. "EMS at the 1984 Olympics." *Emergency Medical Services* 13, no. 2 (March-April 1984).

Feschuk, Dave. "Celtics-Lakers Doc Highlights NBA's Uncivil War." *The Star,* June 10, 2017.

Galanis, Sam. "Charles Barkley on Ex-Agent Lance Luchnick: 'I'd Blow His Damn Brains Out.'" NESN, August 28, 2015.

Gallo, Carmine. "Mac 1984: Steve Jobs Revolutionizes the Art of Corporate Storytelling." *Forbes,* January 24, 2014.

Garrity, John. "The Trade That Made the Cubs." *Sports Illustrated,* September 3, 1984.

Geist, William E. "The Expanding Empire of Donald Trump." *New York Times,* April 8, 1984.

Gleaves, John. "Manufactured Dope: How the 1984 US Olympics Cycling Team Rewrote the Rules on Drugs in Sports." *International Journal of the History of Sport* 32, no. 1 (January 12, 2015).

Goldberg, Michael, and Christopher Connelly. "Michael Jackson: Trouble in Paradise?" *Rolling Stone,* March 15, 1984.

Goldstein, Steve. "Martina Fears Avon's Call If She Talks." *New York Daily News,* July 30, 1981.

Golenbock, Peter. *Wrigleyville: A Magical History Tour of the Chicago Cubs.* New York: St. Martin's, 1996.

Gonzales, Mark. "Game 5 Loss Still Haunts 1984 Cubs." *Chicago Tribune,* January 19, 2014.

"The Great Leap Upward." *Sports Illustrated,* July 18, 1984.

Greenberg, Alan. "Bird (7 of 17): Cooper Gets Help from Friends." *Los Angeles Times,* May 28, 1984.

Greenberg, Jon. "Here's the Pitch." *University of Chicago Magazine,* July 2010.

"Gretzky Recalls Great Rivalry." New York Islanders website, NHL.com, March 8, 2009.

Griggs, Lee, and William Henry III. "Faster, Higher, Stronger: Against the U.S. Basketball Teams, the World Was Second." *Time,* August 20, 1984.

Halberstam, David. *Playing for Keeps: Michael Jordan and the World He Made.* New York: Three Rivers Press, 2000.

Herrick, Dennis F. *Media Management in the Age of Giants: Business Dynamics of Journalism.* Albuquerque: University of New Mexico Press, 2012.

"High Court Hears Case of N.C.A.A. TV Rules." *New York Times,* March 21, 1984.

Hiltzik, Michael. "A Reminder That Apple's '1984' Ad Is the Only Great Super Bowl Commercial Ever—And It's Now 33 Years Old." *Los Angeles Times,* January 31, 2017.

"The History of Michael Jordan's 'Banned' Sneakers." *Complex,* May 3, 2020.

Hoffer, Richard. "Left Is All Right." *Sports Illustrated,* May 9, 2005.

Howard, Dylan. "Never-Before-Seen Medical Records Reveal How Pepsi Fire Started Michael Jackson on the Road to Addiction." *Radar Online,* October 21, 2013.

"The Image Has Altered." *Sports Illustrated,* August 15, 1988.

Isaacson, Walter. *Steve Jobs.* New York: Simon and Schuster, 2011.

Kerr, Peter. "Cable TV's Turn for the Better." *New York Times,* July 28, 1984.

King, Peter. "Kraftwork." *Sports Illustrated,* February 6, 2012.

Kirkpatrick, Curry. "Hooray for the Red, White, Black and Blue!" *Sports Illustrated,* July 23, 1984.

———. "It Was Trial by Fire." *Sports Illustrated,* April 30, 1984.

———. "They Did Their Things." *Sports Illustrated,* September 17, 1984.

———. "They're Second to None." *Sports Illustrated,* February 21, 1983.

———. "Worthy of Really High Fives." *Sports Illustrated,* June 18, 1984.

Klein, William, dir. *The French.* France: Acteurs Auteurs Associés, 1982.

Kleinfield, N. R. "ABC to Acquire ESPN as Texaco Sells Its 72%." *New York Times,* May 1, 1984.

Knight, Bob. *Knight: My Story.* New York: Thomas Dunne, 2002.

Knight, Phil. *Shoe Dog: A Memoir by the Creator of Nike.* New York: Simon and Schuster, 2016.

Knoll, Carolina, and Jeff Gottlieb. "Jackson's Drug Use Started After Pepsi Commercial, Attorney Says." *Los Angeles Times,* April 29, 2013.

Krugel, Mitchell. "Special Report: Michael Jordan. Twist of Fate Makes Koehler." *NWI Times,* November 24, 1991.

La Rocco, Claudia. "Rings of Power: Peter Ueberroth and the 1984 Los Angeles Olympic Games." *Financial History,* Spring 2004.

Lassiter, Jim. "Lewis a Thriller, but Bigger than Jackson?" *Oklahoman,* June 23, 1984.

Lazenby, Roland. *Michael Jordan: The Life.* New York: Back Bay Books, 2015.

Lidz, Franz. "The Ivy's Irish Pug." *Sports Illustrated,* March 19, 1984.

Littwin, Mike. "For Lakers, the Last Chapter in the Series That Got Away." *Los Angeles Times,* June 13, 1984.

Loder, Kurt. "Cyndi Lauper: Dream Girl." *Rolling Stone,* May 24, 1984.

Lublin, Joann S. "Dogfight in Space: Competition Heats Up in Domestic Satellites as Technology Gains." *Wall Street Journal,* September 8, 1978.

Lupica, Mike. "Trump Making Steinbrenner Run Scared in NY." *New York Daily News,* May 4, 1984.

Maeroff, Gene I. "College Students Flock to Computer Science." *New York Times,* January 14, 1985.

Maslin, Janet. "'Karate Kid,' Bane of Bullies." *New York Times,* June 22, 1984.

Mathews, Tom, Janet Huck, Michael Reese, Martin Kasindorf, Daniel Pedersen, and Elisa Williams. "Is Los Angeles Ready?" *Newsweek,* July 30, 1984.

McCallum, Jack. *Dream Team: How Michael, Magic, Larry, Charles, and the Greatest Team of All Time Conquered the World and Changed the Game of Basketball Forever.* New York: Ballantine, 2013.

———. "When L.A. Buried the Garden Ghost: How Magic, Kareem and the Lakers Finally Beat Bird's Celtics." *Sports Illustrated,* June 4, 1985.

McDonough, Will. "Patriots' Records Show Debts Over $75 Million." *Chicago Tribune,* July 27, 1987.

Meacham, John. "Jon Meacham: George H. W. Bush and the Price of Politics." *New York Times,* December 1, 2018.

Meyers, John A. "A Letter from the Publisher." *Time,* January 7, 1985.

Michalopoulos, Demetrios. "New Applications & Recent Research: Olympics Electronic Messaging System Demonstrated." *IEEE Xplore,* November 1983.

"Mike Tyson vs. Henry Milligan 1984-06-09 (Amateur)." Video, 6:08, uploaded by 0gc00l, July 25, 2012. https://www.youtube.com/watch?v=FD8E2bC5TnA.

Miller, James, and Tom Shales. *Those Guys Have All the Fun: Inside the World of ESPN.* New York: Little, Brown, 2011.

Miller, Jim. "The Tour, the Money, the Magic." *Newsweek,* July 16, 1984.

Mitchell, Fred. "Durham's Glove Took Bath in Playoff Before Cubs Did." *Chicago Tribune,* February 22, 1985.

Mitchell, Lincoln. "Which Republican Candidate Is Most Like Ronald Reagan?" *New York Observer,* August 27, 2015.

Mooneyham, Mike, and Shaun Assael. *Sex, Lies, and Headlocks: The Real Story of Vince McMahon and World Wrestling Entertainment.* New York: Broadway Books, 2002.

Moore, Kenny. "Hey, Russia, It's a Heck of Party." *Sports Illustrated,* August 6, 1984.

Moran, Malcolm. "67,596 See Olympians in Hoosier Dome." *New York Times,* July 10, 1984.

———. "Players: A Powerhouse on the Court." *New York Times,* April 24, 1984.

Morrow, Lance. "Feeling Proud Again: Olympic Organizer Peter Ueberroth." *Time,* January 7, 1985.

"Moscow Settles a Score." *New York Times,* May 9, 1984.

Nagle, Dave. "1984 in Review." ESPN, January 2, 1985.

NCAA v. Board of Regents, 468 U.S. 85 (1984).

Newman, Bruce. "Together at Center Stage." *Sports Illustrated,* June 4, 1984.

———. "Who's Kidding Whom?" *Sports Illustrated,* April 29, 1985.

Nocera, Joe, and Ben Strauss. *Indentured: The Inside Story of the Rebellion Against the NCAA.* New York: Portfolio, 2016.

Nofil, Brianna. "The California Activists Who Scared the Soviets Away from the 1984 Olympics." History.com, September 1, 2018.

O'Donnell, Jake. "The Story Behind Barkley's Sour Relationship with His Ex-Agent." *SportsGrid,* August 28, 2019.

"Olympics Sabotage." *New York Times,* August 9, 1984.

Ostler, Scott. "The World Is Coming to See Olympics and Give L.A. Its Best Shot." *Los Angeles Times,* June 27, 1984.

———. "Wrestling Has Gone Hollywood and It's Ruining the Sport." *Los Angeles Times,* March 11, 1985.

Overman, Steven J., and Kelly Boyer Sagert. *Icons of Women's Sport.* Vol. 1. Santa Barbara, CA: Greenwood, 2012.

Pearlman, Jeff. "The Day Donald Trump's Narcissism Killed the USFL." *Guardian,* September 11, 2018.

———. *Football for a Buck: The Crazy Rise and Crazier Demise of the USFL.* New York: Houghton Mifflin Harcourt, 2018.

———. *Showtime: Magic, Kareem, Riley, and the Los Angeles Lakers Dynasty of the 1980s.* New York: Avery, 2014.

Pesca, Mike. *Upon Further Review: The Greatest What-Ifs in Sports History.* New York: Twelve, 2018.

"Peter Ueberroth: The Achievement Was Olympian." *Time,* January 7, 1985.

"Piper's Pit with Cyndi Lauper (06-16-1984)." Video, 4:49, uploaded by All Out of Bubblegum, March 18, 2015. https://www.youtube.com/watch?v=fW0FgLGKa4U.

Podhoretz, Jim, dir. *30 for 30.* Season 3, episode 16, "Celtics/Lakers: Best of Enemies, Part 1." Aired June 13, 2017, on ESPN.

Prewitt, Alex. "The Crane Kick Is Bogus: A Karate Kid Oral History." *Sports Illustrated,* May 1, 2018.

Putnam, Pat. "Their Fists Did All the Talking." *Sports Illustrated,* July 16, 1984.

Reich, Kenneth. "Doleful Day for the Games." *Sports Illustrated,* May 21, 1984.

Reiterman, Tim, and Mitchell Landsberg. "An Olympic Boxer's Long, Hard Fall." *Los Angeles Times,* January 26, 2000.

"Remember When? Bloomington Was the Basketball Capital of America." *Hoosier Times,* August 20, 2018.

"Retton Vaults Past Szabo to Win Gold Medal." *Los Angeles Times,* August 4, 1984.

Rohan, Tim. "Donald Trump and the USFL: A 'Beautiful' Circus." *Sports Illustrated,* July 12, 2016.

Rovell, Darren. "How Nike Landed Michael Jordan." ESPN, February 15, 2013.

Rushin, Steve. *Knights in White Castle: A Memoir.* New York: Little, Brown, 2019.

Ryan, Bob. "In Sweltering Boston Garden, Larry Bird Was On Fire." *Boston Globe,* June 8, 2012.

Sandberg, Ryne. *Second to Home: Ryne Sandberg Opens Up.* Chicago: Bonus Books, 1995.

Saxon, Wolfgang. "Juan Burciaga, 65, Judge Who Ended TV Football 'Cartel.'" *New York Times,* March 17, 1995.

Schickel, Richard. "Cinema: Nothing New Under the Sun." *Time,* Monday, July 2, 1984.

Schoen, Fletcher, and Christopher J. Lamb. "Deception, Disinformation, and Strategic Communications: How One Interagency Group Made a Major Difference." *Strategic Perspectives* 11 (June 2012).

Schoenfield, David. "From Zeroes to Heroes." ESPN, September 24, 2009.

Schope, Dan. "Blood Enhancing Aided U.S. Cyclists." *Morning Call,* January 9, 1985.

Schwartz, Larry. "Martina Was Alone On Top." ESPN, July 7, 1990.

Shea, Jim. "Father-and-Son Dream Team." *Hartford Courant,* September 26, 1993.

Shoemaker, David. *The Squared Circle: Life, Death, and Professional Wrestling.* New York: Avery, 2013.

Simmons, Bill. "Let's Go to Tape." ESPN, July 22, 2002.

Smith, Sam. *The Jordan Rules.* New York: Pocket Books, 1993.

"Smith Says Soviet Forged Threats." *New York Times,* August 7, 1984.

Solomon, Jon. "NCAA Supreme Court Ruling Felt at O'Bannon Trial 30 Years Later." CBS Sports, June 26, 2014.

Springer, Steve. "Bird Blames the Commissioner." *Los Angeles Times*, June 11, 1984.
———. "For Magic, the Mistakes and Loss Won't Wash." *Los Angeles Times*, June 13, 1984.
———. "This Time Magic Lets It Get Away: With Clock at His Disposal, Johnson Uses Too Much of It." *Los Angeles Times*, June 1, 1984.
Steinbreder, John. "The $126 Million Fumble: How Billy Sullivan and His Son Chuck Turned a $25,000 Investment in the Patriots into a Financial Disaster." *Sports Illustrated*, March 14, 1988.
Stenovec, Tim. "Apple's Iconic '1984' Commercial Aired Nationally for the First Time 32 Years Ago Today." *Business Insider*, January 22, 2016.
Stewart, Larry. "ESPN Still Afloat in Uncharted Water." *Los Angeles Times*, May 6, 1992.
———. "Laker-Celtic Game 7 Draws Record 40-Million Viewers." *Los Angeles Times*, June 15, 1984.
Stone, Oliver, dir. *Wall Street*. Los Angeles: Twentieth Century Fox, 1987.
Strauss, Ben. "30-Year-Old Decision Could Serve as Template for N.C.A.A. Antitrust Case." *New York Times*, June 13, 2014.
Swift, E. M. "The Best and Getting Better." *Sports Illustrated*, October 12, 1981.
———. "From Corned Beef to Caviar." *Sports Illustrated*, June 3, 1991.
———. "Greatness Confirmed: Four of the Best Players in NHL History Assess the Supremacy of Wayne Gretzky." *Sports Illustrated*, December 27, 1982.
Swisher, Kara. "Tough Match for Martina." *Washington Post*, May 17, 1993.
Taaffe, William. "How Wrestling Got TV in Its Clutches." *Sports Illustrated*, April 29, 1985.
Taraborrelli, J. Randy. *Michael Jackson: The Magic, the Madness, the Whole Story, 1958–2009*. New York: Grand Central, 2010.
"Tass Mocks Smith Charge." *New York Times*, August 9, 1984.
Thomas, Robert McG., Jr. "The Man at the Center of It All." *New York Times*, July 22, 1984.
Thomsen, Ian. "Memories of Los Angeles Lakers–Boston Celtics Rivalry Come to Mind as 2017 Finals Near." NBA.com, June 1, 2017.
Thorsberg, Frank. "Business Today: What Happens to High-Tech Olympics Hardware Now That the Show Is Over?" United Press International, August 13, 1984.
Tolentino, Jia. *Trick Mirror: Reflections on Self-Delusion*. New York: Random House, 2019.
Tollin, Mike, dir. *30 for 30*. Season 1, episode 3, "Small Potatoes: Who Killed the USFL?" Aired on ESPN, October 20, 2009.
Ueberroth, Peter, Richard Levin, and Amy Quinn. *Made in America: His Own Society*. New York: Horizon Book Promotions, 1988.
Vecsey, George. "Good Cop, Bad Cop." *New York Times*, December 21, 1982.
———. "One Bad Game for Lakers." *New York Times*, June 10, 1984.
Walker, Benjamen. "1984 (the Year Not the Book) Expanded Version." *Benjamen Walker's Theory of Everything*, 2014. https://soundcloud.com/bwalker/1984-the-year-not-the-book.

Wallace, William N. "Trump Would Like to Take On N.F.L." *New York Times,* September 30, 1983.

Weinbach, Jon, and Dan Marks, dirs. *30 for 30.* Season 2, episode 29, "Sole Man." Aired April 16, 2015, on ESPN.

West, Jerry. *West by West: My Charmed, Tormented Life.* New York: Back Bay Books, 2012.

Wharton, David. "Remember When McDonald's Lost Big at 1984 Los Angeles Olympics?" *Morning Call,* June 16, 2017.

White, Gordon W., Jr. "Colleges May Find TV's Golden Egg Tarnished." *New York Times,* August 26, 1984.

Wikipedia, s.v. "Victory Tour (The Jacksons Tour)." Last modified August 9, 2020, https://en.wikipedia.org/wiki/Victory_Tour_(The_Jacksons_tour).

Wiley, Ralph. "The Wranglers Were Star Struck." *Sports Illustrated,* July 23, 1984.

———. "They're Loaded with Trump Cards: The New Jersey Generals Now Have More than Herschel Walker, as They Proved in a Win Against Birmingham." *Sports Illustrated,* March 5, 1984.

Williams, Gregory L. *The Campus Series: California State University, Dominguez Hills.* Charleston, SC: Arcadia, 2010.

Wolff, Alexander. "In the Driver's Seat." *Sports Illustrated,* December 10, 1984.

Wolman, David. "This Man Reinvented Nike, Seduced Adidas, and Helped Make PDX the Sports Gear Capital of the World." *Portland Monthly,* June 13, 2016.

Yesko, Jill, dir. *Tainted Blood: The Untold Story of the 1984 Olympic Doping Scandal.* Baltimore: Baxter World Media, 2018.

Young, Royce. "Video: Larry Bird and Magic Johnson on Letterman." CBS Sports, April 12, 2012.

Zirin, Dave. "Donald Sterling: Slumlord Billionaire." *The Nation,* April 26, 2014.

Index

Page numbers followed by "n" indicate a footnote.